"This book tackles a vitally important field—the relation between music and theological education. Hess pushes us to think hard about what theology in a 'performative' mode might look like. An adventurous and bold book."
—**Jeremy Begbie**
Duke University

"Lisa Hess challenges us to ponder how music and learning actually work to transform our lives. This provocative study draws on diverse sources from history, philosophy, education, and music theory to construct a promising new approach to doing theology in a performative mode. What Hess offers us in this symphonic masterpiece is nothing less than insight, which she identifies as 'music's primary gift.'"
—**Arthur Holder**
Graduate Theological Union

"Lisa Hess introduces her book with three significant questions: how do we learn, do theology, and build a unified community of diverse peoples through music? These questions are intriguing and urgent in a world where the process of knowing and the work of theology both demand full participation of all our human senses. Hess dives deeply into these questions, and she surfaces with a vibrant picture of music as a living, embodied, relational set of practices that simultaneously express, question, and illumine theology. Her presentation is richly textured and integrative, drawing deeply on the fields of history, ethnomusicology, education, music, spirituality, and aesthetics. What lingers after reading Hess's book is a bounty of knowledge composed into the performative mode of music, beckoning readers back into the pages to sing and play with the harmonies until we truly understand the new possibilities that she presents."
—**Mary Elizabeth Moore**
Boston University

"Christian theology, like musicology, uses words to describe realities and experiences that resist explanation. Lisa Hess explores how theologians could better attend to the performative, embodied nature of spirituality in all its various forms. This book is a helpful reminder of how elusive the subject of theology is, and points readers to a variety of voices and questions that are often neglected in theological reflection."
—**John D. Witvliet**
  Calvin College and Calvin Theological Seminary

"Professor Hess takes on a monumental task in her study entitled Learning in a Musical Key, that of an exhaustive investigation into what constitutes an embodied musical experience as celebrated by so many who speak of the life-changing and transcendental elements of the physical act of music making and the implications for those seeking to harness the accompanying learning processes that lead to this state of elevated emotion and consciousness. An amazing resource simply in the amalgamation of the leading voices in education, music philosophy, and theology-all in one binding!"
—**Paul D. Head**
  University of Delaware

Learning in a Musical Key

Princeton Theological Monograph Series

K. C. Hanson, Charles M. Collier, D. Christopher Spinks,
and Robin Parry, Series Editors

Recent volumes in the series:

Michael A. Salmeier
Restoring the Kingdom: The Role of God as the "Ordainer of Times and Seasons" in the Acts of the Apostles

Timothy Hessel-Robinson
*Spirit and Nature:
The Study of Christian Spirituality in a Time of Ecological Urgency*

Paul W. Chilcote
*Making Disciples in a World Parish:
Global Perspectives on Mission and Evangelism*

Nathan Montover
*Luther's Revolution:
The Political Dimensions of Martin Luther's Universal Priesthood*

Alan B. Wheatley
*Patronage in Early Christianity:
Its Use and Transformation from Jesus to Paul of Samosata*

Jon Paul Sydnor
*Ramanuja and Schleiermacher:
Toward a Constructive Comparitive Theology*

Eric G. Flett
*Persons, Powers, and Pluralities:
Toward a Trinitarian Theology of Culture*

Learning in a Musical Key
Insight for Theology in Performative Mode

LISA M. HESS

☙PICKWICK *Publications* · Eugene, Oregon

LEARNING IN A MUSICAL KEY
Insight for Theology in Performative Mode

Princeton Theological Monograph Series 169

Copyright © 2011 Lisa M. Hess. All rights reserved. Except for brief quotations in critical publications or reviews, no part of this book may be reproduced in any manner without prior written permission from the publisher. Write: Permissions, Wipf and Stock Publishers, 199 W. 8th Ave., Suite 3, Eugene, OR 97401.

Pickwick Publications
An Imprint of Wipf and Stock Publishers
199 W. 8th Ave., Suite 3
Eugene, OR 97401

www.wipfandstock.com

isbn 13:978-1-60899-697-1

Cataloging-in-Publication data:

Hess, Lisa M.

    Learning in a musical key : insight for theology in performative mode / Lisa M. Hess

    p. ; 23 cm. —Includes bibliographical references and index.

    Princeton Theological Monograph Series 169

    ISBN 13: 978-1-60899-697-1

    1. Music—Religous aspects. 2. Theology. I. Title. II. Series.

ML3921 .H48 2011

Manufactured in the U.S.A.

Dedicated to
David A. Weadon & James E. Loder
of blessed memory

Contents

Preface / ix

Introduction / 1

1. Hildegard of Bingen and the Letter to the Prelates at Mainz / 28

2. Learning and the Conundrum of Aptitude for the Musical/Non-Musical / 63

3. How We Learn Music / 95

4. Religious Education and the Challenges of Learning in Music / 133

5. Learning in a Musical Key / 167

Conclusion / 208

Bibliography / 213

Index / 229

Preface

ON NOVEMBER 11, 1993, A SEMINARY CHOIR OFFERED ITS FIRST AND only performance of Mendelssohn's *Elijah* oratorio for an audience of about eight hundred in the acoustic, historical space of a university chapel. Like many who are drawn into a deepening study of music, I received a marvelous gift amidst this musical event: transcendent awareness in heightened sensation, an indescribable joy reminiscent of my teacher, Søren Kierkegaard, and a deepened *consciousness of* something I have been driven to articulate ever since. In the terms of this study and as shaped by a transformative logic of another teacher, I received an *insight* into a critical problematic I had not yet begun to conceptualize. The *interlude for scanning* has ensued for over seventeen years, with various *releases of energy* when new connections were made and new *interpretations* could be articulated. This study is only the next portion of this unending interpretative process with the most *congruence*—internal sense-making for me and my understanding—and the best *correspondence*—external sense-making with tools of critical-communal discourse—to the reality of how music teaches when one surrenders to it in a community of struggle and celebration. As a lived quest for assurance driven by this problematic, *Learning in a Musical Key* addresses and finally provides response to two guiding questions instigated by the work of Jeremy Begbie in *Theology, Music, and Time*: "What does learning from music in a performative mode require?" and "How does a disciplinary theologian integrate its performative mode into critical discourse?"

The study is not only driven by a seventeen-year fascination with how music shapes human learning, however. It has been pulled forward to completion today by an increasingly urgent need, which is to conceptualize—even model and foster—traditionally-rooted, theological contributions able to nourish a life-giving wisdom amidst irreconcilable difference and polarized community(ies). Music brings persons together like nothing else,[1] as many of us observe. Yet this very same music is the lightening rod of utter division and communal rupture, in history as it is today. Consider the eighteenth-century, Rankinite Schism and the formation of the Associate Reformed Presbyterian Church, newly constituted of mostly "Old Side" Scotch-Irish who were vehemently *against* the singing of hymns instead of the English-metrical Psalms.[2] Consider music as practice within a faith community today, now the dispute within which it is torn asunder for the inability to sustain divergent musical practices or styles. The living wisdom of historical, religious traditions has contributions to make toward becoming fully alive, fully human, rooted in religious particularity *but integrative of it* amidst even the most trying circumstances of inhumanity. This study follows a bit of that wisdom, ultimately suggesting it's not actually the music, per se, but the *performative mode*, which is the primarily relational, explicitly embodied and multidimensional space in which self-transcendence and new insight ultimately create new communal ways of living together: intimately particular yet differentiated amidst a greater relationality or rule of relation.

Learning in a Musical Key grows out of the historically rooted, Christian theological tradition, claimed through a Chalcedonian christological method within a relational logic of the Spirit made known by God in the name and power of Jesus, who the church and I call the Christ. The scriptural roots of this entire study lodge in Colossians 3:12–17, given repeated expression over years of touring-choir performance of a similarly scriptural anthem, arranged for choral performance by Jane M. Marshall. The experiential warrant for the work deepened through immersion in Christian Protestant, Catholic and Orthodox liturgies, sung Psalms, and centering prayer within Quaker contemplative practice. But music's irrepressible multidimensionality and intercultural complexities have drawn such particularly-identified, indwelt-theological inquiries into broader and broader communities of discourse across faith traditions and philosophical speculation. Music's

---

1. LaMott, *Traveling Mercies*, 65.
2. Westermeyer, *Te Deum*, 252–53.

primarily relational-embodied constitution across generations and diverse human expressions allows nothing less.

As such, this work has been pulled out of purely musical contexts by deepening companionships—with Conservative, Orthodox, and Hasidic Jewish rabbis, with multiple Tibetan Buddhist practitioners, most recently with a Muslim mystic-scientist—who have compassionate claims to make of traditionally-rooted, Christian faith practitioners or disciples. These companionships have fostered new ways for me to enter into and live a traditionally rooted, Christ-centered discipleship, while being shaped into an abundant love of unexpected depths, observant of, and intimate through, our intersecting traditions' particularities. Music in its performative mode, investigated over seventeen years, taught this *method*, if one were to name such a journey or path for disciplinary ears. Therefore, *Learning in a Musical Key* examines learning from music in a performative mode from various angles—learning *from* music, learning *in* music, learning within music's distinct *mode* of expression and agency; but it also aims to articulate, model and foster the *manner in which such critical contribution comes to be made*, at least within the discipline of Christian spirituality. A contemplative empiricism within an artisanal way offers a tried-and-true invitation to others to enter deeply into the primarily relational, explicitly embodied, and multidimensional space in which new insight assuredly arrives for shared human fullness and ultimate value.

I am thankful to Charlie Collier at Pickwick Publications/Wipf & Stock who continued to express interest in the musical work amidst other collaborations. The Wabash Center for Teaching and Learning in Theology and Religion graciously provided a summer research fellowship, not to mention a hospitable collegiality, in which the work grew. Robert E. Alvis asked the right question at precisely the right time, spurring actual completion of the lengthy research and writing. Willie Jennings continues to inspire a confidence and tenacity with critical contributions to theological disciplines, even as I, a member of one of his cohorts, have clearly left the nest. Jason Vickers suggested the particular monograph series as an ideal way to express gratitude for one's disciplinary origins even as the path of scholarship leads away from them. Members of the Society for the Study of Christian Spirituality, especially Arthur Holder, Anita Houck, and Douglas Burton-Christie, continue to sculpt new ways for me to see and engage in deeply rooted and provocative scholarship, for the good of the scholar and the learning communities s/he serves. Hester Higton (http://www.academicedit.co.uk/index.html) was a marvelous, near-conclusion companion to the work, and Jono Sparks-Franklin offered invaluable help with the Index. Heartfelt gratitude goes to all.

In a project with as lengthy a duration as this one, words fail for a complete and just thanksgiving. For all those who live wisdom in ways I could not begin to imagine until we met—Laurie Ferguson, Sharon Trekell, Irwin Kula, Janet Kirchheimer, Brad and Rebecca Hirschfield, Shmuel Klatzkin, the Kiddush Club, the wise women of Yellow Springs, and Natalie Blommel—I am inexpressibly indebted. The study is dedicated to those weighty elders who first taught me music and theology were intimately connected—David A. Weadon and James E. Loder—but deepest thanksgiving goes to the most faithful, steady, and enlivening companion I have ever known, Brian D. Maguire.

Introduction

Learning from Music in a Performative Mode

A Practical Theological Contribution to Christian Spirituality

THE HISTORICAL-THEOLOGICAL DISCIPLINES HAVE MUCH TO LEARN from music in its performative mode. Systematic theologian and noted pianist Jeremy Begbie concludes his *Theology, Music and Time* with the observation: "One of the most obvious challenges music will present is to ask theology if it is prepared to integrate a 'performative mode' into its work. To repeat: music bears its theological fruits most potently by being practised, by enacting possibilities."[1] In contrast to the increasingly textual, deconstructionist, and continental impulses in systematic theology, Begbie challenges theology to find critical rigor at the crossroads of performance and scholarship that is bodily contextualized. This is not surprising within contemporary, (post-)modern[2] thought that shepherds the habitual mind back to its origins, its "I" in context. Even so, readers are left to muse on their own about what learning from music in its performative mode would entail amidst the labyrinthine hallways of specialized, theological disciplines. What does *learning from music in a performative mode* require? How does a theologian, in the disciplinary sense, integrate a performative mode into critical discourse?

---

1. Begbie, *Theology, Music and Time*, 280.

2. Ploeger, *Dare We Observe?* "(Post-)modern" gives symbolic representation of the modernity–postmodernity discourse, articulating observable characteristics of modernity, of postmodernity, and ultimately their symbiotic interrelationship.

These questions have stymied me for over a decade now. The prevalent questions within musical-theological literatures have been unhelpfully formulated, with a high degree of objective–subjective, theory-practice split, which pre-empts Begbie's challenge in the very formulation of the problem. A sampling of the current questions includes the following: What is music? What makes it religious? What kind of music is appropriate in which religious tradition(s)? What is an aesthetic of music in a religious tradition (i.e., Christian, Jewish, Hindi, etc.)? Which has primacy in Christian theological tradition—Word or music—and why? Does music have theological character; if so, what is it? Is music a form of theology or could theology be a form of music? Each of these questions—and those like them—invites critical inquiry, inspired by the fragments of truth within them. Each presupposes an objectivism or "whatness" to the phenomenon of music that is unhelpful for its integrative, embodied, performative realities. As Christopher Small bluntly states, "Those are the wrong questions to ask. There is no such thing as music. Music is not a thing at all, but an activity, something that people do."[3] The unhelpfully formulated questions have misguided my own understanding, not to mention many disciplinary studies of musical phenomena interested in a multidimensional, integrative approach. The freedom to pursue the broader questions of learning from music and within musical events arises with philosopher Susanne Langer, recognized for her contributions to philosophy of mind and art. She acknowledged from the start that formulating the most appropriate question might very well be the necessary innovation.[4]

Music is not only an object to be studied; it is also an inextricable, embodied part of human life and awareness. Music has a subjective force with a shaping agency all its own. As philosopher Aaron Ridley quips, "Music is a part of life. It's a rotten slogan, but it does capture pretty well what I mean."[5] To be studied critically and with integrity in its multidimensionality, music must be understood as a phenomenon with unavoidable self-implication for the scholar and a communally shaped agency organic to the participants and contexts of meaning in which music comes into being as music. This also means that music

---

3. Small, *Musicking*, 2.
4. Langer, *Philosophy in a New Key*, 4.
5. Ridley, *Philosophy of Music*, 1.

in all its dimensions partially shapes what we understand music to be. Critical inquiry into music requires an epistemological humility *and* an ever-widening precision, which seems methodologically impossible. Not surprisingly, most disciplinary perspectives bracket out large portions of musical phenomena—what scholars call *extra-musical* or *extrinsic* elements—in order to investigate the portion of narrowed interest. That is the path of the modern mind. But how much is lost from view as a result? Does one take a cat apart to understand its workings and significance in the same way that one disassembles a car to understand its workings and potential? Of course not. Only recently have we begun to see musicological and methodological perspectives unwilling to take an objectivistic approach. In Ridley's words,

> My point, then, is not that it is wrong to think of music as sound-structure. Music no doubt is that, among other things. The mistake is to assume that music is *essentially* sound-structure; that its character as structured sound is its true, real, ultimate nature.... We do ourselves a disservice if we decide before we start what sort of thing we're going to find in the end, especially if we don't notice that that's what we've done.[6]

Here we arrive at Begbie's systematic theological challenge: the complex, utterly earthy, potentially transcendent dimensions of music are available only within musical possibilities become consciously embodied, music in its performative mode, where an active shaping agency may be bodily received. Ethnomusicologist John Blacking coined a similar notion back in the 1970s with his understanding of music as humanly organized sound *that soundly organizes humanity*,[7] though he only gave it summary attention before his untimely death in 1999.

Receiving music's lessons in primarily embodied fashion myself, I have since learned to become skeptical of "What?" as an interrogative for music. When we view music as a "what," whole swaths of the phenomenon embodied within human consciousness become invisible. We miss the life of the phenomenon that cannot be separated from its sound-based forms, human behaviors, and primarily relational character left implicit. It has taken me years to recognize the disciplinary lens suitable for an investigation of music within its actual parameters

---

6. Ridley, *Philosophy of Music*, 13.
7. Blacking, *How Musical is Man?*, 89ff. Emphasis added.

and realities, of music as humanly organized sound inextricably woven into and able to shape human individuals and communities of practice. Previous forms of this study spoke within the discipline of *practical theology*, an interdisciplinary cohort of theologians working, thinking, contributing to the interpretation of situations in theological praxis.[8] Practical theology describes a multitude of perspectives with performative undertones, though many in the field resist the notion of performance with preference for terms such as *praxis*, practice, *phronēsis*, and action.[9] My persistent investigations have since been welcomed into the academic discipline of Christian spirituality, which offers integrative disciplinary resources beyond those of traditional practical theology. *Learning in a Musical Key* has finally coalesced by means of Christian spirituality's methodological finesse and the clear articulation of self-implication with a horizon of ultimate value required for a study into the role of music in teaching and learning.

Academic Discipline of Christian Spirituality ... for Transformative Learning

"Spirituality" may bring a heavy sigh or rolled eyes within critical discourse, surrounded as it is by popular speculation and self-help volumes aimed at the many fascinations and inconveniences of the human condition. Christian spirituality as academic discipline braves the disdain on behalf of all who yearn for more rigorous, historical-theological-religious resources. Critical suspicion will probably not diminish, considering the term's diverse references within its long history and its popular renditions, but Bernard McGinn has traced the trajectory and potential of "spirituality" in conversation with

---

8. *Praxis* refers to the "purposeful, intentional, and reflectively chosen ethical action" by which "knowing arises through engagement in a social situation." It always includes "twin moments" of action done reflectively and reflection on what is being done. Thus, "knowing arises not from one's inward speculation, but from intentional engagement with and experience of social reality." Groome, *Christian Religious Education*, 152–54. See also his *Sharing Faith, the Way of Shared Praxis*.

9. See Farley, *Theologia*; Browning, *Practical Theology*; Wheeler and Farley, *Shifting Boundaries*; Schweitzer and van der Ven, *Practical Theology*; Chopp, *Saving Work*; Heitink, *Practical Theology*. A more recent volume with musical metaphor is Stevenson-Moessner, *Prelude to Practical Theology*.

other scholars such as Jean Leclerq, Walter Principe, Hans Urs von Balthasar, and Sandra Schneiders.[10]

McGinn places the term's origins within the Hebraic *ruah* or spirit, given further nuance in the Greek *pneuma* (spirit) and *pneumatikos* (spiritual) within foundational Christian documents. The word simply referred to "the quality or condition of being spiritual," as seen in particular behaviors that could be shaped (or misguided) for specific purpose. *Spiritualis*, the Latin translation of *pneumatikos*, occurs 22 times in the Vulgate of Jerome, but the fifth century proffered the record of a noun form, *spiritualitas*, in a letter ascribed to St. Jerome: "Age ut in spiritualitate proficias" ("Act in order to grow in spirituality"). Here the term holds on to its etymological nuances within the original Greek for Christian traditions: "increase your hold on the Spirit of Jesus, the source of the Christian life."[11] The remainder of McGinn's study tracks various evolutions—twelfth century, Scholastic, Old French, seventeenth-century French, then progressively and historically French uses, until arriving in English usage in the early twentieth century. I smiled at the summary given by Gustavo Vinay, an Italian medievalist whom McGinn brings to new attention: spirituality is "a necessary pseudoconcept we don't know how to replace."[12]

Our organizing questions, focused upon learning in music in an enacted mode, lead us to the definition of spirituality articulated by one of the field's primary voices, Sandra M. Schneiders. Spirituality, in her view, is "the actualization of the basic human capacity for transcendence . . . the experience of conscious involvement in the project of life-integration through self-transcendence toward the horizon of ultimate value one perceives."[13] Spirituality here is not a catch-all term for the unclassifiably sacred or the inarticulate mysteries of human experience. Rather it is a conscious and deliberate way of living with integrative knowing, an ongoing project that orients a human being toward growth and learning beyond private gain, toward a perceived good or horizon of value. The definition assumes a "basic human capacity for

---

10. McGinn, "Letter and the Spirit," 26–27. See also LeClercq, "Spiritualitas;" Principe, "Toward Defining Spirituality;" Balthasar, "Spirituality," and Schneiders, "Spirituality in the Academy."

11. McGinn, "Letter and the Spirit," 26.

12. Vinay, "Spiritualità," 706. Cited by McGinn, "Letter and the Spirit," 25.

13. Schneiders, "Approaches to the Study of Christian Spirituality," 16–17.

transcendence," which may (or may not) be actualized in the course of a person's life experience.[14] When it is, there is the problematic for study and continuing research within many fields of human investigation. A concrete expression of spirituality only comes into focus—thus allowing it to become a possibility for critical study—when there is "conscious involvement in the project of life-integration" and "growth." This criterion of *learning* not only distinguishes spirituality from other human pursuits, like addictions, exploitations, aggression or venal concerns with money, power, or pleasure.[15] It is a most compelling criterion for Christian spirituality as disciplinary guide for a study into learning in music. To inquire deeply into how and what human beings may learn within music, musical consciousness, and musical practices, the orienting discipline of inquiry *must* be overtly shaped around questions of self-implication, communal shaping, ultimate values, and mutual learning and integration.

Christian Spirituality, Learning and Integration

Education is a complicated business, of course. This study relies on various nuances of the term and its associates, especially *learning*: learning *from* musical events, learning *in* musical events, and learning *in a musical key*. Each phrase orients learners in a distinct relationship with music in performative mode. They also chart the study's progression from a perspective of objective distance (learning from musical events) toward one in performative mode (learning in musical events) toward an integrated, methodological perspective of theology *in* performative mode (learning in a musical key).

One philosophical overview of education names its processes largely within school contexts, with schools considered to be reproductive agents, agents for social change, and proponents of invitation into the questions of the cosmos.[16] In contrast, this study frames education more

---

14. Wolfhart Pannenberg's "exocentricity," developed from Helmuth Plessner's work, describes this human characteristic as one of the religious impulses observable within the human condition. It refers to human beings' center as something that is simultaneously in their evolved biological form—body—yet also outside of themselves. Pannenberg, *Anthropology in Theological Perspective*, 37ff.

15. Schneiders, "Approaches to the Study of Christian Spirituality," 17.

16. Morris and Pai, *Philosophy of the American School*, 10–18.

within a micro/macro lens of the complex developmental-educational ecologies available for individual learning and growth amidst systemic education.[17] Renown educator John Dewey identifies historical educational thought to be centered in one of two ways. "The history of educational theory is marked by opposition between the idea that education is development from within and that it is formation from without; that it is based upon natural endowments and that education is a process of overcoming natural inclination and substituting in its place habits acquired under external pressure."[18] Broadening historical perspective in helpful fashion for Christian spirituality study, Dewey's sense of education describes development within, by, and for *experience*, understood to be educative if it has the effect of inviting growth toward further experience.[19] Christian spirituality as a discipline wrestles with the (largely hidden) complexities of that word, *experience*, often preferring *consciousness* to describe "new ways of knowing and loving based on states of awareness in which God becomes present in our inner acts, not as an object to be grasped, but as the direct and transforming center of life."[20] As a result, this study leans toward consciousness or awareness when experience arises in description. We cannot avoid the term completely, however. Part of the oral wisdom to come is honoring the *lingua franca*, so to speak, of those with whom musical events lead into transformative learning. Many rely on the word *experience* to describe its performative center.

Theological educator Craig Dykstra crafts a relationship between education and experience well-suited for Christian spirituality in his *Growing in the Life of Faith: Education and Christian Practices*. He identifies education to be "the work of bringing to consciousness the hidden dimensions embedded in and through our actions and relations and institutions, giving these dimensions names, and then helping each

---

17. Bronfenbrenner, *Ecology of Human Development*, 209ff.

18. Dewey, *Experience and Education*, 17.

19. Dewey, *Experience and Education*, 28. Others have referred to Dewey's work as "learning through experience," though learning for him meant the acquisition of what is already incorporated in books and the heads of elders. *Education* incorporates 'learning' and corresponding 'instruction' or 'teaching' into a much more dynamic process of development within, by, and for experience. See Dewey, *Experience and Education*, 19.

20. McGinn, Introduction to *Essential Writing of Christian Mysticism*, xv–xvi.

other take notice and live in their light."[21] He acknowledges that education in faith presupposes and depends upon people's experiences of God, but argues that experience must be distinct. "Education is not the same as experience . . . [although] education is, of course, itself a form of experience."[22] Distinguishing his position somewhat from Dewey, Dykstra describes education as an *investigative* process that guides exploration of experience, a *critical* process that liberates from old patterns of thinking, feeling, or valuing that hinder experience, and a *caring* process through which we invite and are invited to freely explore experience. Instead of aiming toward future experience, Dykstra suggests education to be aimed toward new consciousness, new naming, and new noticing. While education is a form of experience itself, it is not aimed toward experience alone.

Educational perspective for Christian spirituality study aligns well with Dykstra's sense of education. Christian spirituality study aims toward the "actualization of the basic human capacity for transcendence" and the "experience of conscious involvement in the project of life-integration through self-transcendence toward the horizon of ultimate value." *Learning*, at least for Christian spirituality study, refers to what Dykstra would call *investigative-critical* processes exploring both the *material* object of study in the discipline—spirituality as an existential phenomenon—and the *formal* object of study—spirituality as religious experience.[23] The material object, so defined, allows inquiry into an overwhelming diversity of spiritualities expressed within the global community, refusing to universalize any into a descriptive category conditioned by one culture. The formal object focuses critical attention on the lived faith of concrete believing subjects, the "lived experience of the Christian faith." Experience here is not an end to itself or an abstracted object of study, but the *experience of* or *subjective awareness of* a particular person of articulate faith.[24]

Religious consciousness of all kinds re-emerges here as a focus of analytical effort and discriminating interpretation, if only within the artifacts of persons in historical contexts. Christian spirituality focuses

---

21. Dykstra, *Growing in the Life of Faith*, xii.
22. Ibid., xiii.
23. Schneiders, "Approaches to the Study of Christian Spirituality," 16–17.
24. Ibid., 17–18.

its analytical and constructive tools on specific "texts," articulations of particular individuals on their own experience(s) of lived Christian faith. Schneiders brings Paul Ricoeur's imagery to mind when she calls this "the science of the individual,"[25] which opens doors into deeper and deeper understandings of the human condition in every particularity that we have time and effort to research and describe. This is not "spiritual experience" or the human condition as an absolute or universal, but a combination of concrete events and human awarenesses that draws us forward into self-implicating learning toward communally-shaped life-integration.

Furthermore, the sense of *learning* intended here speaks to what Dykstra would call the *caring* dimension of education, though Schneider's "project of life-integration" toward its "horizon of ultimate value" offers broader potential for including both desired and undesired learnings framed by an ultimate value or aim. *Caring* denotes a more static notion too close to "nice" or "enjoyable nurture" for easy reference to the potential disruption in transformative learning from deep investigation and exploration. Caring may intend a kind of "tough love" within it, of course, but the need for clarification here is warrant enough to challenge the term. "The horizon of ultimate value" articulated by Schneiders in her organizing definition establishes an end-state for spirituality's formal study free from emotive referents, free for multidimensional interpretation and invitation toward ultimate value.

For example, the horizon of ultimate value for *Christian* spirituality is described as "the triune God revealed in Jesus Christ to whom Scripture normatively witnesses and whose life is communicated to the believer by the Holy Spirit . . ." Schneiders describes this horizon more concretely to include being made a child of God and living a new life celebrated communally, sacramentally, and in mission in the world toward God's reign.[26] Note the traditional theological formulations *and* the intimate reliance upon a received "new life" that has descriptive shape. Theological specificity *and* particular faith commitment are held together in a critical awareness that is at once self-implicating and historically concrete for collective investigation. An ecological spirituality, let's imagine, would articulate a horizon of ultimate value quite dif-

---

25. Ricoeur, *Interpretation Theory*, 78-79, cited by Schneiders, "Approaches to the Study of Christian Spirituality," 18.

26. Schneiders, "Approaches to the Study of Christian Spirituality," 17.

ferently, of course, with integrity for its contribution to the discipline. One articulation of its horizon of ultimate value could be "the gentle, sustainable care of creation in all its complex biodiversity, allowing the natural, ecological cycles of life, death, and rebirth to evolve within non-human rhythms or preferences."[27] Thus, spirituality becomes particular yet collectively accessible, dependent upon the artifacts of its concrete participants engaged in the project of life-integration toward the horizon of ultimate value.

Robert Kegan's overarching curricular project for modern life provides a helpful lens for viewing Christian spirituality's interrelationship of self-implicating critical study and collective engagement or integration. In his popular text, *In Over Our Heads: The Mental Demands of Modern Life*, Kegan offers an overarching educational perspective for conceiving of learning processes in particular *and* public purview. He invites his readers to imagine North America's contemporary culture as a kind of school, and the complex set of tasks and expectations therein as the "curriculum" of that school. He then suggests that the mental demands of today's "cultural curriculum" require two important things. Each of us needs "a qualitative transformation in the complexity of mind."[28] Through self-transcendence, we are faced with the demands of conscious involvement in life to be transformed or transcended toward a horizon of ultimate value. Second, Kegan argues we need a "transformation that only exists for the individual in a community's collective intelligence."[29] He suggests that this qualitative transformation in mind's complexity only exists for each of us in a community's collective intelligence. Integration therefore means transformation of the individual within the context of a critically shaped, communal investigation. Not only is learning conceived toward a valued end, but the actualization of our capacity for transcendence requires sustained, conscious involvement in intentionally personal and communal interactions. An important methodological contribution by the academic discipline of Christian spirituality toward this sense of integration is a sustained negotiation of self-implication in shared, critical discourse.

27. For recent Christian spirituality contributions with ecological themes, see Frohlich, "Under the Sign of Jonah." A contrasting, interdisciplinary volume is Tucker and Grim, *Worldviews and Ecology*.

28. Kegan, *In Over Our Heads*, 134.

29. Ibid., 134.

Self-Implication

Christian spirituality faces the self-implicating nature of its discourse head on, in some contrast to both (practical) theology and religious studies. "Self-implication" in Christian spirituality allows the intensely personal dimensions of research questions to surface within critical discourse, repeatedly addressed in the methodological and historical-contextual dimensions of its contributions. Schneiders observes, "The only truly critical approach to the knowing process is self-knowledge and honesty about our social location and presuppositions, *and methodological control of their effects*."[30] Scholars must recognize the inherent danger in being personally transformed by their study, in "taking a chance on hearing [one's] name called [by God] at close range." Self-implication in critical inquiry must also be sustained while nevertheless avoiding what Schneiders calls "methodological narcissism"—the attempted use of personal anecdotes as evidence.[31]

The discipline continues to refine its discourse on self-implication, seen in the recent work of another spirituality scholar, Mary Frohlich RSCJ. Within her brief description of Christian spirituality's main concern—"the living and concrete human person in dynamic transformation toward the fullness of life in Christ"[32]—Frohlich calls *critical interiority* the specific methodological principle that guides its interdisciplinary study between the Scylla of uncritical experience and the Charybdis of an objectivity that disregards self-implication. She identifies three methodological implications in critical interiority—what we know, how we know it, and how we deal with events of unknowing "(*démesure*, or "excessiveness")."[33] By this she means that each focus of disciplinary inquiry is not only the item of interest (prayer, artifacts, et al.) but how that item is linked to the lived transformation toward that life's fullness in Christ. What we know in Christian spirituality is both object and a concrete subject's lived consciousness of that object toward fullness. Critical interiority also functions with a sense of mimesis in the case of *how* we know. A scholar can inquire into the lived transformation toward fullness researched in the life of another *if and only if* that

---

30. Schneiders, "Study of Christian Spirituality," 18, emphasis added.
31. Ibid., 20.
32. Frohlich, "Critical Interiority," 77–78.
33. Ibid., 79.

shared consciousness is apprehended and mirrored in the scholar's own life. Frohlich observes this with an impish quip—"it takes one to know one"—but also as a long-standing recognition in the contemplative tradition.[34] Finally, interiority as a methodological principle identifies a fundamental key to understanding transformation in concrete, human lives: "attention to nodal events in which both convicted knowledge and awareness of 'unknowing' are at peak intensity."[35] While these events are not the goal of the spiritual life, they do chart concrete instances of life's fullness as experienced by particular persons in concrete situations, all the while retaining an edge of unknowing or transcendence.

Ultimately, self-implication offers a means for the critique of spiritual phenomena and an honest inclusion of social location and presuppositions into theological or disciplinary inquiry. It establishes a frame in which integration doesn't occur upon conclusion, but is seamlessly a part of critical method, which is a crucial distinction for considering theology in performative mode. Instead of an uncritical tolerance of experience, spirituality scholarship describes a need to discover principles of evaluation within experience and consciousness corresponding to the objective-subject of inquiry. As a scholar's self-awareness and self-knowledge grow, he or she learns to perceive, understand, make judgments, and act toward the fullness of life in both his or her scholarly contributions and in the lived experience of his or her own transformation toward life's fullness. On the one hand, many theological disciplines have disavowed such self-implication as "soft." On the other hand, religious studies habitually takes the self-implication into the private realm of the scholar's personal life, preventing it from informing scholarship. Christian spirituality charts its course in distinction from each of these disciplines, charting renewed ground for historically and theologically-rigorous scholarship that is critically limited by particularity and realistically contextualized for contribution.

Intentionally brief, this disciplinary sketch is well-trodden ground within Christian spirituality scholarship, which has yet to appreciate fully its grounding ballast for contributions to the scholarship of teaching and learning. The discipline's birth and contributions can be seen in the marvelous flowering of fascinating studies and the reissue

---

34. Ibid., 78.
35. Ibid., 80.

of individual volumes of classics in spirituality for contemporary access.³⁶ The centrality of *learning* to this discipline is an under-developed articulation which this study aims to address. Among other contributions, this study intends to show Christian spirituality to be a discipline of transformative learning—first within the scholar, then through the disciplinary community into the world. For the central questions of this book—What does learning from music in a performative mode require, and how does a disciplinary theologian integrate a performative mode into critical discourse?—Christian spirituality offers deeply rooted, historical-theological-anthropological lenses.³⁷

Therefore, this long-standing project is finally conceived as a practical theological contribution to the academic discipline of Christian spirituality. *Learning in a Musical Key* offers a historical, theological examination of learning in music's possibilities and practices, engaged critically as a project of life-integration toward a horizon of ultimate value within Christian traditions. The methodological approach, in Christian spirituality terms, is anthropologically theological, rooted in music's presenting phenomenality: music is within most (if not all) human communities (anthropological) and therefore, for theology's learning, compels historical-theological resourcing for critical disciplinary discourse (theological). The initial result is an interdisciplinary study of learning from music and learning in music. The concluding contribution to theologically disciplinary work is a *contemplative empiricism* within an *artisanal way*, a non-correlational theological method for theology in performative mode shaped by the Chalcedonian formulation and a relational logic of the Spirit palpable in its lived transformative pattern centered around insight. Simultaneously anthropological and theological, required by its origin of music in performative mode, the horizon of ultimate value becomes an expressive theological delight, able to companion the suffering of self and others.

---

36. See Douglas Burton-Christie, *Spiritus: A Journal of Christian Spirituality*. See also *Classics of Western Spirituality* series, edited by Richard J. Payne and the multi-volume work by McGinn, *Presence of God*.

37. Schneiders, "Approaches to the Study of Christian Spirituality," 19–29.

Structure of the Book

The argument opens with a historical inquiry into one composer-theologian's contributions to this problematic before spanning outward into the contemporary challenges and constructive methodological work necessary for disciplinary theologians to learn from music in performative mode. Within the history of Christianity, composer-theologian Hildegard of Bingen (1098–1179) offers an outstanding glimpse into a musical event, theological interpretation, and the crucial importance of music for learning within a historical community of faith. The Interdict of 1178, with her resulting letter to the Prelates at Mainz, constitutes one of the major events of Hildegard's life, as well as a historically accessible glimpse into her lived musical consciousness, given theological interpretation in a text that is available today. An artifact for Christian spirituality study, this letter provides historical-theological resources for learning in music as practiced within a Psalms-centric, Benedictine spirituality.

Even so, Hildegard's historical remove makes her theological interpretation and educational wisdom difficult for today's (post-)modern contexts. One contemporary voice who offers at least two analogous concepts may help. Susanne K. Langer provides a resonant, philosophical voice for understanding Hildegard's thought. Significant, too, is the fact that her work has informed a bulk of theological reflection on music today. Hildegard sees music as first and foremost an incarnate sacramental teaching for lived faith in, and mandated praise of, God made known through *discretio* and *desire* for Jesus Christ in the power of the Spirit—her horizon of ultimate value. Langer's work on mind as *human feeling* and music's primary gift as *insight* gives a more contemporary way to conceive learning amidst music's enacted possibilities. Critical distinctions will be drawn across historical horizons, of course, but such collaboration suggests learning from music in performative mode requires, at the very least, embodied participation in musical activities and a deepening openness to music's unpredictable but assured gift, insight.

Many contemporary challenges emerge when pursuing the contributions of Hildegard and Langer with respect to music and learning in theological discourse. *Chapter Two* addresses a conundrum increasingly present in many North American communities today, especially for scholars of the historical-theological disciplines. Well-established research shows that human musical potential is ubiquitous in the general population. Everyone has at least some musicality, and most have average potential. Yet much of this same population claims to be *nonmusical*, unable to participate in any musical activity, except (perhaps) listening. If these findings are legitimate, then what is required to learn from music when a substantial bulk of a human population professes a lack of musicality or an unwillingness to enter into such learning? Two theorists' works on human musical potential are therefore examined— Edwin Gordon's *music aptitude* and Howard Gardner's *musical intelligence*—in order to assess the claims for normally distributed musical potential and to name any resulting challenges for learning in musical events. We find musicality to be a near-universal in human potential, but one that stabilizes at greater or lesser aptitude by about age ten. Musicality, in other words, is a psychologically-biologically based human potential which, when nourished, results in perceived musicality, but when neglected or stymied before age ten, results in a perceived non-musicality. Challenges and strengths for learning *from* music and learning *in* music, distinct between those who identify as non-musical and those who identify as musical, conclude the chapter.

Chapter Three brings Edwin Gordon's *music learning theory* to bear on the study's central problematic of learning from music in performative mode. Based upon decades of research into how children learn music, Gordon's theory offers a detailed overview of the types, stages, and distinct mode or *world* entailed for human beings to perceive, recognize, and come to understand music. He demonstrates that music learning occurs primarily through the body as a whole and is enacted in various perceptual, unconscious, and conscious activities, including aural perception, imitation, recognition, listening, reading, writing, composing and improvising. Coining the word, *audiation*, Gordon also signals a need for critical distinctions between learning for deep understanding rooted in a mode determined by language and that mode required by music. In contrast to much popular speculation that music is a universal language, Gordon's work compels a renewed investigation of a *performative mode* as a crucial distinction, inaccessible to purely literate investigation. Performative mode is therefore re-examined for a critical appropriation of the term for this study, congruent with Gordon's methodological presuppositions yet theologically shaped for advancing historical-theological scholarship. Guided by the orality studies of Walter J. Ong, S.J., who shares Gordon's methodological presupposition, music's unique integrity or performative mode directs theological discourse toward the potential transformation of consciousness available in a *reflective orality*. Particularly significant for disciplinary theologians, a *performative mode* becomes recognizable through three "marks": primary relationality, explicit embodiment, and irreducible multidimensionality. Such a mode in these terms invites awakening to music as a primarily aural-oral phenomenon, encountered most fruitfully underneath and beyond current (practical) theological and literate habits of mind.

Chapter Four examines one discipline's sustained struggle to articulate (and implement) music's multidimensionality in teaching and learning, finally resolved in the transformative-learning work of educator James E. Loder. Religious education, considered by some to be a sub-discipline of practical theology and by others to be an independent, pluralist discipline of teaching/learning, offers this study an instructive review of twentieth-century contributions to learning *from* music and more recently, learning *in* music. Curricular lenses suggest five facets of music's role within educational theory: *development of cognitive processes, technology* or *method of instruction, consummatory experience* (sometimes called *self-actualization*), *social-relevance* and *social reconstruction*, and lastly, *academic* or *ecclesial rationalism*.[38] As a discipline, religious education continues to wrestle with the objective/subjective captivity of music put to educational ends. In contrast, the transformational logic articulated by educator James Loder moves the study fully into learning *in* music, reliant upon music's primary gift, insight. Similar to the educational wisdom of Hildegard of Bingen, Loder's work forefronts an *embodied* epistemology, enacted through *indwelling* and guided by a pattern or logic of transformation toward one way of learning *in* music. We are reminded that music is an embodied teaching for lived wisdom made known in desire and an openness to its unpredictable but assured gift, insight. Learning *in* music orients participants to the dynamics and dimensions of self-transcendence and a logic or pattern for transformative learning in the project of integration within communal contexts. A fourth "mark" of performative mode emerges

---

38. See Decker and Soltis, *Curriculum and Aims*.

as well: a central role of insight for learning within multidimensional phenomena like music.

Chapter Five offers the methodological fruits of this sustained encounter with music in performative mode toward resolution of the study's second aim—articulating one plausible way for disciplinary theologians to integrate a performative mode into critical discourse. The received insights, ironic as they may be in light of this movement into performative mode, show theology in performative mode with its methodological seeds or marks of *learning in a musical key*, that which is *relationally-formed, explicitly embodied, multidimensional,* and *centered around insight*. In contrast to traditionally critical-correlational methods of practical theology, this spirituality study ends urging a non-correlational theological method called a *contemplative empiricism* within an *artisanal way*. With disciplinary tasks extended beyond interpretation and right action, this method has been shaped through contemplative inquiry toward self-transcendence in compassionate companionship, all of which points to a deeply theological yet non-sectarian horizon of ultimate value: an expressive theological delight able to companion the suffering of self and others.

As practical theological contribution to the academic discipline of Christian spirituality, this method honors the anthropological and theological impulses within critical discourse on music directed toward a deeper understanding of how disciplinary theologians may learn from (and in) music in its performative mode. The study as a whole re-orients contemporary theological disciplines away from any systematic approach to theological method and instead, toward a methodological commitment to relationally-formed, explicitly embodied transformation of the self, one person at a time. Ultimately a trinitarian method, rooted in the relationality of God made known in Chalcedonian christological formulation, this anthropological-theological study urges the expressive theological delight, rooted in but not constrained by religious identity. Music as an intimate and global phenomenon allows nothing less.

These historical-theological resources, guided by the discipline of Christian spirituality into a contemplative empiricist method, have placed this scholar gently within concrete lives (those in history and her own), with contributions brought to bear on the human capacity for transcendence and the yearning for fulfillment in an expressive delight able to companion suffering. There, at the wellspring of human awareness shared between the critically reflective scholar and communities of wisdom, we begin to see again that classical theology unto enacted wisdom *has* been rooted in a performative mode. A musical key simply makes it newly palpable for literate, (post-)modern minds today.

Music Defined or (at Least) Confessed

In order to clarify what is meant by "music" in these pages, a preliminary definition—or better, a confession of the sense developed here—will help. My first sense of music grew out of a Pennsylvania-Deutsch and Irish heritage, in which table grace was sung and one learned to play at least one instrument for communal performance and expressive achievement. Classical music meant the historic repertoire that my father enjoyed. The flute was a primary choice of instrument for community performances by my mother. My instruments were piano and French horn, though eventually voice became my main instrument of musical expression. As I got more interested and encountered new communities and settings, a new choral repertoire emerged in my experience of corporate worship in which we sang classical choral works of Bach, Brahms, Mendelssohn, and more. Music had always been a participatory activity in my experience, and largely Western and tonal in constitution. Then I heard a Tuvan throat-singer. I heard the creativity of two African-American young men, improvising rap on the subway train. Then . . . then . . . then . . . As I became theologically interested, I realized that there was an overwhelming diversity of music, better understood as musics, plural.[39] While I continue to learn a practiced openness to new musics, my conditioned recognition remains largely tonal and Western, with a fascination for global sound and song.

Musical-Historical Perspectives

When I was drawn into musical-theological research, I first looked to those who would know from the inside how to talk or write about music. Igor Stravinsky's *Poetics of Music* opened my eyes and ears, literally: I both see and hear differently because of his recorded composi-

---

39. Begbie, *Resounding Truth*, 29–30.

tions and his prose. He opens a lecture on the phenomenon of music with the great delight experienced in the sounds of nature that are yet only "promises of music."[40] Music actually requires a human being, in his view: "a human being who is sensitive to nature's many voices . . . who . . . feels the need of putting them in order . . ."[41] I then moved to understanding this organization of sound within my own community, through biblically and theologically informed discourse about music in scripture, historical witness, and worship. James McKinnon's classical compilation, *Music in Early Christian Literature*, offers a thorough sampling of scriptural and patristic sources citing music, song, psalm-singing, and musical instruments.[42] But is that the music of ancient Christianity? Well, yes and no. It is a lens, but no real sense of the music as it was. As Stravinsky observes, "We lack an indispensable element of investigation: namely, the sensation of music itself."[43] The closest we can come is a comparison between an archaeological record and the textual sources in antiquity.[44] For biblical music as music—the ancient music of early religious communities—is simply gone.

The historical tension between the "literature of music," whatever that might mean, and the music itself can also be seen in two volumes offering a broad historical perspective on music within the church. Paul Westermeyer, a professor of church music and a recognized church musician within Christian worship settings, offered a first volume on the church and music, or *Te Deum*, which "was stimulated by the need to understand church music itself."[45] Music within theological communities appeared to mean "church music." Pair that volume with his more recent *Let the People Sing: Hymn Tunes in Perspective*, and one immediately becomes aware of the complexity of looking at music as it is within any living community. How *does* one keep historical record of something like ordered sound within diverse communities over time? Organizing a study of such a phenomenon is difficult and lengthy enough—just looking at the 2,787 tunes within fourteen

40. Stravinsky, *Poetics of Music in the Form of Six Lessons*, 23.
41. Ibid.
42. McKinnon, *Music in Early Christian Literature*.
43. Stravinsky, *Poetics of Music*, 26.
44. Braun, *Music in Ancient Israel/Palestine*.
45. Westermeyer, *Te Deum*, ix.

hymnals of English-speaking, Anglo-European churches in North America.[46] "Church music" also has a felt-specificity amidst increasing but hidden diversity of practice. What a congregation considers music appropriate for its worship life varies dramatically, often from practices within classical nuance and organ instrumentation and/or choral performance to those of communities who rely on other musical styles amplified and with a beat, which is how Brian Wren defines "contemporary music."[47] Robin Leaver urges a sense of "liturgical worship" to push critical reflection beyond the limitations of "church music." In an edited compilation on liturgy and music, he defines liturgical music as "the music of worship in the Judeo-Christian tradition, the *Gebrauchsmusik* (functional music) of the gathered congregation at worship." He surveys other operative terms, all attempting to broaden the narrower "church music," including religious music, sacred music, pastoral music, ritual music, Christian ritual music, and liturgical music.[48] Meanwhile, Linda Clark's study, *Music in Churches*, actually brings our attention back to music within local faith communities as "a very ordinary phenomenon" that "relies on the voices of people who sing and play music in church."[49] We get closer once again to music as that which requires human beings to give it form and which requires ordinary sensation in order to be investigated.

Theological Perspectives

Theological views on music in this broader vein vary from the metaphorical to the more systematic. Liturgical theologian Don Saliers identifies music as "the language of the soul made audible," an image that encourages a complex interplay between human speech, spiritual yearning, and an utter physicality of sound and sensation—what he calls a "synesthetic matrix." However music may have been understood within an earlier theological view, it involves body, mind, and spirit— or soul, in Saliers's theological anthropology. The image is not simply metaphorical for poetic beauty, however. Saliers's second thesis is that

---

46. Westermeyer, *Let the People Sing*.
47. Wren, *Praying Twice*, 131.
48. Leaver, "What is Liturgical Music?," 211–19.
49. Clark, *Music in Churches*, v.

music as ordered sound "is intimately related to the narrative quality of human experience, presenting our temporality in symbolic form, but always sensually and bodily perceived."[50] Music offers in its practice, in our hearing, in our shared participation, a pattern of contextual and particular lived experience. It weaves a soundtrack alongside the stories of our lives, connecting at points of celebration or lament, entertainment or work. I am reminded of the hymn that brings back memories of a loved one's funeral, the political silliness around "The Macarena" in 1994, the national song of the civil rights' movement "We Shall Overcome," and the eased experience of hard work when songs are shared.[51] Music, particularly song, is intimately related to the "narrative quality of human experience."[52] More recently, Saliers has aligned his understanding of music as a human practice, something "sounded by voices and/or instruments by means of a disciplined set of embodied skills."[53] This broader frame of reference emerges from moral theory, specifically the work of Alasdair MacIntyre, which was developed by many in the theological disciplines to better articulate theology as "a way of life for a searching people."[54]

The first theologian cited here, Jeremy Begbie, began to reorient musical-theological scholarship with his recognition in *Theology, Music and Time* that music has the staying power and potential to advance theological scholarship. The traditional approach shows theologians working to reveal particular aspects of the sacred in music, interpreted within theological categories.[55] Begbie, however, begins a wonderful and quite fruitful reversal of that trend. Music is not interpreted theologically. Instead, music, in its own constitution and performative mode, challenges theological scholarship. Begbie too describes music as a practice "or better, a multiplicity of practices."[56] His use of the term is much more general than the MacIntyrean–Bass–Volf tradition of thought, suggesting that his approach may be more fruitful

50. Saliers, "Sound Spirituality," 334, 336, 338.

51. Gioia, *Work Songs*.

52. See Crites, "Narrative Quality of Experience," 291–311.

53. Saliers, *Music and Theology*, xi. See also Saliers and Saliers, *A Song to Sing, a Life to Live*.

54. Bass, *Practicing Our Faith*; Volf and Bass, *Practicing Theology*.

55. See, for example, Blackwell, *Sacred in Music*.

56. Begbie, *Theology, Music and Time*, 5.

in the end. Begbie reminds us that, at root, music requires two "interlocking and mutually informative procedures: those which engender music—*music-making*, and those of perception—*music-hearing*."[57] He returns us once again to music as the elemental act(s) of making and receiving sounds. Such embodiment requires a rather intense relationship with time and space, of course. "Time is intrinsically bound up with music's sounds," he observes. "Musical sounds 'pull the strings' of the temporality 'in which' they occur."[58] He notes music's formative agency present within an explicitly performative mode. His work opens new avenues for critical inquiry into theology's practice and what its performative mode may entail.

Religious Studies and Ethnomusicological Perspectives

Across the methodological-disciplinary divide between theology and religious studies, Robin Sylvan offers an ethnographic study of the religious dimensions of popular music with a similar emphasis upon music's performative mode. Drawing on Ninian Smart's model of the seven dimensions of religion, he names the *multidimensionality* of religion, centered on the numinous as the primary ordering structure for human beings. At the conclusion of his theoretical analysis of music (to be examined in more detail below), he emphasizes that each of the dimensions of religion and music take place in the experiential state, which is "a unique, phenomenological and ontological mode of being-in-the-world in which the subject–object, body–mind, and spiritual–material dualities are transcended in a unified field. In this state, the body is the central locus through which experiential integration occurs."[59] No longer is music solely an object with causal or corresponding influences upon human experience; it is a phenomenon whose performative mode invites a particular way of being in the world in which dualities are somehow transcended. Sylvan's work moves religious studies scholars, and I dare say theologians and Christian spirituality scholars, to broach concrete musical experience not as a quagmire of objectivistic captivity but as a continuously fruitful locus for critical study in music through

57. Ibid., 9.
58. Begbie, *Theology, Music and Time*, 26.
59. Sylvan, *Traces of the Spirit*, 5, 43. "Numinous" here refers to Otto, *Idea of the Holy*.

which transcendence and transformational learning repeatedly manifest themselves in human sensation within the human body as a whole.

With this epistemological-ontological commitment, Sylvan argues that music is a "vehicle par excellence" for the transformation of experience and for carrying "the religious impulse."[60] Simply put, just as religion is multidimensional, so music functions simultaneously at many different levels, which embodied consciousness may serve to integrate into a coherent whole. In his words, "Music is one of the most powerful tools for conveying religious meaning known to humankind" because it, like religion, "is capable of functioning simultaneously at many different levels (physiological, psychological, sociocultural, virtual, ritual, and spiritual) and integrating them into a coherent whole."[61] While important distinctions remain to be drawn between his use of "experience" that integrates and the embodied consciousness that comes through the critically reflective task of transformative learning, Sylvan does set the stage to understand music in the breadth and depth of an ethnomusicological perspective, clearly rooted in basic biological, psychological, societal, and cultural social-scientific categories.

Both Begbie and Sylvan refer to an earlier voice within musicological research, impossible to omit even as his voice blends more and more with contemporary ethnomusicology today. A founding voice in ethnomusicology was John Blacking, who described music as *humanly organized sound that soundly organizes humanity*. He thus gave the sociocultural and contextual study of music a dialectical phrasing, rooted in modern sociological-anthropological categories and brought into concrete expression within his studies of the Venda people of southern Africa. He identified the analytical task in ethnomusicology with respect to these categories in his *How Musical is Man?*, with priority on music as a primarily relational or social phenomenon, pregnant with the recognized dimensions of being human in biological, psychological, sociological, and cultural terms. Music is

> a product of the behavior of human groups, whether formal or informal: it is humanly organized sound. And, although different societies tend to have different ideas about what they regard as music, all definitions are based on some consensus

---

60. Sylvan, *Traces of the Spirit*, 5.
61. Ibid., 6.

of opinion about the principles on which the sounds of music should be organized.

His structural-functional framework can be seen here as well:

> At some level of analysis, all musical behavior is structured, whether in relation to biological, psychological, sociological, cultural, or purely musical processes; and it is the task of the ethnomusicologist to identify all processes that are relevant to an explanation of musical sound.[62]

Music, for Blacking in his early work, refers to a primarily societal phenomenon with implicit structural dimensions somehow rooted in the human body. As he observes, "many, if not all, of music's essential processes may be found in the constitution of the human body and in patterns of interaction of human bodies in society." But "[m]usic can never be a thing in itself . . . in the sense that music cannot be transmitted or have meaning without associations between people . . ."[63] Nevertheless, while music is a behavioral and societal product of human groups, musical phenomena are essentially biological—with essential processes found in the physicality of the individual human body—and psychological—with essential processes also found in the patterns of interaction of human bodies in society.

Lastly, his sense of music also refers to a cultural phenomenon of significance and associations between people: it is a societal, biological, psychological, and cultural phenomenon that unifies the objectively perceived sound with its human organizers and the subjectively perceived organizers with their ordered sound. Some ethnomusicologists within Blacking's discipline have extrapolated this sense of music to "music-cultures," or "a group of people's total involvement with music."[64] While helpful in its broadening scope, this sense of music overemphasizes the cultural dimension of humanly organized sound, almost to the exclusion of all other dimensions. Such imperialism by cultural studies is coming under substantial criticism from ethnomusicologists in Blacking's heritage.[65] The more contemporary contributions within

---

62. Blacking, *How Musical is Man?*, 10, 17.
63. Ibid., x, xi.
64. Slobin and Titon, "Music-Culture as a World of Music," 1.
65. See especially Kuckertz, "Introduction: The Problem," 1–7; and Philipp, *Ethnomusicology and the Historical Dimension*.

religious studies perspectives show the continuing validity and influence of Blacking's ethnomusicological perspective on music.

Brief overview of Robyn Sylvan's first four categories in *Traces of the Spirit* shows this reliance upon Blacking's work and fleshes out their significance for understanding music in performative mode. The *physiological* level of music attends to the most fundamental level for inquiry into music as physical vibration and its effects on the physiology of the human body. The *psychological* level notes both the inadequacy of looking at music in purely emotional-affective terms and the contributions of psychological models for understanding music at various levels of human consciousness. The *sociocultural* level examines music's impact within social and group contexts, which is also where Sylvan places John Blacking's initial definition. Sylvan's *semiological* level of music within human experience explores the "complex process of symbolization, or signification, in which structured musical patterns come to be associated with particular resonant meanings."[66] All four dimensions so far sketch the familiar terrain within Blacking's later work, though distinctions and divergences could certainly be offered in more depth than space allows here.

Sylvan's additional categories—virtual, ritual, and spiritual—draw us onward, as they reflect the important contributions of more contemporary resources that were not so readily available to Blacking. *Virtual*, in Sylvan's work, refers to "the world one enters into and through the computer screen, a virtual world not bound by the rules of the physical universe . . ."[67] For musicological scholarship exploring the "worlds of music,"[68] the virtual level of music names the ability of music to create a world with unexpected and ephemeral interrelationships between space, time, and form—a world that is hinted at in Begbie's recognition of music's shaping of temporality. *Ritual*, as Sylvan uses it to describe a dimension of musical experience, refers to the now-established discipline of ritual studies, an area of contribution on "the universality of rites of passage for transitions from one phase of life to the next; the three stages of separation, liminality, and reintegration; and notions of

---

66. Sylvan, *Traces of the Spirit*, 29. See also Langer, *Philosophy in a New Key*, in which symbolization *is* the new key of philosophical discourse in her era.

67. Sylvan, *Traces of the Spirit*, 29

68. Slobin and Titon, "Music-Culture as a World of Music," 1.

structure, antistructure, and communitas."⁶⁹ This level speaks loudly in many of the studies of music in adolescent development, for instance. Music seems to have a holding pattern or logic of development in which identities may be experienced in their felt sense, then let go as the musical styles and preferences change. This level of music, when examined, gives compelling interpretation to the ease of musical use by marketing professionals to hone in on adolescents' identities as they shift in developmental predictability.⁷⁰ Lastly, Sylvan articulates his sense of the *spiritual* dimension of music with an analysis of Rudolph Otto's work, complemented by more recent Western views, and then compelling African and Eastern views, steeped in cosmologies far removed from the Western, Enlightenment mentality. Sylvan's contribution, ultimately, is a critical reminder of music's multidimensionality with each dimension in active and overlapping interrelationship with others.

Conclusion

In sum, any critical study of music faces the task of defining its object of inquiry, even as the integrity of music, in all its diversities, is then transgressed. The discipline of Christian spirituality offers a refreshing and rigorous alternative to this conundrum of musical study, a critical investigation that is articulate in its specification of material and formal objects of study *and* engaged with a self-implicating method toward integration and a horizon of ultimate value. Music as an object *and* as an inextricably communal phenomenon, a concrete-ephemeral object of study *and* a subjective force with a shaping agency all its own, finds full expression for renewed critical theological inquiry, resourced by ethnomusicology and, as we proceed, by music education and religious educational theory. As humanly organized sound that soundly organizes humanity, music may finally begin to advance theological scholarship in its compelling, irrepressibly performative mode.

Literary critic George Steiner offers a poetic argument well-suited to our purpose and conclusion. He places music as the central pin in his wager on transcendence titled *Real Presences*. Music is "central to the

69. Sylvan, *Traces of the Spirit*, 35.

70. See Erikson, *Identity and the Life Cycle*; Ritson and Elliott, "The Social Uses of Advertising: An Ethnographic Study of Adolescent Advertising Audiences," 260–77; McKee and Pardun, "Reading the Video," 110–22.

meanings of man, or man's access to or abstention from metaphysical experience," he writes. It withholds or shapes transcendence, the learning beyond form which is transformation. "In music form is content, content form. Music is at once cerebral in the highest degree . . . and it is at the same time somatic, carnal and a searching out of resonances in our bodies at levels deeper than will or consciousness."[71] Music, in this kind of performative mode, brings us repeatedly face-to-face with the human limitation and particularity necessary if transcendence and transformation are to be bodily-contextualized, real.

> The final paradox which defines our humanity prevails: there is always, there always will be, a sense in which we do not know what it is we are experiencing and talking about when we experience and talk about that which is. There is a sense in which no human discourse, however analytic, can make final sense of sense itself.[72]

In his view, music in ephemeral yet embodied form continues to teach all those willing to listen and learn. It invites the release of valued truths in order to gain new perspectives on those same truths. Here we remember: the task is ultimately not understanding, which will always be preliminary, but *learning within sense*, critical inquiry within a self-implicating, communally-shaped, and receptive embodiment that makes conceivable the deepest wellsprings of life in all its transformations and fullness.

This study, with its cohort of scholars, pursues such penultimate, critical theory toward transformational learning within sense: an embodied, relational path of indwelt contemplative inquiry toward insight, made palpable within musical awareness. This reiterative method urges contemporary theology toward its perichoretic awakening to performative mode. Steiner's words:

> Music makes utterly substantive what I have sought to suggest of the real presence. . . where that presence cannot be analytically shown or paraphrased. Music brings to our daily lives an immediate encounter with a logic of sense other than that of reason.[73]

As we began, so introductions end. In the historical-theological disciplines, we have much to learn from music in its performative mode.

71. Steiner, *Real Presences*, 6, 217.
72. Ibid., 215.
73. Ibid., 218.

Hildegard of Bingen and the Letter to the Prelates at Mainz

Historical-Theological Resources for Learning from Music

WITHIN CHRISTIAN HISTORY, ONE THEOLOGIAN-COMPOSER STANDS out for historical-theological wisdom for conceiving of learning in music, its activities, its particular way of life. Hildegard of Bingen (1098–1179) presents us with an overwhelmingly complex portrait of a visionary leader, woman of privilege, Benedictine abbess, theologian, composer-musician, and, ultimately, a force to be reckoned with in the twelfth-century renaissance.[1] Rare is the historically-recognized theologian who is *also* acclaimed for a substantial record of musical composition. Given her historical legitimation, reclaimed and renewed in the last fifteen years upon the 900th anniversary of her birth, she offers promising theological contribution for understanding learning in music from a theologian who is also a composer.

Her medieval location, however, complicates contemporary interpretation with the challenge of disparate historical horizons. Hildegard sees music as a triune, incarnate teaching for lived faith in, and mandated praise of, God made known through *discretio* and *desire* for Jesus

---

1. See Pernoud, *Hildegard of Bingen*; Blumenfeld-Kosinski, *Poets, Saints, and Visionaries of the Great Schism, 1378–1417*; Newman, *Sister of Wisdom*; Newman, *Voice of the Living Light*; and Madigan, *Mystics, Visionaries and Prophets*. For second-wave critical view, see also King-Lenzmeier, *Hildegard of Bingen*.

Christ in the enfleshed power of the Spirit. What might that say for contemporary understanding today? What does learning in music entail within that theological interpretation? A surprising dance-partner emerges in Susanne K. Langer, a classical philosophical voice of the mid-twentieth century who has informed a bulk of contemporary theological reflection on music. Langer's magnum opus, *Mind: an Essay on Human Feeling*, expands conceptualizations of *human mentality* as *human feeling*. Her *Philosophy in a New Key* argues for the significance of music whose primary gift is *insight*. Not only will a retrieval of Langer's work clarify contemporary theological reliance upon her work, it may lend perspective for Hildegard's historically inaccessible contributions. A creative interplay between these two voices on desire and feeling, discretio and insight, offers a contemporary sense of Hildegard's wisdom in her letter to the prelates at Mainz. After critical distinctions are drawn, we find that learning from music in performative mode, at the very least, requires a participatory, embodied awareness and a deepening openness to unexpected insight.

Historical Background

Hildegard was born in 1098 as the tenth child of a Rhenish nobleman, Hildebert of Bermersheim, and his wife, Mechthild. Respectful to tradition, her parents offered her to God as a tithe in 1106 by giving her into the care of Jutta, an anchoress in religious seclusion near the recently founded monastery of St. Disibod in what is now Germany. Under Jutta's extremely ascetic tutelage, Hildegard became familiar with the Latin Psalter—the center of monastic prayer—and with other books of the Bible. She took to the religious life with relative ease,[2] though her health was always frail and she was touched from infancy by her exceptional gift of *visio*, an unusual and sometimes painful perception of hidden things seen through a radiance she referred to as "the living Light." Upon the death of Jutta in 1136, she was appointed *magistra* and took over the administration and education of her community of faith.

---

2. There is some dispute whether Hildegard took her primary vow as an anchoress before electing to live in community within Benedict's Rule, but, regardless, historical consensus suggests that she took religious vows sometime between 1112 and 1115. She is understood as the founder and first abbess of the Benedictine community of women at Bingen. Newman, "Introduction," in Hildegard, *Scivias*, 9.

Hildegard was fascinated with and wrote extensively about the natural world in which she was immersed. She was dismayed at the need for clergy reform in the Church and yet served within it dutifully as abbess and servant of the Holy Father. She sought wisdom from the "living Light" on behalf of the multitudes who made their way to her doorstep for counsel. She was summoned to and unexpectedly debated with popes who were disarmed by her compelling humility and theological authority. Historian Peter Dronke notes that Hildegard could be seen as stubborn, combative, and willful unto domination. Sometimes she used her illnesses and visionary gift as a weapon to defend her own interests against those of others. He notes her apparent snobbishness in refusing women of poor means into her convent, stemming from the correspondence with her colleague Tengswich of Andernach, who had questioned such exclusiveness. "In short," Dronke writes, "Hildegard could blind herself."[3] She is most popularly known today, however, for her extensive collection of musical chants and responses, or perhaps her primary theological text, *Scivias*, which is short for *Know the Ways of the Lord*, a collection of her visions and corresponding illuminations in theological commentary.[4]

The interdict of 1178–79 constituted one of the major events of Hildegard's life, as well as the impetus for what Dronke calls her greatest letter, written to the prelates at Mainz.[5] The letter not only provides an artifact for Christian spirituality study into the importance of music within a faith community. It also gives us a glimpse of Hildegard as abbess, musician, and theologian, living toward the fullness she perceived amidst a particular historical event of conflict and advocacy.

In 1178, when she was in her eightieth year, she permitted and participated in the burial of a certain nobleman (unknown to us by name) in the consecrated ground of Mount St. Rupert. The dead nobleman had, at one time, been excommunicated. There remained some question as to whether he had been absolved from that status and truly welcomed back into the fold. While the archbishop was away in Rome serving as mediator between Frederick Barbarossa and Pope Alexander III, the prelates of Mainz ordered Hildegard to have the corpse exhumed

---

3. Dronke, *Women Writers of the Middle Ages*, 200.
4. Hildegard, *Scivias*. See also Fox, *Illuminations of Hildegard of Bingen*.
5. Hildegard, "Letter 23," 76–80.

or to fall under pain of excommunication along with her community. Looking to the living Light, she understood her call to be one of refusal to exhume the corpse. As a result, she and her community were placed under ecclesiastical interdict for failure to obey the prelates' orders. Submitting to Church authority, Hildegard and her community abstained from singing the divine praises and from monthly participation in the Mass, as had been their practice. In this context of silenced song and ecclesial exclusion, Hildegard reflected on music and its activities in the formative life of her community. She wrote a most well-known letter in response to this interdict, to argue against it with scriptural and theological authority. The struggle lasted for at least six months and the interdict was lifted only a couple months before Hildegard's death on September 17, 1179.

Hildegard's Worldview: Medieval, Benedictine, Ecclesiastical

Hildegard's frame of reference for understanding music emerged from a medieval context and worldview largely incomprehensible to modern or postmodern sensibilities, though not for lack of effort by contemporary voices.[6] Pythagorean thought, transmitted to the medieval world via the work of Boethius, taught that the human body and soul are structurally united by musical harmony.[7] In this worldview, there are three kinds of music: *musica mundana*, *musica humana*, and *musica instrumentalis*. *Musica mundana* refers to the well-known harmony of the spheres, an inaudible "music" that is produced by the motion of the celestial bodies and that orders the elements and seasons of creation. It bears clear observation: this kind of music is not listened to by the ears, but is a liberal art or science for inquiry, contemplation, theoria. The second kind of music, *musica humana*, is also inaudible and refers to that which binds the rational to the irrational part of the soul and both parts of the soul to the body. Unification and harmonization constitute it, intuited and comprehensible in human understanding. *Musica*

---

6. Fraser, *Music of the Spheres*; much more recently, see James, *Music of the Spheres*; Tame, *Secret Power of Music*; Godwin, *Harmony of the Spheres* and *Harmonies of Heaven and Earth*.

7. Boethius, *De institutione musica*, cited in Newman, "Introduction," in Hildegard, *Symphonia*, 18–19.

instrumentalis, the third kind, refers to the *audible*, organized sound made by humans in human groups. Hildegard names a fourth kind of music, called *musica celestis*: that which is inspired and enfleshed in the Garmented Word of God, manifest in human fullness and divine glory in the heavenly chorus.[8] This medieval worldview undergirds Hildegard's advocacy for music, conceived in all four kinds only within the Church, and described by her as the Garment of the Word of God, a divinely human reflection of celestial harmony through which the symphonic soul is able to reach God in active praise.

More recent literature brings a fascinating perspective to this medieval worldview, centered creatively and prophetically by Hildegard in *embodiment* and *desire*, specifically the female body and the shared desire for God. Bruce Holsinger and Heidi Epstein are the primary theological voices interpreting Hildegard's worldview in this manner. Holsinger identifies Hildegard as the medieval figure "whose work most thoroughly and intensively reflects an awareness of music's corporeality."[9] He traces this theme through Hildegard's written and musical compositions to argue her own conception of the body and its central role in religious devotion.[10] The important distinction here is Holsinger's argument for moving beyond the disciplinary boundaries of traditional medieval musicology, for listening to Hildegard's compositions within *yet beyond* the classical understanding of music in her era. He writes,

> Despite the pervasive somatic significance Hildegard gave to music . . . most studies of her compositions have neglected to examine them as embodiments of her visionary experience, devotional practice, and Christian theology. Instead, scholars have focused primarily on the music's formal attributes without considering the abbess's religious experience, gendered identity, social milieu, and the enormous influence all must have had on her musical creativity.[11]

Hildegard's worldview undergirds her contributions to our understanding of music's teaching/learning roles today, but her own musical and

---

8. See Slocum, "Harmony of Celestial Revelations," in Davidson, *Wisdom Which Encircles Circles*, 82. See also Newman, "Introduction," in Hildegard, *Symphonia*, 20.

9. Holsinger, "Flesh of the Voice," 96.

10. See Holsinger, *Music, Body, and Desire in Medieval Culture*.

11. Holsinger, "Flesh of the Voice," 98–99.

theological compositions move beyond the traditional perspectives on that worldview. More recently, Heidi Epstein has confirmed this trend in Hildegard studies. She relies on her as both resource and norm toward a feminist theology of music because Hildegard, steeped in Boethius's musical-mathematical worldview as she was, nevertheless inverted the Neo-Platonic abstractions and rooted music's theological power in the flesh and in divine breath. "Boethius recognized humanity's essential musicality," Epstein writes, "but metaphysically disembodied this principle in the name of God. By contrast, Hildegard's thoroughly musical conception of the *imago dei* transfuses Word with flesh."[12]

Hildegard's frame of reference for reflecting on music in teaching and learning undoubtedly relies upon the medieval cosmology so prevalent within classical scholarship. However, it is significant for our interest in learning from music in its performative mode that Hildegard also challenges our conceptions of the classically medieval worldview. For Hildegard, this worldview shaped thought and action from the primary site of listening, growth, insight, and understanding: the *human body* and *a desire for God* shared in praise.

Benedictine

Hildegard's musical compositions, illuminations, and writings also come to us from within a monastic spirituality, informed by the Rule of St. Benedict.[13] Many resources offer insight into Benedictine spirituality in historical and contemporary perspectives,[14] but two contemporary voices—those of Laura Swan and Joan Chittister—offer both continuity of historical view and contemporary wisdom.

Benedictine spirituality originates from more than 1500 years of wrestling with the challenges of human life in conversation with and guided by a small text, the Rule of St. Benedict, written by Benedict of

---

12. Epstein, *Melting the Venusberg*, 122.

13. Benedict of Nursia, *Rule of St. Benedict*. See Hildegard, *Explanation of the Rule of Benedict*.

14. See McDonnell, *Benedictine Approach to Lay Spirituality*; Ryelandt, *Quest for God* and *Union with Christ*; Faulkner, "Participation in Being Loved by God"; Chittister, *Rule of St. Benedict*; Stewart, *Prayer and Community*; de Waal, *Living with Contradiction* and de Waal and Norris, *Seeking God*; Marett-Crosby, *Benedictine Handbook*; and Casey, *Unexciting Life*.

Nursia (480–ca. 550) sometime between 530 and 550 CE. Built upon but in contrast to the desert monasticism of his day, Benedict's rule centered in the virtues of *humility* and *hospitality*. "Benedict's humility is about getting really real, becoming increasingly authentic and dropping pretenses and facades," according to Swan. It comes out of the desert monastic tradition but focuses upon a person's journey toward purity of heart: "As we grow in humility, we come to know and understand ourselves as individuals, in community, as members of the human family, and before God."[15] In complementary fashion, *hospitality* opens the human heart to all in communal practices of welcome, wonder, and invitation. A communal virtue, hospitality encourages a receptivity to all as Christ. It deepens engagement beyond the self and leads each person back to a community within which humility may grow. Humility and hospitality therefore challenge and nourish each other. As Swan interprets it, "The common life shapes our hearts: the natural rubbing of edges, learning from one another, and the burden of bearing one another invites us to cultivate inner detachment and to find Christ in our fellow monastics."[16] Within Benedictine tradition, Hildegard's spirituality likewise revolved around this alchemy of individual and communal life in encounter with God made known in Christ in the power of the Spirit. Historical scholarship into Hildegard's spirituality identifies the foundational monastic virtues manifest in her work to be the fear of the Lord, poverty of spirit or humility, obedience, and discretion.[17] Chittister gives these virtues contemporary relevance and understanding by placing them in active or performative mode—listening, prayer and *lectio*, and relationship.[18] It is here in performative mode that we can relate these virtues across historical horizons into our own contexts for understanding.

Listening to four primary realities—the Gospels, the Rule of St. Benedict, one another, and the world—ferments spiritual growth for Benedictines, in Chittister's view.[19] The centrality of listening within Hildegard's spirituality is manifest both in her pervasive musical

---

15. Swan, *Benedictine Tradition*, xix, xx, xvii, ix.
16. Ibid., xviii.
17. Newman, "Introduction," in Hildegard, *Scivias*, 19.
18. Chittister, *Wisdom Distilled From the Daily*, esp. chs 2–4.
19. Ibid., 15.

compositions for her community's prayer and in her own words as a visionary. Again and again, she attests to *hearing* words in her visions.[20] Instead of the expected images within a vision, Hildegard *heard* their significance for guidance. This primary posture of listening, even for a visionary, shaped the life of prayer and lectio as well. Prayer is the "center and centrifuge of life" within Benedictine monasticism. It is regular, universal, converting, reflective, and communal.[21] It is lived out in fixed times of prayer with the Divine Office and Eucharist. As such, listening, prayer and lectio provide a sense of connection to both micro- and macrocosms, personal and communal interrelationships in God's creation. As Chittister cites Benedict's Rule in light of its theology of community, "'The most valiant kind of monk,' Benedict writes in a culture of hermits, 'is not the solitary or the pseudoascetic or the wandering beggar but 'the cenobite' (RB 1:12), the one who has learned to live with others in community."[22] Benedictine spirituality here lives its gift into the world, the primacy of relationship within which all spiritual growth and conversion of spirit occurs. Chittister ultimately describes Benedictine spirituality—Hildegard's spirituality—as one of *awareness*, lived into form through listening, prayer and lectio, and the relationship of common life. Hildegard's advocacy for the fear of the Lord, humility (poverty of spirit), obedience and discretion become more comprehensible when viewed in such performative mode. Hildegard's life and thought would have been Benedictine to the core.

Ecclesiastical

Hildegard's ecclesiastical roles contextualize her diverse contributions to this study as well. Barbara Newman identifies the most crucial ones to be Hildegard as Gregorian reformer, apocalyptic preacher, and Benedictine abbess.[23] Two of these roles, reformer and preacher, frame much of her correspondence and theological contribution to the larger ecclesiastical ecology, significant for the "Letter to the Prelates at Mainz."

20. Hildegard, *Scivias*, "Declaration," 59, and "Vision 13," 525; Hildegard, "Sixth Vision," in *Hildegard of Bingen's* Book of Divine Works *with Letters and Songs*, edited by Fox, 178. See also Caviness, "Artist," in Newman, *Voice of the Living Light*, 110–24.
21. Chittister, *Wisdom Distilled From the Daily*, 29ff.
22. Ibid., 40.
23. Newman, "Introduction," in Hildegard, *Scivias*, 19–22.

They also give ample correction to some popularized misperceptions about Hildegard. She lived and taught and argued *within* ecclesiastical order and the importance of history, not beyond it from some desire to eradicate ecclesiastical authority, which appears in vogue today. Her role as an abbess meant that she shouldered primary responsibility for the care of souls in her community. From this role, we may glean her view of music for strengthening her nuns' faith and understanding with the guidance she received from the living Light.

As Gregorian reformer and apocalyptic preacher, Hildegard offers a necessary corrective to much of the popularist nuance given to her today. Newman reminds us that "although she herself was raised by a recluse, Hildegard was not particularly sympathetic to the eremitic life." Nor can she be seen, historically, to argue for many of the contemporary fashions with her name on them today—feminism, eco- or creation spirituality, and so forth. Hildegard saw herself as a reformer of the Church, not as any radical change-agent or priestess outside the fold. She was an elitist Benedictine from a noble family, whose commitments lay with *order* in standing institutions—Church, secular authority, and obedient subjects—and with prophetic condemnation of clerical sexual promiscuity or marriage, simony, and the surrender of ecclesiastical authority to secular principalities. As Newman writes,

> Hildegard did not call for radical change of social or ecclesiastical structures . . . Her ideal was a Christendom wherein the secular power would be firmly subordinate to the spiritual, princes and prelates would rule with vigilance and justice, and subjects and layfolk would offer prompt obedience.[24]

A classic correspondence between Hildegard and Abbess Tengswich of Andernach and her brother Richard of Springiersbach demonstrates *this* Hildegard. Tengswich and Richard espoused a radical reform toward apostolic poverty and challenged Hildegard for her exclusion of all novices into her community except those from noble, wealthy families. Hildegard responded with a defense of class discrimination. For example, "One would not put beasts of different species in the same stall, and even angels had their hierarchy."[25] The other examples

---

24. Ibid., 20.

25. Hildegard, "Tenxwind von Andernach und Hildegard von Bingen: Zwei 'Weltanschauungen' in der Mitte des 12 Jahrhunderts," cited in Newman, "Introduction,"

in the lengthy exchange follow suit, but the point here is that, while at her tithe Hildegard relinquished material wealth and power, she clearly maintained its institutional, social, and cultural boundaries. As Gregorian reformer, she understood herself to be a "mouthpiece for the pure but continuously imperiled bride of Christ" in the service of "an essentially clerical vision of the church and hierarchical vision of society."[26] Her advocacy of music would therefore fall primarily within ecclesiastical or liturgical senses of its use for a clerical vision of the church and its reform.

Hildegard's apocalyptic preaching, engaged through four preaching tours in the last two decades of her life, shows a clear awareness and avid condemnation of human sin in princes and people alike. Newman aligns Hildegard's voice with that of the Old Testament prophets: "divine judgment inevitably follows on human sin, and especially on the sins of rulers." She did not foresee an imminent Second Coming, nor did she profess a golden age of Spirit.[27] She spoke out against the tumult between popes and secular rulers—particularly acrimonious in her century—and she preached reform and repentance that just might result in last-minute avoidance of damnation. Newman notes that Hildegard's apocalyptic also shows an uncanny concern with history, perceiving the importance of salvation history from creation to final judgment: "In order to understand the present it was necessary to consider the past . . . as well as the future," which in her vision "entails a grim succession of evils that must come to pass before the judgment."[28] Not only does this reshape any Pollyanna popularism about Hildegard's voice for contemporary ears, it lends itself well to an historical appreciation of what Hildegard still has to say to us today. She valued historical perspectives for their witness to God's continuing action in salvation history, regardless of contemporary priorities of modern historical consciousness and critical thought.

Two medieval scholars, Margo Fassler and Margot Schmidt, have provided an overview of Hildegard's role as abbess, responsible for the care of souls in her community. In their view, significantly, music was

in Hildegard, *Scivias*, 20.

26. Newman, "Introduction," in Hildegard, *Scivias*, 20. See also Newman, *Sister of Wisdom*, ch 6.

27. Newman, "Introduction," in Hildegard, *Scivias*, 21.

28. Ibid.

the central link in Hildegard's implementation of educational life for her nuns. Schmidt specifies Hildegard's educational aim further to be an "inner mission of renewal and the strengthening of the proclamation of the faith," and "the care of souls."[29] The goal was the harmony between body and soul in relation to God and the world, to be reached through the search for God via *discretio*. An important term within Benedictine contexts, *discretio* names an ability and practice of making distinctions, in moderation, in both natural and sacred endeavors. It is considered the anchor of the Benedictine Rule and Newman notes Hildegard called it "the mother of virtues."[30] As abbess, Hildegard urged a middle way "between laxity and self-indulgence on the one hand and excessive abstinence on the other." She urged unity in community. Her teaching, Newman observes, "is pervaded with classical monastic themes: spiritual warfare, knowledge of good and evil, the conflict between soul and body, the acquisition of virtues and the special merit of chastity." Music, particularly the *musica humana*, served as regular means for unity and harmonization of body and soul amidst all these forces.

Fassler also argues for the centrality of music for Hildegard's educational work in community. "Singing the Divine Office was the defining action of monastic life for Hildegard of Bingen," she writes. "Her attention to music . . . was part of her intention to lead the nuns entrusted to her care more fully into Benedictine life."[31] As such, music provided the connective tissue between shared liturgies, work in and for the monastery, and faithful learning from treatises and other dramatic and creative arts. Even more provocatively, Fassler views Hildegard's entire corpus as a comprehensive, holistic, and innovative "program" of formation created for the purposes of bringing her nuns more fully into the strength of faith and the Benedictine way of living Christian discipleship. This "program" of theological, musical, and dramatic work is "perhaps the only such educational program surviving in its entirety from the Middle Ages, with the texts, the music, and the explanation of meanings intact, and all organized by the creator's own hands."[32] Music,

---

29. Schmidt, "Hildegard's Care of Souls," 43.

30. Newman, "Introduction," in Hildegard, *Scivias*, 19.

31. Fassler, "Composer and Dramatist," 156.

32. Ibid., 175. As one might expect, there are now a handful of challenges to the authenticity of authorship in Hildegard's musical compositions and artistic illuminations. See Maddock, *Hildegard of Bingen*, esp. ch 12.

for Hildegard in her work of education and reform, offered a holistic and comprehensive vehicle—centered in the liturgy of the Divine Office and the practices of prayer—for teaching and learning the Benedictine way of faith in God by means of the body. Her role as abbess urges a more comprehensive view of music and its role for personal and communal faithfulness to God. With her distinct historical location in mind, addressed in terms of her medieval, Benedictine, and ecclesiastical worldviews, we may now turn to Hildegard's letter to the prelates at Mainz.

Hildegard's Letter to the Prelates at Mainz[33]

Hildegard argues in this letter for release from the interdict and return to the musical activities of her community based upon the canonical authority of the Psalter with scriptural and sacramental warrant. She concludes her argument with the praise of God as purpose focusing all of creation. Not surprisingly in such a letter of advocacy by an abbess, the importance of music for learning and its role for strengthening the faith of community members figure prominently in her prose.

Hildegard argued music to hold a primary place within the context of Christian salvation history. It serves the redemptive and sanctifying work of God, available to all who are penitent and offer praise. Her interpretation of music's place and function in salvation history begins with Adam's original voice, lost through disobedience and regained by Spirit-inspired delight, knowledge, renewal and inner illumination. Adam's original voice "blended fully with the voices of the angels in their praise of God" (77). His rejection of the will of his Creator caused him to fall "asleep to that knowledge which he possessed before his sin, just as a person on waking up only dimly remembers what he had seen in his dreams" (78). Inward ignorance resulted from "his iniquity" (78). Humanity now requires the voice of the living Spirit to learn of inward things. God devised the means to renew the "hearts of many

---

33. Dronke provides a notable historical contribution on the letter's Latin text, citing two surviving documents—*Echtheit*[B] 54rb–56rb, and Roma Vat. Lat. 4030:265–74, 317f. (specifically 308va–309va)—with some slight divergences from the text in the *P.L.* 197. This study relies primarily on the Baird and Ehrman translation, however, with their more contemporary contribution and clearer expertise for translation decisions, nuanced by Dronke's work. Citations are given parenthetically in the text.

with the pouring out of the prophetic spirit" (78). These "holy prophets, inspired by the Spirit which they had received," composed "psalms and canticles (by which the hearts of listeners would be inflamed)" (78). They also constructed musical instruments "to enhance songs of praise with melodic strains" (78). All this was to renew hearts and, through God's interior illumination, regain knowledge lost by Adam at his sin. The prophets "get beyond the music of this exile and recall to mind that divine melody of praise which Adam, in the company with angels, enjoyed in God before his fall" (78). All those of zeal and wisdom, then, may sing for the "the delight of their souls" and accompany such singing with musical instruments, recalling God's loving creation of all (78). The promise of delight, knowledge, renewal, and illumination is simply too much for the devil, however. Humanity's great deceiver seeks to stymie repentance and confession, and therefore any pleasure through divine praise and communal singing. He desires to eradicate goodness through "wicked suggestions, impure thoughts, or various distractions from the heart of man and even from the mouth of the Church itself... through dissension, scandal, or unjust oppression" (78).

Secondly, music serves the triune God's redemptive and sanctifying work by vesting the human body with the Garment of the Word, who infuses human spirits with the Holy Spirit and enlivens the body and harmonizes it with the soul in praise of God. Hildegard here urges consideration of the human body and how God infuses and illumines the bodies of those who are penitent, who praise the Lord, and who participate in the singing of music. "Consider, too, that just as the body of Jesus Christ was born of the purity of the Virgin Mary through the operation of the Holy Spirit, so, too, the canticle of praise, reflecting celestial harmony, is rooted in the Church through the Holy Spirit... The body is the vestment of the spirit, which has a living voice, and so it is proper for the body, in harmony with the soul, to use its voice to sing praises to God" (79). Singing by means of God's breath, given through creation, enlivens the body and harmonizes the body with the soul who sings praises to God. For "all arts pertaining to things useful and necessary for mankind have been created by the breath that God sent into man's body. For this reason, it is proper that God be praised in all things" (79). Hildegard's final image further shapes the redemption and sanctification promised, in the body, through the singing of the divine office: "The prophet... urges us in the psalm [Ps 32.2, 91.4] to confess to the Lord with the harp and to sing a psalm to Him with the ten-stringed psaltery" (79). Typical in the scriptural interpretation of her day, she offers allegorical interpretation of the prophet's psalm: the harp, plucked from below, relates to "the discipline of the body;" the psaltery, plucked from above, pertains to "the exertion of the spirit;" the ten-chords of the harp refers to "the fulfillment of the law" (79).

Ultimately, Hildegard's contributions to our understanding of music and its contributions to her Benedictine community originate from the rhetorical and authoritative moves of her argument. By forcing the community to read the Divine Office instead of singing it, the prelates were causing an incorrect celebration of the holy liturgy. Their order promoted *disorder* within God's Church. Scripture repeatedly commands the faithful to praise the Lord with voice, Psalter, harp, and cymbal. The prelates were failing in Church instruction, for it is precisely the material composition of singing, accompanied by various musical instruments, that instructs human beings in God's praise and turns all convictions of inner being to the same (77).

Hildegard's argument rests on the Psalter as *scriptural* authority within the larger Church and as a community text sung regularly in its entirety. God has commanded her to report the facts of the case surrounding the dead man buried in their consecrated ground, as well as to confess the now "incorrect" celebration of the Divine Office—that is, reading it, instead of singing it. She cites Psalm 150, and then Psalms 32 and 92, as evidence of the divine mandate to give praise to God through singing and musical instruments. She observes the Psalms as compositions offered by the holy prophets, inspired by the Spirit, thereby placing her advocacy in a long line of ecclesial, divine authority. This canonical, rhetorical strategy on her part, of course, emerges from the root of monastic community life. Psalm singing was and continues to be a primary practice for Benedictine communities, as well as for other monastic orders. An interdict against singing within a convent or monastery hacks at the very root of communal understanding and the shared shaping of faith. No church authority could argue for long *against* singing the Psalter. Hildegard's reliance upon the Psalms as canonical authority recognizes this communal foundation in practice, as well as argument. Psalm 150 establishes the framework for her entire argument: "Praise the Lord! . . . Praise him with trumpet sound; praise him with lute and harp! . . . Let everything that breathes praise the Lord!" (77). A canonical source of near-universal communal acceptance commands praise, and praise by every breathing thing, with all kinds of musical instruments.

Hildegard also employs *sacramental* warrant in her advocacy for musical practice(s) to be restored, daring to suggest a sacramental character to music when accompanying communal liturgy, the Divine Office. She hears words of her Living Light in a vision: "It is improper for you to obey human words ordering you to abandon the sacraments of the Garment of the Word of God, Who, born virginally of the Virgin Mary, is your salvation" (77).[34] Music, here, is interwoven somehow with the power and function of the sacraments. It has a sacramental character because it clothes the Word of God, revealed within the Divine Office and at the Eucharistic feast. As such, music and its instruments are "outward, visible things to teach us about inward things" (77). Hildegard repeats this phrasing of argument later in the letter (78), and she only reaches the peak of rhetorical flair after situating the entire conflict within their—hers and the prelates'—advocacy for the sanctity of Christ's sacraments.

Her letter begins with her assurance: "we would not have it appear that, out of feminine harshness, we did injustice to the sacraments of Christ, with which this man had been fortified while he was still alive" (76). Just like the prelates, she desires to protect the sanctity of the sacraments. Just like the prelates, but further, she honors the fortification that communion offers to all who receive, even those now dead, like the buried man under dispute. She artfully cautions the prelates' misunderstanding: silencing music actually dishonors the sacraments and plays into the hands of Satan. Without repentance and the lifting of the interdict, the prelates themselves "will lose their place among the chorus of angels and face harsh judgment" (79) as God falls on them in all might and justice. Well versed in the ecclesial understandings and norms of her day, Hildegard places music in such intimate proximity to the sacraments of Christ that exclusion from music becomes exclusion from the salvation of God, for those who falsely judge and silence the Church's mouth of God's praise.

Hildegard's sacramental warrant would be senseless without a clear, corresponding reliance upon music's physicality in the human

---

34. Note regarding translation: one MS has *mei* in place of *Dei*, hence this could be read as "Garment of my Word." Dronke, *Women Writers of the Middle Ages*, 197 n. 101.

body, through which God sanctifies, instructs, admonishes, arouses, awakens, and harmonizes body and soul to give voice praising the Lord. The original image—music as a Garment—suggests clothing of a body, in this case the Word of God become flesh. Hildegard here proclaims an incarnational theology according to God's plan and Christ's birth in human flesh, through whom corruption is cleansed and communicants are sanctified, all "so that he might remain in them and they in him for their fortification" (77). She resides clearly within the orthodox theology of her Christian tradition. Her argument for the sacramental character of music, however, ties the physicality of voice and instruments into the right administration and celebration of Christ's sacraments. "The material composition and quality of these instruments," she writes, "instruct us how we ought to give form to praise, to turn all convictions of our inner being to the same" (77). Not only is it the music of voices raised in song but also the physicality and material form that communicate and connect earth to heaven:

> Just as the body of Jesus Christ was born of the purity of the Virgin Mary through the operation of the Holy Spirit, so, too, the canticle of praise, reflecting celestial harmony, is rooted in the Church through the Holy Spirit. The body is the vestment of the spirit, which has a living voice, and so it is proper for the body, in harmony with the soul, to use its voice to sing praises to God. (79)

Hildegard concludes her argument with the Psalter image, urging all "to confess to the Lord with the harp and to sing a psalm to [God] with the ten-stringed [lute]" (79). As noted above, the harp refers to the discipline of the body, central to sacramental character because of the incarnation and the centrality of human flesh in processes of sanctification.

The purpose of Hildegard's letter, beyond the clearly theological and rhetorical forces of persuasion, was to return her community to lived musical practices—what this study refers to as music in its performative mode. By so doing, they could fulfill divinely-inspired, human purposes in praise God made known in Jesus Christ in the power of the Spirit, in whom Christian faith is given embodied form and material expression. Music, according to Hildegard's understanding and advocacy, teaches by means of its embodied awakening of the human heart to God's inner illumination, resulting in creation's voiced praise. Again and again, Hildegard reminds the prelates of the primary responsibility for all of creation to give praise to God. Not only does music teach in particularly embodied fashion; it also forms the primary vehicle for praising God in human flesh.

Whatever else the prelates attempted to accomplish in their interdict against Hildegard's community, we have received a historical and wonderfully compelling articulation of the significance of music, lived out in practice by a Benedictine community in the twelfth century. Hildegard's letter to the prelates at Mainz shows an original interpretation, an orthodox theological understanding, and a prophetic passion for music as something quintessentially human, sacramental in character, and absolutely instrumental in the instruction and formation of her community of faith. Right celebration required a discipline of the body, an exertion of the spirit, and the fulfillment of the law. The psalms, canticles, and instruments of the holy prophets are to enhance faith as songs of praise so that we might be taught intimately about inward things and participate in Christ's body, a divinely human reflection of celestial harmony through which the symphonic soul is empowered to reach God in active praise. Within the web of a Benedictine spirituality—structured by a common life, the Divine Office and prayer, and primary monastic virtues of humility, hospitality, and *discretio*—Hildegard posits for us the primacy of relationship, enacted in deep listening, ordered practice, shared prayer and expressed desire for God in song. Contrary to most of the writing in her time, her letter also sets the human body as the instrument and site of harmonization sought within the Benedictine way. When we view this within the lived contexts of her life and work, we begin to see an expansive, educational role of music for teaching and learning inward things by means of embodiment, shared desire, and *discretio*, both natural and sacred. Therefore, despite her historical remove and the resulting critical challenges, Hildegard of Bingen offers us a glimpse into this centrality of music for the educational life of faith in her community.

Much work remains to be done to translate Hildegard's insights about music in the teaching and learning of "inward things." Her primarily medieval, ecclesiastical, and theological perspective presents incongruities that are difficult to articulate within contemporary modes of thought such as secularization, postmodernism, and other facets of post-Enlightenment discourse. Recent theologically oriented resources have appeared for the purpose of guiding musical practices within the church,[35] but few address music as a primarily embodied, communally-shaped phenomenon in the way that Hildegard offers at her historical remove. Margot Schmidt has begun the task of contemporary interpretation through her immersion in Hildegard's creative works but, as we shall see below, an established philosopher who has influenced much twentieth-century theological thinking with respect to music offers a surprisingly resonant conversation partner for clarity in our study. Not only may we flesh out aspects of Hildegard's thought, but contemporary theological reflection on music becomes more clearly situated within its philosophical heritage.

Susanne K. Langer in Contemporary Theological Perspective(s)

A classical, twentieth-century philosophical voice that has shaped much contemporary theological and psychological thought with respect to music provides a promising bridge for understanding Hildegard's impulses and advocacy of music. Susanne K. Langer blew onto the mid-twentieth century, philosophical scene with unexpected force as she described the nature of human understanding transformed through *symbolization* (philosophy's new key) made *palpable* when embodied in the arts and made conceivable within music's gift of *insight*. Her philosophical contributions are wide-ranging; her life's work, however, could be summarized as a multi-disciplinary study of *feeling*, not as a psychological construct or biological synapses but as a form essential to human being, its "mark of mentality."[36] She writes:

> Feeling in the broad sense of whatever is felt in any way, as sensory stimulus or inward tension, pain, emotion, or intent, is the mark of mentality . . . the starting-point of a philosophy of mind. The study of feeling . . . leads one down into biological structure and process until its estimation becomes (for the time) impossible, and upward to the purely human sphere known as "culture."[37]

---

35. See esp. Kroeker, *Music in Christian Worship*; Kimbrough, *Music and Mission*.

36. Langer, cited by Danto in the Foreword to Langer's *Mind: An Essay on Human Feeling*, vi. See also Langer, *Feeling and Form*.

37. Langer, *Mind*, 3, 14.

Feeling as "that which is felt in any way" challenged the easy dichotomies of her day, most often rooted in biogenetic theories of mind and positivistic philosophy. Today *feeling* connotes a continuing debate on philosophical formalism(s) and the interrelationships between embodiment, sensation, perception, cognition, and interpretation much beyond our specific purpose.[38] Langer's work is significant to this study for two main reasons. First, her work has been referenced by innumerable scholars in a variety of disciplines, particularly theology. Much contemporary discourse becomes accessible when examined with due attribution here. Second, Langer places music at the center of her work because it embodies "pure form" without material complications and because its primary gift for human understanding is insight or, as she says, "making things conceivable."[39] Her fascination with feeling as the mark of human mentality and the arts for making things newly conceivable resulted in remarkably generative concepts still important for examining learning in music today.

A cursory review of secondary literature shows a wide spectrum of involvement with Langer's work, from her theory of symbolization to her specific view of music as non-representational form. Howard Gardner, the Multiple Intelligences author whose work is engaged in the next chapter, relies on Langer's work to describe his affective yet inexplicable experiences as a performing pianist and habitual musician. Also significant is his reliance upon her broader theory of mind for his own early theories of symbolization.[40] Don Saliers, working in theological-liturgical circles, relies on her to articulate music's power to affect sensual experience within a *synesthetic* matrix through devotional practice(s).[41] Ethnomusicologist John Blacking references her work in his own "Biology of Music-Making," as well as in many of his other works.[42] Jeremy Begbie references both Langer's concept of the logical

---

38. "Connotes" is a precise term here in Langer's work, which as a whole redresses the kind of symbolism *denoted* by language toward a more expansive theory of mind able to explicate "unspeakable" things within a *connotational* semantic, whose highest type is music. See Langer, *Philosophy in a New Key*, 101ff.

39. Langer, *Philosophy in a New Key*, 244.

40. See Gardner, *Intelligence Reframed*, 29 and 65; and Gardner, *Unschooled Mind*, 71–79.

41. Saliers, "Music and Spirituality," 10–12; "Sound Spirituality," 334.

42. Blacking, "Biology of Music-Making," 306. See also Blacking, *Music, Culture, &*

form of feeling and her work on meaning grasped as a single *Gestalt*.[43] David Hargreaves cites Langer's work, specifically relating to discursive and presentational symbols, in *The Developmental Psychology of Music*.[44] Thus we can see that Langer's work has nuanced much twentieth-century reflection on mentality and musical understanding across disciplines. Critical studies of her work can be found in a variety of fields, as further testament to the continuing fruitfulness of her scholarship.[45] A brief review of symbolization as the transformation of experience and music's pivotal role as *pure form* or *unconsummated symbol* will contextualize her work for our purposes. A conversation between Langer and Hildegard on two potentially intersecting themes—desire and feeling, discretio and insight—may then proceed for critical theological perspective on music's role in learning from music in performative mode.

Langer's Symbolization, Music as Unconsummated Symbol, Gift of Insight

Before George Steiner ever wrote *Real Presences*, his own "wager on transcendence," Langer had placed music as the central hinge in her argument for *symbolization* as the transformation of human experience, conceivable within a broader theory of mind through music's *pure form* as an *unconsummated symbol*. In these terms, Langer confronted largely bio-genetic theories of mind unable to account for significant, human phenomena like folly, artistic endeavors, and dreams. Outside of the traditional, evolutionary-linguistic purview, these common phenom-

---

Experience, 36, 152, 239.

43. Begbie, *Voicing Creation's Praise*, 75 and 244ff.

44. Hargreaves, *Developmental Psychology of Music*, 9.

45. Lassegue, "Poles of Meaning," 20–26; Kotchetkova, Evans, and Langer "Articulating Contextualized Knowledge: Focus Groups and/as Public Participation?" Two symposia have been conducted as well, a recent one within speculative philosophy and an earlier one by the Charles Pierce Society. See Innis, "Introduction" and "Placing Langer's Philosophical Project," Kruse, "Vital Rhythm and Temporal Form," and Dryden, "Philosopher as Prophet and Visionary," 1–43; McDermott, "Symposium on Susanne K. Langer," Campbell, "Langer's Understanding of Philosophy," Liddy, "Susanne K. Langer's Philosophy of Mind," Dryden, "Susanne K. Langer and American Philosophic Naturalism," and Hart, "Langer's Aesthetics of Poetry," 131–200. For international interest, see Richter and Bahr, *Naturalisierung des Geistes und Symbolisierung des Fuhlens*; and Brentari, *La nascita della coscienza simbolica*.

ena urged a broader philosophical perspective able to confront them toward human sense-making or significance.

Langer began by observing that scientific interest, and therefore the various disciplines within its claims to rationality, had moved (in largely unaware fashion) beyond a "thoroughgoing empiricism" of seeing the world through its dichotomy of outer world and inner experience. Instead, human inquiry had become *seeing and calculating, seeing and translating*.[46] As such, *sense-data* had become *primarily symbols*. "[I]t becomes apparent," argues Langer, "that the age of science has begotten a new philosophical issue, inestimably more profound than its original empiricism:. . .the edifice of human knowledge stands before us, not as a vast collection of sense reports, but as a structure of *facts that are symbols* and *laws that are their meanings*."[47] So begins her new theory of mind centered in *feeling* as the mark of human mentality and *symbolization* as the transformation of human experience into symbols and meanings.

Symbolization, for Langer, names the pre-rationative and formal means by which human beings transform experience into new and understandable streams of cognition. Then-current theories suggested the human mind as a simple transmitter of perceptions into cognition followed by action, but symbolization relies upon the image of a transformer.

> The current of experience that passes through [the brain] undergoes a change of character, not through the agency of the sense by which the perception entered, but by virtue of a primary use which is made of it immediately: it is sucked into the stream of symbols which constitutes a human mind.[48]

Cognitive thought, traditionally viewed as a transmission of information, does not encompass human reason. Symbolization is the pre-rationative—not irrational or pre-rational, but fully felt-and-cognitive—act of mind transforms human experience within a stream of symbols of previous and contemporary significance. Trevor Hart notes that this symbolization is also the root of new learning because it presents things not directly perceivable within the current experiencing of the world.

46. Langer, *Philosophy in a New Key*, 20.
47. Ibid., 21.
48. Ibid., 42.

"Symbolisation [sic] . . . characteristically goes beyond what is given to or in our experience of the world in any given moment. . .[a] characteristic trespassing beyond the given."[49] Symbolization, in other words, names the pre-rationative, felt-cognitive process in which human experience is transformed into symbolic sense-data with assigned significance and import for learning. Langer thereby challenges any theory of mind that attends to only the portion of human experience visible within evolutionary presuppositions and the distinction of humanity rooted in language. She proposes in their place a more encompassing survey of human behavior found within a theory of felt-mind in which symbolization is the definitive need and the essential act of mind.

At the center of this work, which took the bulk of her life and resulted in her three-volume *Mind: An Essay on Human Feeling*, rests music as *pure form* and *unconsummated symbol* whose gift is *insight*. In order to explore and substantiate further her understanding of symbolization as the transformation of experience, she examined "that which makes *symbols* out of anything" or "the quality of *meaning*, in its several aspects and forms."[50] Her work was informed by theories of art, which are more attuned to the broad swaths of human behaviors considered and through which she pursued the significance of logic, language, sacrament, and myth.[51] All of this leads to the pivotal chapter in *Philosophy in a New Key*, "On the Significance of Music," which establishes the central function of *perfect form* for an artistic—not simply affective, logical, or traditional—identification of meaning. Any theory of art, she reasons, must look "to what every artist knows as the real problem—the *perfection of form*, which makes this form 'significant' in the artistic sense."[52] She postulates a study of pure design[53] but ultimately recognizes the undesirable impact of representation and literal content upon such philosophical investigation. She concludes that music, amongst all the arts, offers philosophical discourse an essentially non-representative form, attached to no literal content that might disrupt critical investigation. "Music," she writes, "is preeminently non-representative

49. Hart, "Through the Arts," 4–5.
50. Langer, *Philosophy in a New Key*, 42.
51. Ibid., chs 5–7, respectively.
52. Ibid., 208.
53. Ibid., 203–7.

even in its classical production, its highest attainments. It exhibits pure form not as an embellishment, but as its very essence; . . . That is a great aid to our chosen preoccupation with form. There is no obvious, literal content in our way."[54]

Nestled between two then-current, emotive theories of musical meaning—music as self-expression of emotion and music as logical expression of emotion—Langer's understanding of music as a "form of human feeling" suggests it to be, even more provocatively, an *unconsummated symbol*. Jeremy Begbie lodges his argument against Langer's work here, though I suspect he colludes the warrant of her argument with the claim itself, argued below. In Langer's description, *"music at its highest, though clearly a symbolic form, is an unconsummated symbol. Articulation is its life, but not assertion; expressiveness, not expression. The actual function of meaning, which calls for permanent contents, is not fulfilled."*[55] As pure form, music is a non-representational, non-discursive, presentational symbol, by which she means it defies linguistic projection, logical sequence, and linear formulation, including being understood as a piece of work. It has an order within it—a pre-rationative, graspable or felt significance determinative within processes of symbolization—but it is not primarily logical, as conventionally understood.

Langer describes this non-discursive, presentational symbolism in some detail:

> The recognition of presentational symbolism as a normal and prevalent vehicle of meaning widens our conception of rationality far beyond the traditional boundaries, yet never breaks faith with logic in the strictest sense. Wherever a symbol operates, there is meaning; and conversely, different classes of experience—say, reason, intuition, appreciation—correspond to different types of symbolic mediation. No symbol is exempt from the office of logical formulation, of conceptualizing what it conveys.[56]

Music as unconsummated symbol holds to logic in the strictest sense of an order and graspable significance as symbolic form. No symbol is exempt from this pre-rationative kind of formulation. But its formulation

54. Ibid., 209.
55. Ibid., 240.
56. Ibid., 97.

is non-discursive, simultaneous with innumerable presentations that are eventually abstractable and combinatory within empiricist reason. "Clearly," Langer concludes, "a symbolism with so many elements, such myriad relationships, cannot be broken up into basic units."[57] It rests on "total reference," not "general reference;" "presentational" symbolism of artistic forms, not "representational" symbolism of language or a mathematical kind of logic.[58]

Here Langer locates music's gift of *insight*, a phenomenon of intuition and imagination received within the "total reference" or non-discursiveness of music as presentational symbolism.

> The imagination that responds to music is personal and associative and logical, tinged with affect, tinged with bodily rhythm, tinged with dream, but *concerned* with a wealth of formulations for its wealth of wordless knowledge, its whole knowledge of emotional and organic experience, of vital impulse, balance, conflict, the *ways* of living and dying and feeling. . . . The lasting effect is . . . to *make things conceivable* rather than to store up propositions. Not communication but insight is the gift of music.[59]

Langer argues that the gift of music is "to make things conceivable," not as propositional or linear thought but through the coordination and complex integration of human sensation and awareness. In insight, Langer identifies music's capacity to accompany human mentality into experience, with all its complexity, transforming it through symbolization into assigned significance and meaning. This non-discursive, presentational form of symbolism argued within music as pure form or unconsummated symbol, honors the multidimensionality of human experience without getting overly caught in its complexity. Insight arrives, given various form in reason, rite and art. In the end, music as pure form or unconsummated symbol is a non-discursive, non-representational "form of human feeling" with a determinative and graspable order, but one quite distinct from the more conventional or mathematical logic(s).

---

57. Ibid., 95.
58. Ibid., 96.
59. Ibid., 244.

Langer in Contemporary Theological Perspectives

Amongst those in other disciplines, many have mis-interpreted, or perhaps narrowly mis-read music's presentational symbolism, which is much more expansive and complex than the oft-repeated phrase, "music as a logical form of human feeling," suggests. Music educator, Mary Reichling, reminds us that Langer classified her intentions with *form* in various ways, though many focus upon one to the exclusion of others. Reichling identifies Langer's *forms of human feeling* to include 1) the dynamic and living qualities of forms, 2) an abstractness and logicality of forms, and 3) qualities of human expressiveness.[60] Jeremy Begbie limits Langer's contributions in his *Theology Music and Time* to expressiveness, centered in human emotional life. He records Langer's work as the "much-discussed theory of musical emotion," in which she "speaks of an analogy of dynamic structure between emotion and music and argues that music is an iconic symbol of mental states."[61] As any compelling misreading does, this interpretation offers an assessment accurate within a specific work's context, but one incongruent with Langer's larger theoretical contributions in *feeling* as the mark of human mentality. Langer's original description of music as an unconsummated symbol *does* use the previous contributions of musical-expression theories to interpret music as a form of human feeling. These musical-expression theories of emotion create the warrant for her philosophical claims extending music's symbolism into realms of feeling beyond the discursive logics within biogenetic theories of mind shaped by evolutionary-linguistic presuppositions. But substantial volumes of subsequent work show Langer's fuller intentions of distinguishing the kind of presentational symbolism music embodies from that constrained by facile dichotomies of logic/emotion, seen when "emotional life" and the plural form of feelings is used instead of Langer's more expansive *feeling*. Begbie's assessment of Langer's thought: "Music conveys not the content of specific feelings but the *form* of feelings."[62] Within his understanding of presentational

---

60. Reichling, "Intersections," cited by Packalén, "In Dialogue," 208.

61. Begbie, *Theology, Music, and Time*, 16 n. 20. See also *Resounding Truth*, 358 n. 56, where he describes more overtly "one of the weaknesses" of her "much discussed theory of musical emotion."

62. Langer, *Feeling and Form*, cited in Begbie, *Theology, Music, and Time*, 16 n. 20.

symbolism, Begbie fairly represents Langer's work. The categorization of "emotional life" and "feelings," however, belies a misreading of Langer's comprehensive sense of *feeling*. Such narrowed misreadings can be found in multiple interpretations reliant upon the phrase "a logical form of human feeling."[63] Instead of Langer's more expansive, holistic, and biologically-unto-culturally nuanced sense of feeling as "that which is felt in any way," music's symbolism is misconstrued as emotional, in contrast to logical; about feelings, instead of "emotions, moods, mental tensions and resolutions—a 'logical picture' of sentient, responsive life, a source of insight, not a plea for sympathy."[64]

Don Saliers, another theologian-musician more interested in music's *embodied* phenomenality, moves closer to Langer's precise meaning than Begbie does, though he still colludes interpretations that Langer carefully distinguishes. Saliers describes music's presentation and symbolizing of "the patterns of how we live and experience the world" through Langer's phrase, the "morphology of human sentience."[65] This is accurate to Langer's project in its entirety. Yet he ultimately neglects her crucial distinction within the very same context by relying upon music as a "language of sound."[66] Langer's careful distinction of music as a form of human feeling with an order beneath and beyond that within linguistic habits of mind gets lost within contemporary theological reflection.[67]

Music's non-discursiveness or indivisible multidimensionality gets a short shrift within contemporary theological discussions as well. Begbie imputes his own literate-training's presumptions into Langer's presentational sense of music. He writes, "A piece of music, Langer believes, is a nonlinguistic presentational symbol. It symbolizes human feelings, not by ostensive denotation, but through possessing the same temporal structure as some segment or segments of emotional life."[68] Good support for his conceptual interests, yet music is telescoped

63. See Piechowski, "Logical and the Empirical Form of Feeling."
64. Langer, *Philosophy in a New Key*, 222. Cited in Storr, *Music and the Mind*, 145.
65. Saliers, *Music and Theology*, 6–7. See also Saliers, "Music and Spirituality," 10.
66. Saliers, *Music and Theology*, 6–7.
67. See also Hess, "Toward a Full Fledged Action Theory," 529, written before deeper immersion in Langer's authorship as a whole.
68. Begbie, *Theology, Music and Time*, 16 n. 20. See also *Resounding Truth*, 358 n. 56.

into a "piece of work," in contradiction to Langer's insistence upon its *total reference*. Music as a non-discursive, non-representational, and unconsummated symbol cannot be dissected without disregarding its non-discursive symbolism. Its significance lies in the felt-multidimensionality, unrefracted and indivisible, out of which insight may arrive. The very nature of contemporary theological reflection makes this category-mistake unavoidable in a sense. Each theologian who contributes to greater understanding about music's multidimensionality has to commit this offense against music's non-discursive whole. Nonetheless, it is illustrative of how easy misinterpretations or misreadings are within theological discourse today. Langer's sense of music as an unconsummated symbol challenges contemporary theological disciplines in the persistent contrast with the reigning referents of mathematically-logical form in contrast to a broader sense of order or pattern. Her contribution of a theory of mind, rooted in *feeling* as the *mark of human mentality* and *symbolization* as the *transformation of experience* suggests an ongoing fruitfulness sufficient for a study into learning from music in its performative mode.

Langer has ultimately contributed a compelling, pre-rationative, and embodied-cognitive model for understanding cognition and significance, generally, and musical cognition and awareness specifically, beyond the traditionally linguistic and narrowly cognitive models of Enlightenment persuasion. The understanding of symbolization as the transformation of experience, and of music as "unconsummated symbol," proposes a dynamic, often apophatic but sensuous form of human activity in music that is cognitive but not necessarily utilitarian; personally communicative but not linguistically, rationally confined. Symbolization as the transformation of experience also acknowledges the primary character of human embodiment that underlies the operation of the mind in basic ways. Underneath or logically prior to the cognitive functioning of the mind noted in biogenetic, linguistic thought is the pre-rationative, symbolic, sensuous, and intensely meaningful cognitive activity that exhibits itself in rite and art—specifically music—in addition to human reason, more narrowly conceived. Music as unconsummated symbol is "consummated" again and again in particular performances or enacted possibilities.

Langer wrestles her own limitations, of course. She ultimately, if artfully, avoids the specifics of significance in lived human experience by a philosophical tautology within symbolization. In her redefinition of human need away from evolutionary superiority through language and reason, Langer argues what is most human is symbolization and therefore humans most need to symbolize. She does not directly address *why* humans symbolize, transforming experience into cognition and beyond, hiding the quagmires of motivation and intention in her pre-rationative yet cognitive constructs. Langer redefines the basic human need as symbolization and places *any* question of significance in reason, rite, art—and especially in music—nicely *within* that framework of need as it has been defined.

Historical Horizons and Learning from One's Forbears

When Hildegard of Bingen first claimed my attention for a deeper, more critically-theological understanding of learning from music in all its complexities, respected historians dear to me dissuaded more than aided the inquiry. Understandably. Too often, historical figures *are* forced to legitimate interpretations and understandings with which they would have substantially disagreed in their own lifetime. Yet contemporary theological scholarship faces a multitude of challenges in any investigation of music within its diverse practices and forms. The literature is daunting, expressive of innumerable sides in (post-)modern disciplinary discourses, with no clear direction in sight and little opportunity to refine the problematic helpful for deeper understandings with "teeth," with traction in the whirlwind of (post-)modernity. Anyone seeking to advance theological scholarship by means of encounter with music in its performative mode faces this seemingly irreconcilable Gordian knot. So what to do?

We "rush in," as the saying goes, in order to learn from our forbears, well aware that others may not "tread" so lightly across historical horizons. Hildegard's claims arise from the warrant of what she called "salvation history," which authorizes at least a glimpse into the historical-theological interpretations she offers for learning in music. She respected history enough to locate her argument for music in practice within it; so does this study respect the possibility of historical wisdom from an established theologian who was also a composer. Langer's theory of mind and conceptualization of music undergirds many recent voices within contemporary theological discourse today. Anyone pursuing critical-theological contribution to a well-defined problem cannot neglect her work, as appropriated by such voices. This study begins the theological appropriation of historical-theological resources with review of her contributions. Narrowing the historical examination of Hildegard's contribution to a specific artifact for Christian spirituality study, such as the "Letter to the Prelates at Mainz," minimizes the risk of uncritical appropriation, but does not eradicate it. Placing Langer's work in conversation with Hildegard will indubitably favor contemporary sense-making over Hildegard's intentions. Nonetheless, a couple themes of interest emerge when Hildegard's Letter and Langer's thought are brought together toward a deeper understanding of learning from music in performative mode.

Hildegard of Bingen and Susanne Langer meet in the centrality of music for their work(s) and the pivotal place of insight in conceptualizations of music's significance.[69] Hildegard lived into this centrality through her work as an abbess and her musical creativity as a composer. Susanne, learning to play both the cello and piano amidst her substantial philosophical pursuits, centered her philosophical contributions within a conceptualization of music appropriate to her interest and argument for a more expansive theory of mind. Hildegard's advocacy for music in confrontation with the interdict of 1178 persuades from conviction that music serves to combat human ignorance resulting from Adam's disobedience. It renews human hearts and, through God's interior illumination, regains knowledge previously lost. Susanne's advocacy for music as pure form or unconsummated symbol is the pinnacle of her argument for presentational symbolism whose non-discursive, total reference posits a means for receiving its greatest gift, insight. Hildegard's argument, at least within the most recent interpretations of Holsinger and Epstein, places music's sacramental participation in the redemptive and sanctifying work of God within the human body, specifically desire. Susanne's theory of mind locates the mark of human mentality in *feeling*, which she defined as "that which can be felt in any way." Hildegard of Bingen and Susanne Langer devoted their energies to entirely different purposes, yet music is arguably the functional center, focused by means of interior illumination or insight, and the human body with desire or feeling. These

---

69. For parity, the rest of the discussion will reference both women by their first names, in contrast to the modern, critical custom of formalized last names.

two distinct themes—interior illumination/insight and desire/feeling—outline a refreshingly historical yet contemporary way to think about learning from music in performative mode.

Interior Illumination/Insight

In the twofold concept and practice of *discretio*, Benedictine spirituality contextualizes one interpretation of Hildegard's "interior illumination" in music's activities within her community. Margot Schmidt identifies Hildegard's aim as abbess and reformer to be the renewal and strengthening of faith through the care of souls, accomplished in the harmonization of body and soul in relation to God and the world. This aim was advanced through the comprehensive and creative interweaving of music in the liturgy, learning within and beyond the liturgical center of the Divine Office, and the expression of theological knowledge by means of illuminations, drama, and the natural world. Schmidt clarifies that the renewal and strengthened faith understood in Hildegard's educational work was to be accomplished through harmonization of body and soul in heightened sensation and an increasing desire for God. "As one who is knowledgeable about souls, [Hildegard] knows that proximity and possession of God cannot be taken for granted and these are not necessarily permanent. God requires to be searched for diligently again and again, and thus he can be found."[70] As such, *discretio* in its natural/sacred meanings and disciplined practice guides a person's journey to God within communal shaping of God's Word revealed, written, and proclaimed, yet hidden in the veiled revelation of nature and history.

Discretio in Hildegard's sense carries dual meanings as an ability to make distinctions in natural and sacred endeavors and as a practiced discipline of moderation. Natural *discretio* comes through the force of reason and will, acting as the provider of acquired learning and experience of life.[71] This *discretio* does not penetrate to the innermost spirit and soul, however. Hildegard therefore articulates the supernatural gift of *discretio* available in the light of grace alone. In Schmidt's words,

> For the perfection of the image of God and for sanctification, human beings need "sacred *discretio*" (*sancta discretio*), illumi-

---

70. Schmidt, "Hildegard's Care of Souls," 45–46.
71. Ibid.

> nated by the Holy Spirit as a supernatural force. . . . "Sacred *discretio*" makes distinctions and gains its insights not through logical thinking but through the supernatural light of grace. As this grace is given, thus grows the supernatural gift of *discretio*, which is displayed in insight, judiciousness, and moderation.[72]

Here Hildegard stresses *discretio* as judiciousness and moderation, a second nuance to the term in Benedictine context. Well aware that a person's journey to God entails listening and definite action within community, so also does Hildegard urge a moderation of boundless inquiry. Schmidt writes, "Just as Hildegard speaks of the engagement of the individual in seeking God—she understands that when one poses no questions there can be no answer from the Holy Spirit—so also does she forcefully castigate the presumption of boundless inquiry . . . Immoderation in this form destroys harmony . . ."[73] Hildegard's educational work as abbess and composer relied upon the interior illumination gifted by God within musical consciousness amidst natural and sacred endeavors, enacted in moderation. Music most aptly served the renewal and strengthening of faith through the harmonization of body and soul, in relation to God and the world, dependent upon a notion not unlike Susanne Langer's *insight*.

Susanne's articulation of insight as music's gift offers much less a communal context, much more a conceptual habitat within her theory of mind in terms of human feeling. Insight, for her, means "making things conceivable." With respect to music, it is "personal and associative and logical," tinged with affect and bodily rhythm and dream.[74] It is the product of non-discursive symbolism, whose totality instigates combinatory sensation and integrates complex human experience through symbolization. Music, as a non-discursive symbolism, instigates insight through its indivisible multidimensionality. In this sense, insight is concerned with an indefinite wealth of formulations and knowledge, regardless of specified educational aims, characters or qualities. *Whatever the human mind can conceive* (in its felt-mind, one might say) is the focal point of insight. Whereas Hildegard's interpretation appears to place insight as a product of personal and communal *discretio*,

---

72. Ibid.
73. Ibid.
74. Langer, *Philosophy in a New Key*, 244.

in natural/sacred terms and a disciplined moderation, Susanne's *insight* emphasizes a broader conceptuality, descriptive in terms of sensation and feeling, or experience transformed through symbolization into assigned significance.

Desire/Feeling

Hildegard and Susanne both advocate for music's significance via illumination or insight located a broader context of sensation, whether explicitly embodied or implicitly described in feeling. Hildegard urges the scriptural injunction of Psalm 32 and 91: Confess to the Lord with the harp and sing a psalm to Him with the ten-stringed psaltery."[75] The harp, plucked from below, relates to the "discipline of the body;" the psaltery, plucked from above, pertains to "the exertion of the spirit;" the ten-chords of the harp refers to "the fulfillment of the law."[76] Though neglected in much traditional scholarship on Hildegard's medieval worldview, Hildegard prioritizes here the physicality of the body and its importance for God's redemptive and sanctifying work. Susanne's creative description of music as an *unconsummated* symbol attests to a more implicit, but no less significant, embodiment which *feeling* subsumes within its definition as the mark of human mentality. Her definition of *feeling* retained a faith that the word logic would hold within it sensations and sentience broader than purely scientific or mathematical logic. Whether that faith remains justified is a determination for another day. But unexpectedly, these themes placed side by side not only instruct us about learning from music; they also highlight a contribution that Hildegard's impassioned advocacy makes to Susanne's reluctance to specify embodiment more explicitly, seen in the tautology with symbolization.

Hildegard's sense of *interior illumination* relies fully upon the physicality of the human body, enlivened and harmonized (as she would say) when vested with the Garment of the Word and infused with the Holy Spirit. In this way, Hildegard thoroughly integrates form and force of human experience with respect to music. She moved beyond the classical medieval worldview of Boethian musical-cosmology

---

75. Hildegard, "Letter to the Prelates at Mainz," 79.
76. Ibid.

into the primary site of listening, growth, insight, and understanding: the human body and a shared desire for God expressed in relational community. Bruce Holsinger's early work introduced and then further developed this understanding of Hildegard's musical compositions and their emphases on music's corporeality. "Hildegard's musical compositions exemplify her own conceptions of body . . . and its central role in religious devotion," he argues. Thus, music, by means of divine agency and heightened desire, makes "sensual physicality integral to religious devotion."[77] Hildegard brings the human body explicitly into music's form and significance, whereas Langer omits it in her need for "pure form." Hildegard also offers awareness of the inevitability of desire within musical participation and yearnings for clarity about its significance. Again, Holsinger: "Hildegard's direct encounter with divinity . . . takes place in and through the physical body, involving many of the same kinds of corporeal pains and devotional pleasures."[78] Hildegard shows a fundamental force of music to be the shaping and potential sanctification of the human body in all its desires. Toward an end of expressive praise, music offers communal form and intimate participation which subtly shape human mentality and action. When given careful consideration and traditional guidance via *discretio*, this subtle shaping through desire sanctifies and harmonizes human being in community of sung praise.

In contrast, Susanne aims for clarity about the transformation of human experience while de-emphasizing or even omitting what is "particularly human," not to mention any specific motivation or determinative aim. As stated above, she redefines human need as symbolization itself, away from the evolutionary-linguistic determination of human being. Unable to make explicit connections to embodiment without de-legitimizing her theory of mind as irrational, she offers this philosophical tautology: what is most human is symbolization and humans most need to symbolize. She offers substantial contributions for understanding a human mentality that includes rite, sacrament, and the arts, yet she ultimately demurs from human particularity, from the pleasure and pain of being an embodied human being, driven inward or outward by desire. Langer ironically omits the power of desire as

---

77. Holsinger, "Flesh of the Voice," 96.
78. Ibid., 97.

shaped in community from the significance of music. Seen side by side with Hildegard's advocacy for music's utter corporeality within a Benedictine spirituality, symbolization becomes a more realistic, relational, and interactive transformation of experience, even for contemporary ears beyond diverse historical locations.

Conclusion

Hildegard of Bingen, as composer-theologian and Benedictine abbess, demonstrates a Christian theological wisdom about the crucial role music played in her community and in the reform of the Church, in this case specifically the right administration of liturgy and the sacraments. She offers in her own terms an impassioned argument for music as a primarily embodied, sacramental teaching for the renewal and strengthening of faith through the sanctifying harmonization of body and soul in communion with and praise of God. Her insistence upon music's corporeality and its ordained expressions of shared desire for God still challenges scholars today, if for widely varying reasons.

Historical remove needs careful attention, of course, but her invitation to consider why music is important within a particular community and how it teaches or instructs its participants continues to resound. She spoke of music's purpose to teach of inward things by outward means, language that exudes a sacramental hue. My own disciplinary lens hears her contribution within the defined object of study, which is the "actualization of the basic human capacity for transcendence," inward capacity and transcendent purpose. Hildegard insists upon the centrality of the human body, and we are witnesses to the force of desire in the experience and enacted possibilities of musical phenomena. *Discretio* unto insight thus offers its conceptual hardware for understanding music's potential role in teaching and learning. Susanne Langer's work, in its own right and in its contemporary appropriations within theological discourse, offers a feasible way for understanding Hildegard's interior illumination and heightened desire for God in music's redemptive and sanctifying work. A creative interplay between them deepens awareness about the various dimensions involved for learning from music in performative mode.

At the very least, both Hildegard of Bingen and Susanne Langer argue music's significance for learning is rooted in its explicitly embodied or felt phenomenality and its capacity for making the transformation of experience palpable within sensation. In this way, music instigates interior illumination or insight from a non-discursive symbolism and indivisible multidimensionality. Chapters 2, 3, and 4 establish the problematic for today and a potential model for greater understanding about how we learn from and in music, in its performative mode.

2

Learning and the Conundrum of Aptitude for the Musical/Non-Musical

Learning in Music and Learning from Music

As conceived today, musicality appears to be a capacity or talent either genetically inherited or professionally trained. Many of us—particularly within Western, Anglo- or Eurocentric groups—profess to being completely non-musical, meaning we have little or no aptitude for participation in musical activities. There are those who love to sing—the musically inclined—and those who prefer, or have been asked, to "just listen"—the non-musically inclined. Yet in global perspective, viewed across geographical location, economic difference, and cultural specificities, musicality appears to be a ubiquitous part of human life and communal interaction. Music "lets us meet in places we couldn't get to any other way,"[1] so the saying goes. It mysteriously opens human beings to one another, even when culture commodifies it as "world music"[2] or musical styles are points of animated disputes.[3] South African educator, Joyce Scott, sums it up well in the opening sentences of her *Tuning in to a Different Song: Using a Music Bridge to Cross Cultural Differences*: "'Music is a universal language.' This sounds

---

1. LaMott, *Traveling Mercies*, 65.
2. Byrne, "I Hate World Music."
3. Byars, *Future of Protestant Worship* and Dawn and Taylor, *How Shall We Worship?*

a warm and comforting thing to say. But in fact it is a myth, and almost the exact opposite is true."[4]

Liturgical reformer and Scottish minister, John L. Bell, identifies this disparity in his little volume, *The Singing Thing: A Case for Congregational Song*. He names several possible causes for this musical/non-musical divide,[5] speaking with characteristic wit and grace. The first cause he names is *early vocal disenfranchisement*: someone in authority told someone else not to sing, that they "could not sing." The memory lodges deeply, resulting in being *non-musical*. A *performance culture* creates this split too. The rise of professionalism of all kinds—church musicians, organists, choir directors, vocal specialists—results in implicit assumptions that good music comes only from professionals. Third, Bell observes that many places and spaces within contemporary faith communities insure musical performance-activities are obstructed, due to *architecture* and *acoustics*. Attention to acoustics and the seating arrangements of human voices that would encourage singing or musical expression gets distracted to sanctuary carpets, pew cushions, sound-dampening tiles, or stately historical architecture. While well suited and advantageous in its own right, the rise of amplified and digital music practices does remove humanly enacted, embodied characteristics of musical sound even further from communal awareness. Bell names *bad leadership* as a fourth cause of the musical/non-musical split, with various expressions of it: musicians arriving late and leaving early, postured professionalism, unrehearsed hymn-playing, overly loud singing within congregational songs, and so forth. Whatever the cause may be, musicality, within a wide variety of communities, raises questions today of musical capacity, ability, and performance, all of which become significant when considering learning from music in a performative mode.

We who give the sciences authority to challenge our perceptions about the truth of such matters must negotiate findings that contradict this perceived split between the musical and non-musical populations. Across the globe, human beings have been identified again and again as an innately musical species. Rooted in biology but expressed in multiple psychological, sociological, and cultural dimensions, music and

---

4. Scott, *Tuning in to a Different Song*, 8.
5. Bell, *Singing Thing*, 95ff.

musical expressionism therefore appear to be limited in some fashion by human will, perception, and imagination or more. To explore the research and challenge the perception, this chapter investigates some of the dimensions of innate musical potential in scientific and popular writing. Delving more deeply, we then examine the work of two theorists who suggest in research and practice that human beings do, indeed, have an innate musicality. The chapter concludes with an examination of the challenges to be faced when one is inclined to learn *from* music, with a sense of objective distance, or when one is more inclined to learn *in* music, in its participatory-performative mode.

Science-Writing on Musicality as a Universal Feature of Humanity

Scientists from diverse specializations have investigated the human fascination with music and come to a burgeoning consensus that musical expression is a universal feature of humankind. *New York Times* science writer Natalie Angier introduced the public to current scientific perspective on the biological bases of cognitive musical activity and behavior in her article entitled "Sonata for Humans, Birds, and Humpback Whales." She points to two contemporary articles in *Science* and concludes that

> the love of music, that unslakable, unshakable, indescribable desire to sing and rejoice, rattle and roll, is not only a universal feature of the human species, found in every society known to anthropology, but is also deeply embedded in multiple structures of the human brain, and is far more ancient than previously suspected.[6]

These articles argue for musicality as not only a human species' trait particular to its neurobiological structures but also a phenomenon witnessed in nature generally and therefore older than human language. In the *Music Educator's Journal*, Franz L. Roehmann similarly notes the increase of attention in the 1980s to connections between music and neurology, medicine, and psychological therapy.[7]

---

6. Angier, "Sonata for Humans, Birds, and Humpback Whales."
7. Roehmann, "Making the Connection: Music and Medicine," 21.

"Music of the Hemispheres," one of the *Science* articles, argues for a universal, biological basis to musical capacity and then summarizes current neurobiological perspectives on music, musical perception, and musical cognition. Mark Tramo writes,

> All of us are born with the capacity to apprehend emotion and meaning in music, regardless of whether we understand music theory or read musical notation. Without conscious effort, the human brain is able to translate spectral and temporal patterns of acoustic energy into music's basic perceptual elements: melody, harmony, and rhythm.... Universal among human cultures, music binds us in a collective identity as members of nations, religions, and other groups.[8]

Tramo further observes that rats and starlings can distinguish between consonant and dissonant chords and suggests that the prevalence of common intervals in human music-cultures "may be a consequence of the way that our ears and brains are built."[9] Though the right hemisphere has been traditionally viewed as the "musical hemisphere," Tramo argues that there is no such music center in the brain at all. Functional imaging studies track perception of music emerging from an interplay of neural pathways in both right and left hemispheres, some specific to music, others not.[10] He details more of the neurobiological studies, but he concludes: all of the structures of the brain that participate in the processing of music contribute to other forms of cognition as well. There appears to be no identifiable or specific neurological area of the brain for musical cognition, per se, but neurobiological multiplicity and diversity.

Six researchers at the BioMusic Program in Washington, D.C. also suggest a universality of music based upon work with "repeated rhythmic utterances" observed similarly in humpback whales' song, bird song, and human symphonies. In "The Music of Nature and the Nature

8. Tramo, "Music of the Hemispheres," 54.

9. Ibid. He cites Zentner and Kagan, "Infants' Perception of Consonance and Dissonance in Music;" and Hulse, Bernard, and Braaten, "Auditory Discrimination of Chord-based Spectral Structures by European Starlings (*Sturnus vulgaris*)."

10. Tramo, "Music of the Hemispheres," 54. He cites Sidtis, and Volpe, "Selective Loss of Complex-Pitch or Speech Discrimination after Unilateral Cerebral Lesion," 235–45; Zatorre, "Pitch Perception of Complex Tones and Human Temporal-Lobe Function," 566–72; and Peretz, "Processing of Local and Global Musical Information by Unilateral Brain-Damaged Patients," 1185–1205.

of Music," they note several interesting phenomena in humpback-whale "songs." Singing humpbacks use rhythms similar to those in human music, though they could just as easily use arrhythmic sounds. They use phrases of similar length and create themes out of several phrases, similar to patterns in human music. More overtly, the authors write, "Whale songs fall between the length of a modern ballad and that of a movement of a symphony. Perhaps they have chosen the same length of performance as we have because, with their large cerebral cortex, they have a similar attention span to humans."[11] Even though whales have a range of over seven octaves, they use musical intervals that are similar to those in human tonal scales. They mix "percussive or noisy elements" in their songs with relatively pure tones in similar ratio to that of Western symphonic music. Finally, and most surprisingly, "humpback songs contain repeating refrains that form rhymes. This suggests that whales use rhyme in the same way that we do . . ." They review bird song and the oral tradition of the Sami (the indigenous people of the northern Scandinavian peninsula), and suggest that there is a deep human need to create, perform, and listen to music because of this deep biological heritage. With a gentle skepticism, they write, "The similarities among human music, bird song, and whale song tempt one to speculate that the Platonic alternative may exist—that there is a universal music awaiting discovery."[12] These contemporary biological perspectives show that widely varying biological forms share behaviors of patterning sounds, suggestive of universal human musical potential (and behavior), which connect humanity to the biological world in a fundamental manner.

Musicality as a broadly human feature does not deny the very particular and internal dimension of music to which humanity also witnesses. Music educator Franz Roehmann, in his article "Making the Connection: Music and Medicine," considers this very particularity of music in human experience, given voice by "Edith," a patient of renowned neurologist Oliver Sacks. Sacks worked with Edith, who described her own struggling with that disease as "being unmusicked." Roehmann cites Sacks's words written in the book, *Awakenings*:

---

11. Gray, Krause, Atema, Payner, Drumhansl, and Baptista, "Music of Nature and the Nature of Music," 53.

12. Ibid., 54.

> She said that she had become graceless... that her movements had become wooden, mechanical, like a robot... that, in a word, she had been "unmusicked."... She would find herself frozen, utterly motionless, deprived of the power, the impulse, the thought of any motion... until the music came [to mind] ... And then with [the] imagining of music... the power of motion, action, would suddenly return... Just as suddenly, [her] inner music would cease and she would fall instantly, once again, into a Parkinsonian abyss.[13]

Something utterly biological yet utterly integrated into the mental and bodily functioning of Edith would come and go, operative only from the inside. Sacks's work further suggested that neither overwhelming musical sound nor intimate "shapeless crooning" from the outside produced this effect in Edith. Only the music that came to her mind from the inside affected her liberation. This observed behavior and experience leads Roehmann to ask, "Is there an inner music within us; if so, what is it and how can it be accessed?"[14] These two questions about a potentially universal music into which humanity is drawn and an inner, quintessentially human music offer provocative propositions about what it is to be human and what it is to explore human musicality.

Edwin Gordon on Music Aptitude and Howard Gardner on Musical Intelligence

The empirical evaluation of musicality[15] presents a rather formidable history, begun in the late nineteenth century.[16] As we might expect, the first evaluations of musical aptitude—the innate, genetic potential for musical achievement and recognized talent—were largely subjective. Early researchers named everything from toil and sweat, to genetic heritage, to the use of imagery for perceiving musical sound as critical

---

13. Sacks, *Awakenings*, 294–95. Cited in Roehmann, "Making the Connection," 21. See more recently, Sacks, *Musicophilia*, 105ff.

14. Roehmann, "Making the Connection," 5.

15. The use of terms—musicality, aptitude, potential, competence, and more—will be necessarily diffuse at this stage of the discussion. Eventually, *musicality* will be interchangeable with *music* or *musical aptitude* (Gordon), crafted for educational discourse with *musical intelligence* (Gardner).

16. Gordon *Psychology of Music Teaching* and *Introduction to Research and the Psychology of Music*.

elements in human musical potential.[17] The need for more verifiable means with which to support conflicting hypotheses quickly arose. The musical test battery was created, originally in the form of the Seashore Measures of Musical Talent. This test represented the empirical efforts of Carl E. Seashore, a proponent of musical aptitude's innate, multiple, and distinct characteristics. The Wing Standardized Tests of Musical Intelligence, published in 1958, constituted another approach to the empirical investigation of musical aptitude, reliant upon the hypothesis of musical aptitude as a unitary phenomenon, unable to be understood in dissected or distinct capabilities.

The ensuing testing tradition therefore roughly revolved around two theoretical stances—many distinct capacities or a unitary capacity. Edwin Gordon streamlined this testing tradition with respect to evaluations of test reliability and validity through critical assessments and the creation of his own Musical Aptitude Profile, now a common instrument for evaluating musical potential with the goal of improving teaching strategies. His mature understanding of music aptitude emerges from both this testing tradition and his own research contributions. His work moved research into musical aptitude toward a more flexible and sensitive reliance upon testing for an integrative, individual-centered, music learning theory, to be examined more fully in chapter 3. After a brief review of his empirical-critical approach to human musical potential illustrated in his own assessment of his Musical Aptitude Profile, we will examine his qualification and quantification of music aptitude.

Gordon's Empirical-Critical Approach to Musical Aptitude

Edwin Gordon began in the musical disciplines with his string bass performance degree from Eastman School of Music. He then entered the specific discipline of music education through his initial research, a critical evaluation of the musical testing tradition, and his eventual construction of several test batteries. His goal was a more sensitive identification and quantification of musical aptitude as opposed to

---

17. Gordon, *Psychology of Music Teaching*, 11. He cites Squires, "Creative Psychology of Carl Maria von Weber," 203–17; Vernon, "Personality of the Composer," 38–48; and Gross and Seashore, "Psychological Characteristics of Student and Professional Musical Composers," 159–70. See also Gordon, *Introduction to Research and The Psychology of Music*, 18–19.

musical achievement, training, or formal skill. This initial research into music education can be laid out in roughly four movements. He surveyed the previous test batteries and examined them in light of their empirical validity, identifying weaknesses in their empirical strategies and their use of validity measures. He constructed his own test battery, the Musical Aptitude Profile (or MAP), which more closely connected his understanding of and educational approach to music with schoolchildren. His commitment to predictive longitudinal validity—a validity assessment over a period of years—resulted in more substantive and more persuasive research on how human beings learn music over time. Finally, he compared the validity measures of his test battery with those in use and revised the MAP accordingly, particularly with respect to developmental concerns.

Methodologically, Gordon reframed the problem of musical aptitude away from the extant framework of unified capacity versus distinct capacities. Instead, he focused upon empirical research in which he was both interested and adept. He thereby established himself professionally by arguing for more empirically precise methods of investigation, especially with respect to test validity and reliability. After all, if musical-aptitude tests were found to be empirically invalid or unreliable, their contributions to an understanding of musical aptitude were moot. From this unusual research agenda (for music education, at least), he argued for *musical aptitude* as a normally distributed product of innate potential and early environmental influences that fluctuates developmentally in the early years and stabilizes as potential by about age ten. Gordon's contribution here, however, is a conceptually tight and empirically researched understanding of musical aptitude, broadly distributed across the human population regardless of ethnicity, race, gender, or perceived musicality.

Definition of Music Aptitude

Gordon's Musical Aptitude Profile (MAP) maximized certain features of aptitude—musical expression, aural perception, and kinesthetic musical feeling—while minimizing aspects of music achievement—previous musical experience, notation, theory, or repertory. Accordingly, it demonstrates an objective assessment tool, to be used in conjunction with a music teacher's holistic evaluation. "Test scores cannot replace human judgment and understanding," Gordon argues, "but can only supplement and objectively reinforce human judgment and understanding."[18] Constituted by three major divisions—tonal, rhythmic, and expressive elements—the MAP prefigures an understanding of music aptitude constructed out of musical structures—tonal imagery (melody, harmony), rhythmic imagery (tempo and meter)—and human sensitivity or interaction—musical sensitivity subtests, measuring responsiveness or preference for phrasing, balance, and style. These seven factors determine Gordon's conceptualization of music aptitude, empirically researched in both short-term and longitudinal studies. His work with the MAP was confirmed by its high predictive validity as well.

> In a three-year longitudinal study, the pretraining *MAP* composite score predicted success in elementary instrumental music with unusually high precision. Furthermore, after three years of typical musical practice and training, it was found that students' *MAP* scores did not significantly improve upon readministration.[19]

This interpretation was confirmed after the five-year longitudinal study was completed and published.[20] A huge body of empirical studies suggests that Gordon created a test battery that met his goal of maximizing musical aptitude characteristics and minimizing the musical achievement characteristics that clouded much of the previous testing traditions' efforts. As his work progressed, he also pursued aptitude-test development specific to age-ranges and other human developmental concerns. Each phase contributed to his summary definition of music aptitude.

According to Gordon, *music aptitude* is

> a product of innate potential and early environmental influences [that] is normally distributed among students of all ages. The main dimensions of musical aptitude are rhythmic, tonal, and aesthetic-interpretive. Although [it] fluctuates throughout the primary grades, it becomes impervious to practice and training at about age ten.[21]

18. Gordon, *Musical Aptitude Profile Manual*, 1–2.

19. Gordon, *Psychology of Music Teaching*, 24.

20. Gordon, *A Three-year Longitudinal Predictive Validity Study of the Musical Aptitude Profile*.

21. Gordon, *Psychology of Music Teaching*, 7.

He sees it as the basis for musical sensitivity and achievement, with both *developmental* and *stabilized* forms.[22] Developmental aptitude describes the musical potential of those children under the age of ten; stabilized aptitude refers to those whose potential has solidified and who are older than ten years.

Gordon observes a ubiquity of human music aptitude across race, religion, personality, or cultural settings. He begins with the empirical studies that suggest that musical aptitude is normally distributed: everyone has at least some musical aptitude.[23] An examination of score distributions provided with musical aptitude tests point to the fact that "the great majority of persons have average musical aptitude, fewer persons have above or below average musical aptitude, and only a very few persons have very little or exceptionally high musical aptitude."[24] Everyone has at least some musical potential that may be nurtured intentionally during early childhood development. Musical *achievement*—the complementary construct to aptitude that describes skill development in more formal instruction—is the more overt phenomenon. While achievement varies according to the availability of resources and educational advantage, aptitude, even stabilized aptitude, is generally distributed across human population. Even more startling is the information available within Gordon's studies on music and various human differences.

"We can only conclude from our [available] information," he observes, "that race, nationality, religion, and sex are not systematically associated with musical aptitude, with the possible specific exception of rhythm aptitude."[25] Neither cultural advantage (or disadvantage)[26] nor

---

22. Gordon, *Music Learning Theory for Newborn and Young Children*, 11.
23. Gordon, *Psychology of Music Teaching*, 5.
24. Ibid.
25. Ibid., 35.
26. Ibid., 36. His point is about musical *aptitude*, not achievement or success in music. See also Gordon, "First-year Results of a Five-year Longitudinal Study of the Musical Achievement of Culturally Disadvantaged Students," 195–213; Gordon, *Second-year Results of a Five-year Longitudinal Study of the Musical Achievement of Culturally Disadvantaged Students*; Gordon, *Third-Year Results of a Five-Year Longitudinal Study of the Musical Achievement of Culturally-Disadvantaged Students*; and Gordon, *Fourth-Year and Fifth-Year Final Results of a Longitudinal Study of the Musical Achievement of Culturally-Disadvantaged Students*.

personality characteristics[27] show a marked relationship to musical aptitude. Informed by both longitudinal and latitudinal studies, Gordon argues that human musical potential—differentiated from training, success, or achievement in music—shows no direct correlation to the wide diversity of human experience. Music aptitude for him is therefore defined as the product of a universal innate human potential and early environmental influences. It is comprised of rhythmic, tonal, and aesthetic or expressive-interpretive aptitudes. It is not affected by race, religion, nationality, personality, or cultural setting.

These preliminary findings regarding social or cultural influences as being of little or no import do not erase the importance of the immediate early environment for the sustenance of music aptitude received by a young child at birth.

> A child's music aptitude is innate, but it is affected by his environment. Because the music environment for only a few newborns is appropriate and as rich as it should be, it is reasoned that the level of music aptitude with which a child is born begins to decrease shortly after birth. A child's music aptitude continues to decrease until his music environment becomes appropriate. When the music environment becomes appropriate, a child's music aptitude will begin to increase toward its birth level. Regardless of how positive the quality of the music environment becomes, however, a child's music aptitude will never rise above its birth level.[28]

Current research does not prove or disprove that claim, but it coheres with the remainder of Gordon's empirical-theoretical work.

In sum, music aptitude is described as the product of universal innate human potential and early environmental influences. Distinct from music achievement, aptitude is not affected by race, religion, nationality, personality, or culture. The main dimensions are rhythmic, tonal, and aesthetic-interpretive. It fluctuates throughout early childhood, when it must be nurtured toward its theoretically highest

---

27. Gordon, *Psychology of Music Teaching*, 36–37. Here Gordon refers to Schleuter, "An Investigation of the Interrelation of Personality Traits, Musical Aptitude, and Musical Achievement." Gordon does not directly address personality, but he does intimate "personality" similar to "social intelligence," which is not be positively or negatively affected by stabilized potential. See Kilhstrom and Cantor, "Social Intelligence," 359–79.

28. Gordon, *A Music Learning Theory for Newborn and Young Children*, 9–10.

(birth) level, and becomes impervious to such nurture at about age ten. Gordon describes the early form of music aptitude as developmental aptitude and the later form (after age ten) as stabilized aptitude. His later work in *Learning Sequences in Music* gives a narrative description of music aptitude that fills out his earlier, empirical approaches to it. Music aptitude is "a measure of a student's potential to learn music [that] points beyond itself" to future learning and musical experience.[29] He describes it as a hunger, a capacity to learn, that is spontaneous, is associated more with intuition, and is located in the genes and cells, or primarily in the entire body.[30]

Edwin Gordon Meets Howard Gardner

As Edwin Gordon researched and theorized about musical aptitude from the 1960s to the present day, another theorist explored *musical intelligence* within interdisciplinary, cognitive-science explorations of human intelligence. Howard Gardner of Harvard University became fascinated with human potential and cognition, creating a body of literature intended for the cognitive science world but now deeply rooted within educational theory and reform, the central plank being his *Frames of Mind: The Theory of Multiple Intelligences*. Gordon and Gardner's similarities and differences suggest each as a resonant conversation partner of the other, and both as good contributors for our purposes here of identifying ways that persons learn from music in musical events.

Both Gardner and Gordon explore human potential with respect to music, each providing an understanding that is oriented toward ongoing development of learning processes. Both also posit the need for educational reform toward an education where understanding is valued in broader contexts of human disciplinary thought and in the existential questions of life. Gardner campaigns for deep understanding in disciplinary thought as the primary educational aim for schools today. He writes, "I take a stand in favor of a certain kind of education, one that yields 'generative' or 'deep' or 'genuine' understanding."[31] Gordon

---

29. Gordon, *Learning Sequences in Music*, 41.
30. Ibid., 41–42.
31. Gardner, *Unschooled Mind*, 16. See also chapters 10–13.

argues that one cannot truly appreciate music without understanding it, although much of current music educational thought aims its pedagogy towards a more superficial music appreciation. He writes, "All but possibly purely emotional reactions to tone quality and dynamics in music depend on understanding. When persons understand, they are able to control and to maximize their advantageous relation to music."[32]

Third, Gardner and Gordon share a similar focus in the substance of their educational reform: learning in a performative mode of specific practices. Gardner's educational reflections based upon his Multiple Intelligences theory have centered largely upon the need to foster deep understanding by beginning with the individual interests and abilities of the child. He writes, "What is the alternative [to uniform schooling]? One possibility is individually configured education—an education that takes individual differences seriously and, insofar as possible, crafts activities that serve different kinds of minds equally well."[33] Meanwhile, from his extensive research and the eventual construction of the MAP, Gordon developed a comprehensive and developmentally sensitive music learning theory that articulates a pedagogy directed toward students' individual differences. He notes that

> By teaching to students' individual differences, teachers lessen the risk of boring students with high potential and frustrating students with lower potential. . . . Music Learning Theory is unique among music teaching methods in accounting directly for students' differing potentials to achieve in music.[34]

Gardner and Gordon's mutual interest in individual-centered educational pedagogies legitimates at the very least their compatibility as educational allies with respect to human musical potential and learning music as an aid toward deepened understanding. The disciplinary distinctiveness between these two—Gardner in developmental psychology and Gordon in music education—allows each to strengthen and supplement the work of the other, doing so from positions of disciplinary expertise.

---

32. Gordon, *Learning Sequences in Music*, 31.
33. Gardner, *Intelligence Reframed*, 150–51.
34. Gordon, "About Music Learning Theory."

The Intelligence Tradition

The intelligence tradition has been organized and assessed by a variety of authors in the last twenty years, but finds its roots at the very least in the early work of Francis Galton, Alfred Binet, and Charles Spearman. David Pyle, a psychologist within a British frame of reference, arranges the substantial intelligence tradition into psychometric, test-based models of human intelligence and the critical models that directly oppose psychometric testing of human intelligence.[35] Nathan Brody offers a standard textbook on human intelligence, which traces this tradition's development through its chronological history.[36] Robert Sternberg provides a current, comprehensive collection of perspectives on the study of human intelligence in his edited volume, *Handbook of Intelligence*.[37] Each of these resources offers a valuable perspective on the study of human intelligence and contributes to the following sketch of "intelligence" developments within which to place Gardner's contributions and challenges.

Chronological overview

Francis Galton originated the modern study of human intelligence in the South Kensington Museum in London in 1882, where he measured individual sensory/cognition differences of those who visited. He was of the British empiricist school that placed primary importance on knowledge derived from sensations, the foundation for complex cognitive functioning and transmission of sense to knowledge.[38] Binet's original intelligence test, or IQ test, birthed the more popular notion of g, a numerical assessment of human intelligence, normally distributed over a bell-curve representing the general population. He is often named the father of the IQ test, but he was more interested than popular assessment suggests in the "remarkable diversity of intelligence."[39] James McKeen Cattell, an American student of Wilhelm Wundt, published a paper en-

---

35. Pyle, *Intelligence*.
36. Brody, *Intelligence*.
37. Sternberg, *Handbook of Intelligence*.
38. Brody, "History of Theories and Measurements of Intelligence," 16.
39. See Siegler, "Other Alfred Binet," 175–202.

titled "Mental Tests and Measurements" that was endorsed by Galton and that began the use of "mental tests" in the study of intelligence.[40]

Charles Spearman built the empirical foundations of the study of human intelligence with his factor analysis and two-factor model of human intelligence— *g* as a measure of general human intelligence and several special factors, *s*, which were measures of differentiated human capabilities. His use of factor analysis to determine probability and strength of correlation between measured mental faculties further proliferated "intelligence" as a two-level phenomenon directly relating sensory discrimination and academic achievement. In 1949, D.O. Hebb articulated a hypothesis that human intelligence consisted of two dimensions: intelligence A, which was an innate potential; and intelligence B, which was the interaction between intelligence A and environment, or the measurement of the actual functioning of neurons and schemata. C. Burt and P.E. Vernon developed Charles Spearman's work further into a two-factor, hierarchical model of human intelligence, which grouped the special abilities and suggested that intelligence changes in its organization throughout development. "Intelligence" was a general cognitive competence with specialized abilities that altered their organization over time and development.

Jean Piaget argued that human intelligence is a structural, functional, and dynamic process of adaptation (assimilation and accommodation) and organization, through which a child constructs her world, a model almost completely distinct from any psychometric or experimentally psychological research approach. "Intelligence" here refers to a scientifically nuanced, genetic-epistemological ability to construct a sensible world. L.L. Thurstone researched and argued an allegedly more useful, "many types" model of human intelligence in terms of "primary mental abilities." Raymond Cattell and A.R. Jensen posited a two-part model of intelligence, divided into fluid and crystallized intelligences, the first of which described the biological, inherited, and non-cultural influences, and the second described the educational and cultural experiences affecting human intelligence. In 1967, J.P. Guilford built upon Thurstone's work with a structural model of human intelligence that identified up to 120 abilities, each with three major faces or dimensions: content, operations, and products of human intelligence. David Pyle

---

40. Brody, "History of Theories and Measurements of Intelligence," 16.

summarizes a consensus conclusion from this chronologically ordered survey pretty well: intelligence is not only a capacity to learn, nor only an entity or substance, nor only unitary in nature, nor only the explanatory concept that it is often taken to be. It is multifaceted, multisided, impossible to directly measure, and potentially flexible in expression.[41]

Tradition: Metaphorical Overview

Robert Sternberg's organization of the conceptions of intelligence in terms of governing metaphors gives another helpful overview within which to place Gardner's work. Sternberg gives seven metaphors within which experts in the field have conceptualized intelligence: geographic, computational, biological, genetic-epistemological, anthropological, sociological, and systems metaphors. The geographic metaphor simply refers to intelligence as a "map of the mind"; Sternberg places Spearman, Thurstone, Guilford, Cattell, and Vernon as conceiving intelligence in this manner: "The basic unit of analysis in this metaphor is the factor that typically is alleged to be a source of individual differences among people."[42] Sternberg identifies his own work in terms of the computational metaphor, in which the basic unit of analysis is the elementary information process or component, measured by reaction-time analysis and computer simulation. A biological metaphor governs the work of Hebb, among others. Although the basic unit of analysis varies across theories, Hebb conceptualized "intelligence" to be dependent upon cell assembly. Others have researched intelligence through neuronal conduction and various biochemical processes of the brain. The genetic-epistemological metaphor in Piaget's work describes intelligence in terms of the basic unit, a schema. The world constructed and organized by the child is built from elementary patterns or units—schemas.

The much more recent anthropological and sociological metaphors identify intelligence in terms of cultural and societal influences. The anthropological conceptualization of intelligence is as a cultural interaction: the basic unit of analysis is the individual in interaction with her cultural context. Sternberg cites theorists J.W. Berry, M. Cole,

---

41. Pyle, *Intelligence*, 18–19.
42. Sternberg, "Concept of Intelligence," 10.

and P.M. Greenfield who work within this metaphor.[43] The sociological metaphor emphasizes the importance of socialization in "intelligence"; Vygotsky and Feuerstein promote this understanding, the former through his notion of "internalization" and the latter through "mediated learning."[44] The final metaphor described by Sternberg is the systems metaphor, in which he places both his more recent work and that of Howard Gardner. Sternberg writes, "The systems metaphor is based on the notion that intelligence is a complex system that integrates many levels of analysis, including geographic, computational, biological, anthropological, sociological, and others. The unit of analysis is the system and its elements in interaction."[45] *Intelligence* from this perspective is a complex, dynamic phenomenon that must account for a variety of impulses within and beyond the human body and mind.

Howard Gardner and Musical Intelligence

Gardner's multiple intelligences—a multifaceted, differentiated group of human competencies that demonstrates functional content, information processing, and cultural products—finds its own history in the critical, "many types" strand of human intelligence studies seen also in the work of Burt and Vernon, as well as Guilford.[46] Burt and Vernon's hierarchical model that groups human abilities into differentiated sets suggests early roots for Gardner's work with grouped abilities corresponding to external media, be it language, music, interpersonal interactions, or other stimuli. Guilford's functional and structural model of human intelligence that posits a multitude of human abilities with three dimensions of content, operations, and products also sets the stage for Gardner's work with intelligence as a potential with a core set of op-

---

43. See Berry, "Towards a Universal Psychology of Cognitive Competence;" M. Cole, *Cultural Psychology*; and Greenfield, "You Can't Take it With You," 1115–24.

44. Sternberg, "Concept of Intelligence," 11. See Vygotsky, *Mind in Society*; and Feuerstein, *Instrumental Enrichment*.

45. Sternberg, "Concept of Intelligence," 12.

46. Gardner contextualizes his own work too. See Gardner, "Intelligence in Seven Steps," 1ff. See also "M.I. after Twenty Years" and "25th Anniversary of the Publication of Howard Gardner's *Frames of Mind: the Theory of Multiple Intelligences*"; "Who Owns Intelligence?"; "Multiple Intelligences," and "Borders of Intelligence." See also Gardner et al., *Intelligence*; and Gardner, "Reflections on Multiple Intelligences," 200–209.

erations toward culturally valuable products.[47] In addition, MI theory emerged from Gardner's felt dissonance with the psychometrically influenced, developmental conceptualizations of intelligence that denied or at the very least ignored artistic abilities and achievements.

In *Intelligence Reframed*, Gardner argues against traditional theories of intelligence dominated by linguistic or mathematical reasoning and instead for the "intelligent" person as society's referent term for an "ideal human being."[48] Intelligence in this sense is the construct that describes what a society most values. Western technological cultures have valued scientific thinking and expertise, so *intelligence* has referred to logical-mathematical reasoning and scientific accomplishments. Gardner argues, in contrast, for eight intelligences, in which eight different expressions of expertise reference the "ideal human being" for that particular competence: composers for musical intelligence, performers such as dancers or athletes for bodily/kinesthetic intelligences, and so forth. He gives a broader, systems-theory definition of "intelligence" determined through interdisciplinary criteria.

The criteria through which Gardner identifies multiple human capabilities as intelligences emerge from four major areas of human thought: biological science, logical analysis, developmental psychology, and psychometric or psychological experimentation. In *Frames of Mind*, he examines the various strands of thought on human cognitive development in terms of these criteria and articulates his definition of "intelligence." A thorough look at his *musical intelligence* will flesh out his definition of an intelligence, his intentions with the eight criteria, and the end-state of composing for a *musical* intelligence.

Musical Intelligence

Relying upon eight criteria, Gardner posits that an *intelligence* is "a biopsychological potential to process information that can be activated in a cultural setting to solve problems or create products that are of value to a culture."[49] In *Frames of Mind*, he argues for seven human capabilities corresponding to various media of human activity: language,

---

47. Gardner, *Frames of Mind*, 12–30.
48. Gardner, *Intelligence Reframed*, 28.
49. Gardner, *Multiple Intelligences*, 33–34.

numbers/abstract relations, music, body, space, consciousness, and community, corresponding to *linguistic, logical-mathematical, musical, bodily/kinesthetic, spatial, interpersonal,* and *intrapersonal* intelligences, respectively. In his more recent *Intelligence Reframed*, Gardner adds an eighth intelligence, a *naturalist* intelligence that corresponds to the natural world: the human potential to catalogue and investigate relations in nature. He later explores the possibilities of an *existential* or *spiritual* intelligence and a *moral* intelligence, but he ultimately argues against both of these as a ninth human intelligence. Humorously, he posits "8 ½ intelligences."[50]

Musical intelligence meets all of Gardner's established criteria. The distinctiveness of musical intelligence in human experience is suggested by potential isolation in brain damage and an evolutionary history that implies a long line of particularly musical ability evolved from and through other species (criteria one and two). Gardner writes,

> This specialness of musical perception is confirmed dramatically by studies of individuals whose brains have been damaged as a result of stroke or other kinds of trauma. . . . the key finding of this research is that one can suffer significant aphasia without any discernible musical impairment, even as one can become disabled musically while still retaining one's fundamental linguistic competences.[51]

Musical intelligence must therefore be a distinct human competency because it can be differentiated from others at a basic neurobiological level (criterion one). Gardner also observes a plausible genetic heritage in human musicality, which arguably resembles the heritage and development witnessed in bird song. The families of Bach, Mozart, and Haydn suggest a strong genetic component to human musical competence. Non-genetic factors such as value systems and training procedures may account for some familial traditions of musical competence, but the presence of some genetic factors cannot be disputed.[52] This leads Gardner to posit an evolutionary plausibility, at the very least (criterion two).

---

50. Gardner, *Intelligence Reframed*, 66.
51. Ibid., 118.
52. Ibid., 112.

Criteria three and four require an identifiable core operation, or set of operations (criterion three), demonstrating a susceptibility to encoding in a symbol system (criterion four). Musical intelligence displays a set of operations in the realm of music as sound-structure and in its expression of human emotions. Gardner states, "There is relatively little dispute about the principal constituent elements of music, though experts will differ on the precise definition of each aspect."[53] He describes the basic elements of music as pitch (or melody)—organized both horizontally over time and vertically in harmonic relationship—rhythm, and the timbre or characteristic quality of a tone. The role of audition cannot be denied, although Gardner does observe that the second central aspect to music, rhythmic structure, can be felt more than heard.[54] He also notes that some composers, such as Roger Sessions, place the affective qualities of music close to its core operations. In that vein, Gardner articulates in the now traditional terms of Susanne Langer that music can capture the forms of human emotion and symbolize them.[55] Gardner names a "central puzzle surrounding music":

> [I]t would seem preferable to describe music purely in terms of objective, physical terms: to stress the pitch and rhythmic aspects of music . . . Yet hardly anyone who has been intimately associated with music can forbear to mention its emotional implications: the effects it has upon individuals.[56]

In response to this puzzle, he cites both "bottom-up" and "top-down" approaches to music's core set of operations. "Bottom-up" folks name these operations as the tonal, rhythmic, and affective building blocks; "top-down" folks emphasize complete musical segments instead of any individual tonal, rhythmic, or affective components.

---

53. Gardner, *Frames of Mind*, 104.

54. Research has been done into the positive role that music has even in a deaf or non-hearing culture. See "Role of Music in Deaf Culture." Preliminary findings suggest that cultural identification is a major factor in deaf individuals' involvement with music and therefore that music can have an important role in the education of most hearing-impaired students.

55. Ibid., 106. See also Langer, *Philosophy in a New Key*.

56. Gardner, *Frames of Mind*, 105–6. Note Gardner arguably misreads Langer's more comprehensive sense of *feeling* too, as he locates support for his argument, without distinction, in affective, emotional terms.

Criteria five and six emerge out of the psychological sciences that focus upon a human developmental history (criterion five) and a definable set of expert "end-state" performances (criterion six). Gardner identifies musical intelligence as the earliest human competence to emerge. He writes, "Of all the gifts with which individuals may be endowed, none emerges earlier than musical talent."[57] This is borne out by research showing that musical potential and musical behavior appear in humans during the early stages of infancy, if not earlier.[58] Gardner then names the height or ideal end-state of musical activity to be composition (criterion six). His claim for musical intelligence developing in progression toward an end-state of composition alternates between anecdotal and more researched support. He paints a portrait of early musical competence that mirrors the work of Mechthild and Hanus Papousek, who noted infants' ability at two months to match the pitch, loudness, and melodic contour of their mother's songs, and at four months to match the rhythmic structures as well.[59] He observes the important transition that happens in the middle of the second year of life: exploration of various small intervals and the invention of spontaneous songs. By age three or four, the melodies of the dominant culture win and such spontaneous play tends to wane. Little further musical development occurs after the school years begin, although there may be an increase in knowledge about music. Gardner continues by identifying a school-period crisis between sheer talented energy expressed in a "figural" approach to music (as demonstrated from birth to approximately age eight) and the propositional, conceptually ordered understanding of musical phenomena in a formal approach, which appears during early adolescence.[60] Ultimately, his sources suggest that musical competency does indeed illustrate a distinct developmental history (criterion five).

---

57. Ibid., 99.
58. See Fridman, "Proto-Rhythms," 181–98.
59. Gardner, *Frames of Mind*, 108–9.
60. Ibid. See Bamberger, *Mind Behind the Musical Ear* and *Developing Musical Intuitions*. She makes a similar distinction between figural—know-how processing—and formal processing—know-that processing—in her description of musical development. She argues for stage-development through an early period, a developmental crisis, then more formal skill building periods afterward. For developmental crisis or "crystallizing experience," see Freeman, "Crystallizing Experience," 75–85.

Gardner posits support of a human musical intelligence from psychometric research and experimental psychological tasks (criteria seven and eight, respectively). *Frames of Mind* was written in direct opposition to the sole psychometric evaluation of human intelligence, so its presentation of psychometric research in support of his claim for a musical intelligence is nearly non-existent. *Multiple Intelligences* cites the need for tests of musical intelligence that would examine the individual's ability to analyze a work of music or to create one, not simply to compare two single tones on the basis of relative pitch.[61] In his later work, Gardner suggests an intelligence-fair and exemplary means for supporting his musical intelligence in the work of Project Spectrum, an assessment and curriculum program for preschool children. He writes, "For example, we sample musical intelligence by letting them explore melodies on attractive Montessori bells and by having them learn new songs."[62] Further detailed support for musical intelligence from either psychometric research or experimental psychology cannot be found easily in Gardner's authorship, though the educational ideal of a musical intelligence has blossomed. Despite the lack of hard evidence in psychometric or experimentally psychological terms, his conceptualization of musical intelligence has found an established, popularly accepted venue for further discourse. Musical intelligence as a description for a distinct human competency is here to stay.

MI in Critical Review

The seed of critical reactions to MI theory can be found in Gardner's rather courageous interdisciplinary perspective, with its resulting, and necessarily descriptive, parameters. For example, the more strictly defined psychological disciplines have attempted to discredit Gardner's work through rationales of disciplinary definitions and methods. Perry Klein argues that MI theory with its eight intelligences simply multiplies the problems of intelligence conceptualization by eight.[63] From this perspective, the act of making intelligence a conceptually multiple phenomenon only confuses further the terminology and issues at hand

---

61. Gardner, *Multiple Intelligences*, 39.
62. Gardner, *Intelligence Reframed*, 81.
63. See Klein, "Multiplying the Problems of Intelligence by Eight," and Gardner, "Reply to Perry D. Klein," 96–102.

in scientific inquiry. The huge response from the professional educational community has intensified interdisciplinary tensions. Gardner acknowledges at the very beginning of *Multiple Intelligences: The Theory in Practice* that most psychologists ignored *Frames of Mind*, though a few took the time to dislike it.[64] The audience for which *Frames of Mind* did meet an apparent need was one that he had not anticipated: professional educators. As a result, professional educators and the broader public have begun to appropriate a theory that strictly psychological science has yet to accept or refute. Gardner's interdisciplinary perspective fits an interdisciplinary, practical profession in descriptive ways within which a more narrowly defined discipline does not seek to contribute.

To his credit, Gardner summarizes the most common questions or critiques against his work in both *Multiple Intelligences* and *Intelligence Reframed*.[65] Critics have argued that MI theory is not a theory at all because it can be neither proved, disproved, nor contrasted with competing theories. Others reject MI theory's claims because it makes no reference to g, the generalized trait of human intelligence, so cannot claim to organize a large body of data about intelligence. Still others have criticized its descriptive, not prescriptive, character: MI theory describes human intelligences but gives no mechanisms through which they operate. And others have questioned whether intelligences represent the right-sized unit of analysis. Perhaps intelligences could be indefinitely reduced into smaller composite pieces more easily empirically investigated. Additionally, capacities that cut across the aforementioned human intelligences, such as memory or perception or even motivation, challenge the more vertically described capacities argued by Gardner. The similarity between intelligences and "learning styles" or "working styles" has also been suggested as a critique of MI theory.

Gardner responds to each of his common critiques in due course. He argues that MI theory does not consider all data because that would be impossible. It remains to be comprehensively proved, disproved, and contrasted with other theories, but such fledgling status does not delegitimate its status as a theory. In this respect, Gardner's notion of a theory is broader than a strictly empirical or traditionally "objective" one: "The theory is a product of the synthesis of this survey [of the

64. Gardner, *Multiple Intelligences*, xii.

65. See in particular Gardner, *Multiple Intelligences*, 35–48 and Gardner, *Intelligence Reframed*, 93–114.

independent research traditions of neurology, special populations, development, psychometrics, anthropology, evolution]."[66] Secondly, he has confronted the notion of *g* again and again, questioning not its existence but its explanatory importance.[67] Regarding the mechanisms of each intelligence, he suggests that there is more work to be done; just because the work is not completed, however, does not mean that the theory of multiple intelligences itself does not describe the manners of human knowing.[68]

Regarding the best unit of analysis for intelligence investigations, Gardner admits his doubt that there actually is one single and correct unit of analysis. He notes the limitations of one construct, musical intelligence, for representing adequately the various tasks of conducting, performing, or composing music; in response, he argues for several musical, linguistic, and spatial subintelligences and allows some dissection of musical intelligence into smaller pieces.[69] He further admits his skepticism about the existence of horizontal faculties such as memory or perception that cut across his vertically described intelligences. He writes, "One of the most important discoveries in the cognitive and brain sciences is that the mind is better viewed in a vertical way, as a set of faculties geared to particular contents in the external world and in human phenomenal experience."[70] In other words, any conceptualization of human faculties should be in direct correspondence with the external world—vertically described—and not within its own parameters—horizontally described. Lastly, Gardner eschews a comparison between his multiple intelligences and learning or working styles noted by professional educators; he argues that there is a systematic, scientific organization to his theory that stylistic assessments do not entail.[71] Other critiques and responses from Gardner can be pursued further in the literature.

The educational fascination with and extensive appropriation of MI theory bring both caution and an urgency to a critical understanding

66. Gardner, *Multiple Intelligences*, 38.
67. Ibid., 28
68. Ibid., 41.
69. Ibid., 103.
70. Ibid., 104.
71. Ibid., 44.

of its strengths and limitations. It is not a well-accepted, developmental psychological theory in the sense of Piaget's genetic-epistemological model of intelligence in its structurally, functionally dynamic terms. It does not provide detailed mechanisms through which each intelligence operates toward its solved problem or created product of cultural value. Nonetheless, it is a body of work that offers a systems approach to human intelligence finally broad enough to include recognized areas of competence beyond scientific or logical-mathematical models. For our purposes here, Howard Gardner provides an interdisciplinary, descriptive framework of human intelligence within which a critical understanding of human musicality may develop, with support in disciplinary perspective.

Human Musicality, Critically Appropriated

Through a juxtaposition of the perspectives of Howard Gardner and Edwin Gordon, we may now shape a working understanding of musicality for the purposes of learning within music and musical events. Both authors define their construct in terms of a biologically based human potential—either innate (Gordon) or biopsychological (Gardner). This potential, able to be assessed and gradually distinguished from musical achievement, is the human capacity to learn music or to process information in musical phenomena to solve problems and create products of value. Both disciplinary perspectives here stem from individual-centered or individually configured educational practice and are to be directed toward understanding, thus suggesting that they can be applied in a complementary manner. Gardner's descriptive assessment of a human intelligence provides a *systems* perspective and contour of the definition that is given further shape in his specifically *musical intelligence*. Gordon's empirical assessments of *musical aptitude*, as opposed to musical achievement or human intelligence in general, substantiate the more descriptive outlines of Gardner's work.

For all that follows, musicality is a biologically based, psychologically significant human capacity. Gordon argues it to be associated more with intuition, located primarily in the body in its entirety. Gardner concurs, recognizing musical intelligence does not rely solely upon hearing or audition. A biopsychological potential, by very definition, implies a biological and psychological integration, a unity in human experience that begins with the body and develops through unconscious and conscious processes of awareness and understanding.

Gordon identifies a normal (bell-curve) distribution of musical aptitude across the human population—some have very little, the majority have an average amount, and some have a high level of aptitude, with very few having none. If you have a body, you have some, and probably average, musical aptitude. Gordon's work also suggests that musical aptitude is not influenced by sociocultural factors such as race, nationality, or religion. Gardner's work suggests musical intelligence will be manifest in sociocultural systems that value music and solve problems with its cultural products. Gordon's understanding of musical aptitude less explicitly addresses the sociocultural context in which children learn music. He does articulate a model for musical understanding that integrates an individual's capacities, the music itself, and particular forms of embodied behavior, through all of which understanding takes place. This model therefore suggests an implicit social presence of either audience or represented performers and audience, each of which points to a broader social and cultural context in which musical aptitude operates.

In conclusion, the above science writing and musical aptitude research give a preliminary response here to our opening inquiry about musicality over against non-musicality. The fragments of truth in each perception find confirmation, leaving us with greater complexity and particular challenges to articulate if we are to identify opportunities for learning from and in music. First of all, the conviction that musicality is a universal feature of humanity is supported by scientific, popular, and musical educational research. More human beings than profess it are musically-inclined. Yet non-musicality—perhaps more accurately described now as lesser musicality—is not *just* a human perception or incapacity. *Less musicality* describes a potentially stabilized aptitude, lower than the birth aptitude, resulting from lack of nurture and valuing of music. Any examination of learning from music in performative mode must take heed of these findings, as people entering into teaching/learning encounters are greatly influenced by what they perceive music to be alongside the level of (perceived) aptitude they may have within musical activities.

Distinct Challenges

Learning from music in a performative mode requires awareness and redress of the contemporary polarization here identified as "those identifying as musical" and "those identifying as non-musical." Such polarization and tensions may be conceived in a variety of ways, of course. Often attention focuses upon the *kind* of music or aesthetic style. Think sacred versus secular, popular versus classic, traditional or classical versus contemporary, and congregational song versus choral performance. Music in performative mode necessarily moves the focus away from such objectively distanced kinds or styles of music into a space of behavior and personhood within musical activities.

Miriam Therese Winter defines this polarization in her study of Catholic church music, *Why Sing?*. She provides a compelling conceptual resolution that prefigures a move into the performative, though she remains somewhat captive to music form. "Catholic church music today," she writes,

> is beset by tensions and polarizations. Perhaps the most critical problem is its failure to achieve unity amid a pluriformity of styles and forms. Instead of a growing tolerance and understanding of differing viewpoints, there is opposition, even antagonism, expressed by proponents of what seems to be two divergent musical streams. It is difficult to define these positions precisely. For now they might be broadly classified as an emphasis on the song of the people and the artist's song. This categorization would eliminate the "folk-song/guitar song" designation that ordinarily adheres to the former, as well as the criterion of professionalism that usually defines the latter.[72]

Winter refers specifically to Catholic church music, but this polarization is similarly identified by Protestant John Carl Ylvisaker as "two streams of congregational music."[73] As formally trained musicians, both Winter and Ylvisaker define the polarization in terms of the music itself. Winter makes the additional, crucial move to identifying music in terms of the persons who embody it, who participate in it. She uses the *song of the artist* to name those musical activities in which primary criteria of aesthetics, professionalism, even formal training apply. The

---

72. Winter, *Why Sing?* 3.
73. Ylvisaker, "Two Streams of Congregational Music."

song of the people refers to those musical activities with primary criteria rooted in communal hospitality, participation, equanimity, and accessibility, regardless of formal training or perceived musicality. This is not to say that artists are disinterested in accessibility or communal hospitality. Nor does this mean that the song of the people has no aesthetic or performative criteria. But the distinction honors something true about musical activities today, significant when one considers learning from music and learning in music in performative mode. John L. Bell further confirms such a distinction.[74] In *The Singing Thing Too: Enabling Congregations to Sing*, he aims to encourage singing, regardless of experience or familiarity, by drawing a clear distinction between a choir and a congregation. One must teach a congregation differently than one would teach a choir. However one conceptualizes the musical polarizations of today, learning from music in performative mode requires different tasks, awarenesses, and objectives, dependent upon whether participants identify themselves to be musical or non-musical.

Having taught simple songs of worship in a wide variety of settings, some of which were *not* self-selected for musical participation, I see two orientations to music in performative mode: those who prefer to learn *from* music (if they have any willingness at all) and those who enjoy learning *in* music. Non-musicality—what the literature suggests is actually musicality, lessened or undernourished—prefigures a more objective-distance from musical activities, hence learning *from*. Those who identify in this fashion do not want to participate in musical behaviors, except perhaps passive listening. They may be avid partakers of musical commodities—CDs, musical tracks, etc.—and know intimately the intense emotional experiences available within musical performances or recordings. They may engage others in conversations about the music they love, but they rarely, if ever, would actively participate via voice or instrument in performances of musical repertoire of any kind. They may have been told they cannot sing and probably cannot read musical notation. They would never be caught making musical sounds in any public setting. No matter how much they may love particular musical styles or even sing privately to themselves in the shower, entering into musical behaviors *themselves* is fraught with shyness, professed inability, defensiveness, and various resistance. When faced with unexpected

---

74. Bell, *Singing Thing Too*.

invitations to participate in musical behaviors beyond passive listening, they may express anything from outright anger to embarrassment to sadness, verbally (afterwards) or nonverbally. Therefore, those with lesser musicality tend to maintain an objectively-distanced relationship to music in its performative aspect, for reasons as diverse as early vocal disenfranchisement (as Bell has suggested), lack of opportunity, or lack of desire and enjoyment.

Those who demonstrate a clear musicality, in contrast, show a real ease with music in performative mode, hence learning *in* music. For the simple pleasure of the arts to the complex associations received in the affirmation of others, the musically-inclined love to be in this space of musical participation. They know intimately music's ability to invite intense emotional experience, and have discovered that participation in actual performances with voice or instrument can intensify it further. Many have pursued more formal training in the musical arts by learning to play an instrument or how to sing for performance. Many have learned to read musical notation, and have been trained in the literate arts of musicological analysis within their teachers' traditions. If they succeed beyond the local musical community's expectation, they may even pursue professional training in musical performance, education, or administration. In these contexts, their participation in musical behaviors becomes even more formalized, offering varying levels of expertise on music in community life—conducting, teaching, composing, and organizing performances within the concert-hall traditions of orchestra and chorus. Others who are musically-inclined may pursue a *non-literate* path of musical performance, simply learning how to perform well by playing for other people and finding affirmation in doing so. Think jazz musicians or those who seem to just sit down and play by ear. One of my favorite artists in Pennsylvania could play *any* showtune, without any musical score; I never heard one named he couldn't play, especially if the one asking could sing a little of the main melody. All those gathered would enter into one song after another, for hours, around his piano. For those identified as musical, music in its performative mode brings a sense of competence, achievement, and social affirmation, within and beyond any sheer delight in expressing human awareness and cultural products in a particular musical style.

The less musically-inclined have offered unexpected perspective into the phenomenality of music, unavailable to those formally trained within it. Those who profess to be non-musical often see the potentially-destructive or alienating dimensions of musical traditions better than most. They often play the role of "other" within musical activities, so they know the shadow sides of its communal power more intimately. Because they have fewer sensate experiences of performing particular musical styles, they may be more open to broader swaths of musical expression across the globe. In some cases, they can be more musically tolerant than those whose musicality led to extensive formal training or formation in music conceived in a certain way, i.e. the Western canon of composers and musical works. Regardless, this kind of learner requires strategies of approach vastly different from those who feel at ease with the subject of music or who are already well-versed in its theoretical and practical aspects.

The musically-inclined, on the other hand, tend to find resistance to music in its performative mode confusing, even frustrating. They rationalize the cognitive-dissonance with claims for music's universality and its complete accessibility for everyone. "But everyone can sing!" and "Music is a human universal!" are the common refrains, which may be scientifically supportable but still untrue for a sizeable portion of human communities. The musically inclined can also be the most recalcitrant in shared musical behaviors, simply because they are so accustomed to already knowing or assuming a previous understanding. Music in performative mode may, *or may not* be what was performed before. That's part of its educational sway, even seduction. If the musically-inclined have pursued formal training in musical performance, education, or administration, they may also be so adept at the literate dimensions of musical traditions that their enjoyment derives from the musical *literature*, alongside its performative presence. I remember an András Schiff performance of Beethoven sonatas, where a woman listened avidly *through the printed score in her lap*. Her entrance into music's performative aspect, in this case, required a literate accompaniment. Educators know a musically-inclined learner requires strategies of approach vastly different from those who have little desire for, or felt-competence in, music in its participatory mode.

In the end, learning from music in its performative mode requires negotiating extensive research into human musicality as a ubiquitous human potential *and* confronting the unavoidable conundrum of the non-musical within many Westernized cultures. Learning *from* music involves different attitudes, abilities, and experiences of music, so understood, than learning *in* music. John Bell's later work spells it out from his perspective of teaching congregations, which are often perceived to be non-musical, especially when compared with a choir.[75] Congregations often believe they cannot sing, and have had this belief confirmed in a lack of participation in the choir. In my terms, music is something they must learn from, but rarely, actively, *in*. Choirs, the musically-inclined, perform; congregations, less-musically inclined, listen. Choirs receive social affirmation and respect. They are considered more significant or knowledgeable than the congregation. Choirs bond regularly in weekly performances, rehearsing even more often with printed scores of musical notation. Congregations face musical notation, which many of them are unable to decipher, and they are asked to enter into music's performative mode from this felt-inability. Choirs sit together for performances while congregations are dispersed across the room as the audience. Choirs usually have a musical leader while congregations rarely do. Bell's global and local travels have taught him well: the musically-inclined learn differently than those less-musically inclined. Choirs learn *in* music while congregations learn *from*. He aims to redress this imbalance by enabling congregations to sing.

Given these practical dimensions, quite diverse between those learning from music and those learning in music, we can only begin to imagine the conceptually distinct and primarily embodied world to which we are headed, named by Begbie as the performative mode. Some disciplinary theologians perceive themselves to be absolutely non-musical. They appreciate the human fascination with music, particularly within religious experience. They may even thrive in the musical heritage of their own theological tradition, ascribing their own beliefs to the hymns sung by their communities of worship. They will maintain an objective-distance to music, however, and retain more objectivistic conceptualizations of music, to be understood in terms of aesthetics, styles, histories, etc. Music in performative mode may even be conceptually unavailable to them. Formally trained in a discipline of expertise, an academic rationalism may prevent awareness that music *has* another world in which to learn and to advance theological scholarship.

---

75. Bell, *Singing Thing Too*, 11ff.

Other disciplinary theologians consider themselves to be musical. They will thrive in the challenges of the performative, and make easy associations with its centrality for transformative learning. Their work may even make explicit use of musical styles, imagery, expressions, and aesthetics for theological interpretation. Their contributions will integrate literate expressions of musical disciplines. Sometimes this musical professionalism distracts recall about music's performative mode, or how music might be experienced by others without their facility with it. But by and large, learning *in* music comes naturally for both musical learning and theological reflection. Music in performative mode, for the musically-inclined theologian, heightens a sense of competence, achievement, and social affirmation, within and beyond any sheer delight in making theological contributions informed by music.

Learning from music in a performative mode requires more than acknowledgement of potential and redress of the attitudes, practiced abilities, and previous experiences/settings of musical phenomena. This chapter's scientific and music-psychological strands of literature offer perspective on the educational challenges to be considered based in musical aptitude. Chapter Three moves into Edwin Gordon's *music learning theory* for critical understanding in how human beings hear and comprehend music. His work provides an established model for human learning of music, from extensive research into how children actually learn music and somewhat independent of assessed levels of musicality. Unexpectedly, Gordon's research led him to conceptualize a distinct mode or world for music-learning, which then urges much deeper analysis of *performative mode* and what it might mean, eventually, for critical theological discourse.

3

How We Learn Music

Music Learning Theory and Music's Distinct Mode

A CLOSER LOOK INTO HOW HUMAN BEINGS LEARN IN MUSIC PROVIDES not only a theoretical model that deepens understandings of such learning, but also a more critical assessment of *performative mode* for our two questions from the first page of Chapter One. Gordon's *music learning theory* articulates a model for the comprehensive, distinctly musical-cognitive processes through which humans make sound intelligible as music. It entails a detailed overview of the types, stages, and distinct world required for human beings to perceive, recognize, and come to understand music. Gordon's empirical research and years of observing children learning in music also led him to coin a new word for distinctly musical understanding, *audiation*. According to Gordon, *audiation* is observable in specific behaviors, signaling entrance into a distinct world or mode, related to but independent of language. As simple as that may sound, the reality of musical thinking, in such distinction from literate habits of mind, is exceedingly difficult. It requires an awakening of sorts, a felt-shift into an awareness without primarily linguistic reference. This finding urges a closer examination of Begbie's *performative* mode, its contributions amidst practical theological perspectives but its irreconcilable limitations within Christian theological discourse dependent upon philosophical traditions of the *logos*, or Word. When conceived in some distinction from, but relation to, this philosophical-theological heritage, as in the orality studies of Walter J. Ong, SJ, *performative mode* promises a more generative concept for critical theological discourse and theological method, congruent with Gordon's music learning theory and more responsible to music's indivisible multidimensionality and its primarily aural-oral phenomena.

Music Learning Theory

Gordon's *music learning theory* builds upon his contributions surrounding music aptitude for an embodied, comprehensive overview for how human beings perceive and come to understand music. He coins the term, audiation, to describe a perceptual and educational model rooted in various embodied activities often considered extramusical but which Gordon argues are essential to learning in music. *Audiation* cannot be found in a dictionary, though its etymological roots point to its meaning. The Latin root, *audire*—to hear—leads us to words related to hearing: *audial* (of or relating to the sense of hearing), *audible* (that which is heard or can be heard), or *audience* (the spectators or listeners assembled at a performance). *Audiation* is therefore the hearing and comprehending of music. Gordon coins his new word from neurobiological and educational findings that linguistic and imagistic approaches to music education have limited our understanding, our participation in music education, and therefore, the human creation and delight in music. Others have coined new terms or phrases to make this very distinction. Christopher Small and William Benzon, for example, use the term *musicking* to prioritize the dynamism of musical phenomena over the more objectivistic music, easily commodified and dissected.[1]

To clarify his sense of audiation, and to prevent popular misunderstandings feasible when engaging any new word, Gordon defines audiation in some contrast to *aural perception* and *imitation*. Aural perception is that hearing of music in which the sound is physically present.[2] Audiation, however, refers to an embodied, pre-rationative, and cognitive process in which sound may or may not have ever been present. It is possible to imagine music or to get a tune stuck in one's head while the sound itself is not physically present. Comprehending

---

1. Benzon, *Beethoven's Anvil*, 3.

2. Gordon, *Music Learning Theory for Newborn and Young Children*, 18. See also Gordon, *Learning Sequences in Music*, xii.

music as referred by audiation differs from imitation as well. "Be clear," Gordon writes, that "it is possible, and unfortunately too often the case, for one to perform a piece of music by imitation without engaging in audiation. It is not possible to imitate and to audiate at the same time. Learning by rote is not the same as learning by understanding. . ."[3] In this sense, imitation is a product of learning by rote, whereas audiation describes learning through understanding. Educators of all stripes recognize the challenge in determining the difference here in students' performances. Gordon's suggestion for identifying whether a student is audiating or imitating is to have them sing alone. Those who are audiating will sing as if it is a solo, and "if for some reason they forget the exact notes, they will improvise convincing substitutes." [4] Audiation therefore involves *cognitive participation* in the performance and creation of music, whereas imitation only requires a mimicking participation with others involved. Gordon describes imitation as tracing paper to draw a picture, whereas audiation is analogous to visualizing and then drawing a picture.

Theory of Audiation: World, Types, Stages

Gordon's theory involves eight different types of audiation, each of which relates a person, sound, and a specific form of embodied practice. This comprehensive approach to embodied participation in musical cognition is one of his most substantive contributions to music education. Previously, with few exceptions,[5] musical activity had been perceived as involving largely the organized sound itself that ought to be taught (instrumentation, dynamic character, form from historical period, etc.). Perhaps ethnic or aesthetic communal settings were added as adjectival descriptors of the music being taught, like learning Celtic, church, folk, or Scandinavian music. Gordon, however, emphasizes a fundamental relationship between a human person, organized sound, and specific forms of practice through which sound is organized and received by others. While his written works are quite dense, he offers a

---

3. Gordon, *Learning Sequences in Music*, 9.

4. Ibid.

5. Orff, *Music for Children*; or, more recently, Orff and Regner, *Orff-Schulwerk in der Welt von Morgen*. See also Frazee and Kreuter, *Discovering Orff* and Ramseth, *Keep In Mind*.

fairly straightforward description of audiation constituted by types and stages of activity.

Audiation can be divided into eight basic types of musical activity, from the least active form of listening (type 1) to the most accomplished or interactive form of creating and improvising (type 8). Table 1 lists the types in succinct fashion.

TABLE 1: TYPES OF AUDIATION

Type 1	Listening to	Familiar or unfamiliar music
Type 2	Reading	Familiar or unfamiliar music
Type 3	Writing	Familiar or unfamiliar music, dictation
Type 4	Recalling and performing	Familiar music from memory
Type 5	Recalling and writing	Familiar music from memory
Type 6	Creating and improvising	Unfamiliar music
Type 7	Creating and improvising	Unfamiliar music while reading
Type 8	Creating and improvising	Unfamiliar music while writing

A review of types of musical understanding urges consideration of perhaps obvious but distinct contributions. Understanding of any kind builds upon what is already familiar. Noting familiar or unfamiliar music, audiation theory accounts for one's previous sociocultural and artistic formation with respect to music, regardless of musicality or aptitude, formal training or stance within the debates of musical styles and aesthetics. Simply—Have you heard something like this before? Does it strike you as unfamiliar?—is where one's understanding begins. The omnipresence of musical notation within today's music educational circles also figures into his theoretical work. Though he prioritizes music as a primarily oral-aural phenomenon, today's musical cultures rely upon systems of writing and reading. Types 2 and 3 describe these secondary aspects of music learning. The role of memory plays into Gordon's music learning theory. Types 4 and 5 name the activities of recalling-performing and recalling-writing familiar music from memory. Types 6–8 show the diversity of activity embedded within creating and improvising music, whether performing (or thinking) from imagination, while reading, or while writing. The hearing and comprehending of music given shape in Gordon's audiation theory reminds all of us how complex and implicitly embodied music is within human community.

Each of these types of audiation also shows six stages of progression—the embodied, prerationative, and cognitive pathway for music learning. Table 2 names the stages observable within each type of musical understanding.

TABLE 2: STAGES OF AUDIATION

Stage 1	Momentary retention
Stage 2	Initiating and audiating tonal patterns and rhythm patterns AND recognizing and identifying a tonal center and macrobeats
Stage 3	Establishing objective or subjective tonality and meter
Stage 4	Consciously retaining in audiation tonal patterns and rhythm patterns that we have organized
Stage 5	Consciously recalling patterns organized and audiated in other pieces of music
Stage 6	Conscious prediction of patterns

Several factors stand out in this progression. When one first receives musical phenomena, there is a physically-sustained, momentary retention of the sound within one's body as a whole. These sounds are kept momentarily and not organized until later stages. This means that there is no fully conscious present but only an immediate past that is held within conscious awareness. We are not conscious of the initial aural perceptions when they first occur. Stage 2 names the initiation of pattern-recognition both for familiarity and a general sense of the sounds as music, what musicians often refer to as its tonality, harmonic structure (if any), beat and rhythmic patterns, style of flow, instrumentation and more. Gordon describes this stage as a preconscious and pre-meaning stage of scanning what we know against what our bodies are retaining as sound impressions. Identifying the tonal center and rhythmic structure of sound phenomena helps us organize the sound amidst previous musics we have encountered. Gordon explains, "The process becomes a continuous interaction between the recognition and identification of tonal centers and macrobeats, on the one hand, and the organization of musical essentials, on the other."[6]

Stage 3 describes the next level of sound-organization in interaction with the larger psychological, societal, and cultural settings. Gordon calls this stage "establishing objective or subjective tonality and meter," a phrase with philosophical nuances specific to his own work. *Objective*, in his theory, means that there is a general consensus from the outside about how the sounded, cognitive patterns are to be organized. Take, for example, nineteenth-century hymnody in Protestant churches. "For All the Saints" has a well-established major tonality[7] and an immediately recognizable meter of 4/4—four beats per measure, primary and secondary pulses in each measure. Most people in Protestant, churched communities would immediately recognize the sense of tonality and meter. When the hymn is sung, the tonality and meter are objectively established within this communal consensus; there is an established manner in which the hymn is to be sung. *Subjective*, on the other hand, is defined precisely by its lack of communal definition or consensus. Upon listening, one may begin to discern a meter and tonality within which to organize sounds, but the harmonic structure and lack of predictable pulses require a subjective determination of patterning. Gordon is less clear about the role of the individual in this subjective establishment of tonality and meter, but makes a clear distinction between the commonly recognized objective frame of reference and the more subjective, internally organized tonality and meter that is more fluid than well-established, socially structured musical patterns/frames of reference.

Stages 4–6 offer contour for what we normally think of as listening to music. Stages 4 and 5, for example, mark the *conscious* retention of tonal and rhythm patterns which are then brought into a *conscious* recall of other pieces of music. These stages often compel the explicit conversations between listeners—Doesn't this sound like. . .? Do you hear how the horns in this section make you think of. . .? An important

---

6. Gordon, *Learning Sequences in Music*, 18–19.

7. Gordon defines a "tonality" as that which is determined by the resting tone. If *doh* is the resting tone, the tonality is major; if *la* is the resting tone, the tonality is harmonic minor or Aeolian. Musical specifics here are less important than the overall progression, but a glossary is provided for further study in Gordon, *Learning Sequences in Music*, 378, 369.

contribution of Gordon's theory, however, is that these are only the final stages of a process begun when the first sounds were received in embodied sensation, well before becoming conscious of any particular organization of those sounds. The final stage Gordon names is the conscious prediction of patterns, or Stage 6. One can demonstrate an audiation of music when not only is there sustained encounter and recognition, conscious retention and recall, but also a sense of anticipating correctly the conclusion of musical patterns. As Gordon argues,

> The more accurately we anticipate and make predictions, the better we will understand the music we are hearing. If our anticipations and predictions are not borne out in the music, we will encounter difficulty in understanding the music, but if only a few of our anticipations and predictions are inaccurate, we can continue the cyclical process of audiation and will make the necessary simple alterations in our further anticipations and predictions. Should our predictions be grossly inaccurate or should we not be able to anticipate or make predictions at all, the audiation process will revert to and probably remain at stage one, and the music will have at best only little meaning for us.[8]

Ultimately, audiation aims to articulate how we hear and comprehend music. It names a cyclical process begun with the aural perception of sound and coursing through the unconscious and conscious interactions between previous and present musical knowledge, all of which then leads to an embodied musical understanding within the individual's societal and cultural settings. And remember: this entire exposition of the stages only addresses the most familiar, Type 1 of audiation—listening to familiar or unfamiliar music. Each of these stages could be recounted and differentiated for the other seven types of audiation listed in Table 1.

Suffice it to say for our purposes, Gordon's music learning theory outlines a perceptual, unconscious, and conscious answer to the question of how we hear and comprehend music in its performative mode. In its eight types and six stages, audiation describes the primarily embodied, systematic, and interactive process whereby human beings organize sounds into musical patterns—both recognizable and unfamiliar. When the anticipation or prediction of patterns is increasingly accurate, the music is understood and made intelligible to and by the

8. Gordon, *Learning Sequences in Music*, 22.

listener. When little accurate anticipation or prediction occurs, the music is unintelligible—not music at all—but sound or noise.

Critical Examination of Gordon's Theory of Audiation

Gordon's theoretical work here presents many strengths and weaknesses, each of which points toward his biggest advantage and disadvantage: an individualistic reliance upon a neologism that methodically coheres with neurobiological findings and educational convictions, which simultaneously demonstrates a willful resistance to engage other scholars or established theoretical discourse. The strengths in Gordon's theoretical work stem from this daring willingness to chart new ground with audiation, musical research, and learning theory, all of which point toward a more holistic, theoretical, and integrated praxis framework for understanding human musical cognition. The difficulties emerge in the solitary will that, for whatever reason, refuses to participate in disciplinarily anticipated, constructively critical, and intentionally public discourse.

The strengths of Gordon's theoretical work and his standing in the discipline of music education cannot be denied. Current audiation theory is the systematic outworking of four decades of research observing children learning. In his own doctoral studies, Gordon decided that he would approach music teaching from the perspective of children learning, a progressive and nontraditional approach compared to those more intent upon top-down pedagogies for music education. He then integrated this research focus and musical acuity (further developed in his own string bass performance work) into the creation of the Musical Aptitude Profile, the most common musical aptitude test used today, in such music schools as Westminster Choir College, recently affiliated with Rider University, in Princeton, New Jersey. However, audiation theory does not originate solely from Gordon's own extensive and professional musical experience and the progressive educational commitments that focused his research. He also exhibited an ultimate knack for statistical analysis in his research that led to the MAP (and all its age-specific evolved forms) and established him as an expert in the psychology of music and music-education disciplines.

The end result has been a theory of musical understanding that distinguishes yet integrates the individual person (and his/her potential), the music as an object, and the form of embodied practice involved (listening, reading, writing, performing, and improvising music) into a coherent model for how human beings hear and comprehend music toward deeper understanding of music and life. Audiation describes the human organization of sound through cognitive and embodied activity from an established musical, educational, and psychological perspective.

Gordon's solitary, neologistic theory of musical understanding simultaneously creates audiation theory's greatest disadvantage. Audiation theory exhibits an individualism that appears to disregard broader interdisciplinary or even disciplinary discourse, which results in two similarly themed difficulties. First, since Gordon engages audiation theory in no broader, critical, or public discourse, its constitutive processes (of retention, imitation, recognition, and identification leading toward anticipation and prediction) have no other helpful fields of reference through which a precise interpretation becomes feasible.

For example, how are human levels of consciousness expressed or employed in the integral processes of imitation, recognition, and identification in Stage 2 of audiation and by what theories of cognition and social action has Gordon been influenced? Momentary retention in Stage 1 of audiation is clearly an unconscious or perhaps even autonomic process, but when we recognize and identify tonal centers and macrobeats in Stage 2, are those completely unconscious? What cognitive theoretical understanding underlies Gordon's imitation of patterns, which precedes this recognition and identification of tonal centers and macrobeats? Does he intend a structural musical cognition or is his understanding of imitation more fluid? Similarly, why does he include person, music, and form of practice in his theory of musical understanding? What understanding of social theory underpins his decision to include all these realms of human action in the musical realm? More concretely, when the objective or subjective tonality and meter are determined in Stage 3 of audiation, is that a conscious decision based in individual experiences or preferences, or an unconscious process with more of a social constructionist nuance? He states clearly that Stages 5 and 6 are conscious processes, but leaves the earlier stages indeterminate with respect to conscious participation by the individual. All stages are left indeterminate with respect to theoretical intentions in cognitive and social theory that yet appear to inform his work.

Second, Gordon devotes the entire last chapter of *Learning Sequences in Music* to the proclamation of the need to value music in American society—to know why children ought to learn music—yet his narrow disciplinary focus on music education and his individualistic approach to human musical cognition prevent him from substantively addressing the issues of value or meaning in his audiation theory. He shares an innovative perspective on musical meaning when he writes, "We don't *take* meaning from music. We give meaning to music, and in return music sensitively guides us to a better understanding of our total selves and our environment."[9] His understanding of musical meaning offers a clearly dynamic, musical, and interactive possibility of powerful educational praxis in the things that matter most: our total selves and our environment. But audiation theory has no inherent process, motivation, or claim for human value or significance. One is reminded of Susanne Langer's philosophical tautology—humans most need to symbolize and what makes them human is symbolization—alongside Hildegard's more compelling rationale or urge to consider the irrepressible force of human yearning or desire, one's urgent drive to reach outside the self into the world.

Gordon does speak of this process of giving meaning to music as either diachronic or synchronic audiation, both of which are intrinsic and extrinsic in human musical activities. Again, he fails to connect these attributional, very technical terms to possible meanings in and through music for total selves and environment.[10] Although audiation addresses the human organization of sound in embodied human practice, Gordon essentially neglects any integrated commentary on why we audiate, why we are drawn to music, and how vastly different

---

9. Ibid., 33.

10. Ibid., 138. Under tonality and tonal syntax, he identifies Stages 1–4 as synchronic audiation, which gives meaning to music *being heard*; Stage 6 is diachronic audiation, which gives meaning to music that has been heard, read, or written, or will be heard, read, or written. Stage 5 appears to have no function in either synchronic or diachronic audiation. Gordon describes intrinsic meaning as syntactical and given to the music by the listener. Extrinsic meaning is taken from music by the listener. It is programmatic, suggesting external events and images. He also describes physiognomic and chromesthetic responses to music that associate an object and a color with music, respectively, thereby giving meaning to music from extrinsic sources perceived affectively or visually. Both of these types of response suggest primarily extrinsic meaning but are not evaluated or interpreted for any connection to meaning "for total selves and environment."

understandings emerge from the exact same combination of pitches, tones, and rhythms.

If he had not avoided larger communal discourse in elaborating the theory of audiation, he would have confronted a plethora of multidisciplinary discussions on the significance of music occurring at the exact same time, though they were largely linguistic or more narrowly cognitive. A real spurt of contributions to the field's literature appeared during the mid-eighties, at precisely the time when Gordon's *Learning Sequences in Music* was being printed and reprinted.[11] Closer to home, if he had looked beyond music education's more narrow focus on learning and teaching humanly organized sound itself and had pursued further the view of musical activity as he already comprehensively identifies it (person, music, communal practice), he might have identified in his own theory *why* people want to learn music and how it encourages or hinders learning "in order to further understandings of 'total selves and environment.'"[12] The limitations of audiation theory are clear for interdisciplinary purpose, but its contributions cannot be disregarded, in light of the strengths of Gordon's empiricism, learning theory, and its explanatory power for human beings hearing and comprehending music, rooted in educational observation and longitudinal research. For our purposes of understanding more deeply *what learning in music* requires, his work provides a compellingly researched and established avenue.

Music's Mode

Gordon's work ultimately invites deeper investigation into the mode or world specific to music learning, even as his insistence upon the neologism, *audiation*, complicates the inquiry. A neologism, by definition, contributes through disruption and *dis*continuity, not critical adaptation and continuity. Critical appropriation of Gordon's work within new studies on learning in music becomes exceedingly difficult,

---

11. Sloboda, *Musical Mind*; Dowling and Harwood, *Music Cognition*; Hargreaves, *Developmental Psychology of Music*—this text actually references Gordon's work, but only in the context of Gordon's Musical Aptitude Profile; Peery, Peery, and Draper, *Music and Child Development*; Serafine, *Music as Cognition*; Jones and Holleran, *Cognitive Bases of Musical Communication*.

12. Gordon, *Learning Sequences in Music*, 33.

plausible only with an intentional bridge-building, not some imagined continuity with previous or contemporary antecedent.

Begbie's foundational work for this study hints at music's distinct way or mode, which he calls a *performative* mode with unique integrity. His approach brings its own complications for critical appropriation, however, both in interdisciplinary overwhelm and in an increasingly incongruent, (practical) theological problematic. Various definitions of performative mode in interdisciplinary view come from wildly diverse literatures, including speech-act theory, ritual studies, feminist philosophy, gender studies, anthropology, ethnography, cultural studies, post-colonial criticism, and more.[13] Any overview of *performative mode* in interdisciplinary source-work wilts in the "domination of the secondary."[14] Begbie's sense offers an optimistic precision, because it originates in critical, Christian theological discourse, specifically an Aristotelian-nuanced understanding of *phronēsis* (practical wisdom) and *practices*. His work reframes music's unique mode in ways more suited to its distinctiveness and more hopeful than current (practical) theological discourse, often limited by objectivist, correlational dichotomies. Optimistic hopes are quickly dashed, however, in light of Gordon's refusal to work within linguistic or language-based models or interpretation. Christian theological discourse evolves out of centuries of living, Platonic-Aristotelian traditions—meant here in Alasdair MacIntyre's "historically extended, socially embodied argument"[15]— crystallized by the *logos*, the Word.[16] Very little could be more *in*congruent for a critical appropriation of Gordon's work. Furthermore, the (practical) theological tradition of *phronēsis* and *practice* often qualify through an *analytic distinction* what music's mode *broadens into primary relation*, indivisible and inseparable. What Begbie calls music's "unique and irreducible integrity."[17] The interpretive schemas at play within such Aristotelian (practical) theological discourse disregard

---

13. See Austin, *How to Do Things with Words*; Bell, "Performance"; Butler, *Excitable Speech: a Politics of the Performative*. See also McKenzie, *Perform or Else*; Carlson, *Performance*. Marcia Hermansen's work gave some introduction to interdisciplinary sourcework here. Hermansen, "Muslims in the Performative Mode."

14. Steiner, *Real Presences*, 6–7.

15. MacIntyre, *After Virtue*, 222.

16. Allen and Springstead, *Philosophy for Understanding Theology*.

17. Begbie, *Theology, Music, and Time*, 19.

music's primary relationality, often for functional and fascinating purpose, yet in a fashion incongruent with music's irreducibly multidimensional phenomenality.

What follows here must be much more circumspect than either Gordon's disruptive discontinuity or Begbie's important theological contributions, rooted as they are in traditions of the *logos* that are radically incongruent with Gordon's work. The orality studies of Walter Ong contribute a compelling bridge or lens with which to see—or better, to *receive*—Gordon's wisdom in his *world of audiation* and its resonances with Jeremy Begbie's authorship. We begin with warrant for the validity of Gordon's contributions, critically appropriated when interpreted in a literature that shares its presupposition: a distinction from but relation to language, understood broadly as human communication with both written and oral expressions. *Performative mode* becomes critically available, then, as a distinct but related mode of human communication-in-relationality, recognizable in 1) the primacy of the auditory or aural, which makes it congruent with Gordon's theory; and 2) its identifiable, psychodynamic characteristics, which attest to a primary relationality enacted in a participatory, oral-aural phenomenon. Marks of a performative mode become increasingly intelligible within music's phenomena: relational-formation, explicit embodiment, irreducible multidimensionality, and a central role for insight in new awarenesses amidst music.

World of Audiation

Gordon's work grows out of neurobiological findings for a cognitive distinctiveness in musical understanding, independent of, if related to, language. Howard Gardner's work, examined in Chapter 2, corroborates such a distinction. He even shares Gordon's developmental perspective on such a mode in music, differentiated between a *figural* approach to music (as demonstrated from birth to approximately age eight) and a propositional, conceptually ordered understanding of musical phenomena in a *formal* approach, which appears during early adolescence.[18] Gordon makes his claim for the *world of audiation* out

18. Gardner, *Frames of Mind*, 108–9. See also Bamberger, *Mind Behind the Musical Ear* and *Developing Musical Intuitions*, for her similar distinction between formal processing—know-that processing—and figural—know-how processing.

of repeated observations of human behavior. He identifies what he calls an *audiation stare*, described more fully below, which signals a dawning awareness of an *other* mode of learning and understanding. Other musicological research affirms such proposition, adding weight to its validity.[19] From a critical theological perspective, developed in intimate conversation with piano performance, Begbie insists upon a distinctive mode for music as well, its way of "enacting theological wisdom" and its unique integrity. Just the presence and diversity of such overwhelming interdisciplinary literature supports Gordon's argument for an observably unique mode of human understanding, in relation to but distinct from linguistic thought and speech. Therefore, a critical engagement with Gordon's *world of audiation* is warranted, from multiple directions, despite his use of discontinuity to stake his claim.

Gordon's research led him to describe what he called a *world of audiation* through which a child demonstrates distinct entrance into musical comprehension. He even identifies a particular behavior, what he calls an *audiation stare*, signaling entrance into this world. Toward the later stages of his work, he developed a portion of music learning theory specific to newborn and early childhood musical development. *Preparatory audiation* describes this early musical development, articulated in great detail as a multi-stage process of acculturation, imitation, and assimilation by and into the musical behaviors and attitudes of a particular sociocultural setting. This theory offers its own contributions to music education but is outside the more basic theory of human musical understanding for our purposes. It is only significant here because Gordon uses *preparatory audiation* to describe an *audiation stare* in some detail as entrance into a *world of audiation*. "There are signs that the child gives when he is ready to leave preparatory audiation [and enter into audiation proper]," Gordon writes,

> The child will stare for a few seconds at the parent, teacher, or another person as the awareness comes that there is a difference between his singing or chanting or moving and someone else's. That is the first glimpse of discrimination; the realization of same or different. The child may also open his mouth and tilt his head. In a sense, the child is attempting to enter the world of audiation. He knows only that something is not quite

---

19. For the developmental event Gordon observes, sometimes called a "crystallizing experience," see Freeman, "Crystallizing Experience," 75–85.

right. That may be the most important moment in the child's music education.[20]

In this behavior, Gordon argues entrance into a distinct mode for learning in music. The deep understanding named by audiation signifies a mode of understanding-learning-being specific to musical understanding, which is to be distinguished, in his view, from other modes of learning shaped primarily by language or narrowly perceived cognition.

At root in this claim is Gordon's conviction that music cannot be fruitfully understood as a universal language or within primarily linguistic modes of thinking. In line with neurobiological findings in evolutionary and neurobiological science, Gordon observes the cognitive distinctiveness of human musical understanding and behavior. He observes that music, like a logographic language with no alphabet or words but only word pictures, invites logographic thought that is neurobiologically distinguished from alphabetical, linguistic thought.[21] It should also be noted that Howard Gardner relied on this neurobiological information to distinguish musical intelligence as a distinct intellectual capacity in his *Frames of Mind*. He writes, "Investigators working with both normal and brain-damaged humans have demonstrated beyond a reasonable doubt that the processes and mechanisms subserving human music and language are distinctive from one another."[22] Neurobiological evidence suggests that musical thought activity is biologically differentiated from linguistic thought and speech, though not in the sense of spatial location with the brain.[23]

Gordon also gives primary emphasis to the auditory, non-visual experience of music for a critical understanding of learning in music. He argues that "all learning of music begins with the ear, not the eye"[24] and thereby confronts the portion of music education tradition that has placed heavy emphasis upon the notation and theory of music in its praxis. Here Gordon contends that music learned through the eye in notation, theory, or historical expression is neither music nor learning. One may appreciate music that is well-notated and historically

---

20. Gordon, *Music Learning Theory*, 72.
21. Gordon, *Learning Sequences in Music*, ix–x.
22. Gardner, *Frames of Mind*, 117.
23. Tramo, "Music of the Hemispheres."
24. Gordon, *Learning Sequences in Music*, 27.

described, but one cannot understand music unless it is experienced. "Music 'hears' us," he writes, "we do not hear music. We *give* meaning to music, and music in return sensitively guides us to a better understanding of our total selves and our environment."[25] Unless music is in its audible and immediate form(s) of expression, it cannot "hear" us into new understanding, new experience, or new confrontations with self and other. Music through visual learning or linguistic (historical) interpretation is not music, as Gordon argues it. And music so learned is not truly learned, nor understood, nor therefore significant for learning that transforms. In this sense, then, largely linguistic and imagistic educational approaches to music have limited the understanding of music and the educational import it could have across disciplines of inquiry. Another scholar in a disparate field of inquiry argues for a distinctiveness of consciousness, transformed from oral into literate and then secondarily oral habits of mind. Theological scholar and literary critic, Walter J. Ong, devoted substantial energies to reclaiming and configuring the implications of a mode of consciousness similarly distinct from but in relation to language, or literacy.

Walter Ong's Orality

Orality is a term of awakening for critical discourse that is available only upon the advent of the electronic age. With the rise of digital communications that interweave sound and print, spoken and imagistic communication alongside language, contrasts have arisen that suggest new awarenesses and ways of knowing distinct from purely literary expression and historical consciousness. Orality is best summarized in Walter Ong's *Orality and Literacy*, though it was first articulated in previous essays and his original volume, *The Presence of the Word*. There begins a radical distinction between what Ong calls "the shifting sensorium" in which an oral consciousness originates, and "the Word," from which *literate* consciousness arises.[26] One potentially immediate misunderstanding is conceiving *orality* only over and against *literacy*—a false dichotomy with the misconception that literacy refers to an ability to read. What Ong intends, however, is a contrast between

---

25. Ibid., 33.
26. See Ong, *Faith and Contexts*, vols. 1–3.

the *consciousness of a literate mind*, well-developed through centuries of writing and historical record, and the *consciousness of an oral mind*, retrievable when considered within the *secondary orality* of digital media.[27] The sense of *oral* refers to the earliest forms of human-being-in-communication, unavailable to human sensate-awareness in the written historical record.

For this study, aware of the irreducible dichotomies inherited within Greek-philosophical and Christian theological habits of mind, Ong's orality studies provide a generative concept of *performative mode* congruent with Gordon's music learning theory and previously unavailable in (practical) theological discourse. Orality signals a primarily oral-aural phenomenon distinct from but in obvious relation to language in today's digital-cultures. A thorough investigation of Ong's work would require more than feasible here, but even a glimpse into how he conceives orality promises much toward a critical appropriation of Gordon's work. Music in his theory, after all, is a primarily oral-aural phenomenon whose mode has a unique integrity, distinct from language. Orality became significant within the early Homeric studies of Milman Parry (1902–1935), investigating structural form and composition of epic poetry. A brief overview of Ong's work within such disciplinary antecedents will contextualize *orality* before delving more deeply into its *psychodynamic characteristics* and contributions to a critical understanding of *performative mode*.

Development of Orality: Brief Overview for its Rediscovery & a Helpful Illustration

Walter Ong locates the scholarly rediscovery of orality in an extensive history beginning as early as *Qoheleth*, the so-named assembly speaker of early Hebrew wisdom literature. "Besides being wise, Qoheleth taught the people knowledge, and weighed, scrutinized, and arranged many proverbs. Qoheleth sought to find pleasing sayings, and to write

---

27. Ong names the development of human consciousness here as *primary orality*, *literacy*, and *secondary orality* observable today. Primarily oral cultures—those which have had absolutely *no* contact with writing of any kind—are obviously scarce, if even in existence today, amidst the prevalence of digital communications. Secondary orality refers to that communication and its corresponding consciousness, dependent upon an integration of orality and literacy. Ong, *Presence of the Word*, 17ff.

down true sayings with precision."[28] Wisdom connotes a primary orality, while knowledge and writing down true sayings denotes the cultural advance of literacy. Ong attributes the modern awareness of orality, however, to twentieth-century work on the *Iliad* and the *Odyssey* by the (North) American classicist, Milman Parry (1902–1935).[29] Parry was the one to enter into epic poetry within its own terms and within an appreciative hermeneutic, less tainted by the "cultural chauvinism" of modernist presuppositions and a prolonged, rather antagonistic history of interpretation wrestling with demonstrations of "progress" and "evolved" sensibilities.[30] Parry's discovery of orality's force is summarized by Ong, relatively free of such value judgment and modernist presupposition: "Virtually every distinctive feature of Homeric poetry is due to the economy enforced on it by oral methods of composition."[31] Ong traces the precise developments of this contribution within twentieth century literary theory, especially as Parry's work was furthered by Albert B. Lord and Eric A. Havelock (due to Parry's untimely death in 1935) and traced in more ethnographic detail by Parry's son, Adam.[32] He then describes as *revolutionary* the disciplinary impact of Parry's work in Homeric studies. He pursues this with traces of the interdisciplinary impact, rippling outward into broader literary studies and then anthropology, cultural studies, even psychology and studies of consciousness.[33] Sufficient to our interest, Parry's work and the disciplinary-interdisciplinary developments to follow, legitimate a sizeable, critical viability of *orality* for generative, interdisciplinary contribution.

Ong offers a plausible rationale for orality's *rediscovery* and a suitable illustration in which to awaken to its promise for reconceiving *performative mode* in terms congruent with both Gordon and

28. Ecclesiastes 12:9–10, cited by Ong, *Orality and Literacy*, 16.
29. Ong, *Orality and Literacy*, 16.
30. Ibid., 18.
31. Ibid., 21.
32. Ibid., 6. See Lord, *Singer of Tales* and "Perspectives on Recent Work in Oral Literature"; Havelock, *Origins of Western Literacy* and "Ancient Art of Oral Poetry"; Havelock and Herschell, *Communication Arts in the Ancient World*; and Parry, *Making of Homeric Verse*.
33. Ong, *Orality and Literacy*, 22–30. Significant to this study is Ong's connection of interdisciplinary impact to Jaynes, *Origins of Consciousness in the Breakdown of the Bicameral Mind*, which contributed to the work of James E. Loder, developed and critiqued in chapters 4 and 5.

Begbie's contributions. A certain irony emerges, Ong's work suggests, when scholars rediscover something that is otherwise patently obvious: language is primarily an oral phenomenon within human awareness. Language has been deemed the evolutionarily significant qualifier of *human being*, who communicates in linguistic complexities in significant contrast to the communicative behaviors of most of the rest of the natural world. It is the audible water within which human beings swim, communicating wants, needs, desires, and ideas with one another. As Ong writes, "Human beings communicate in countless ways, making use of all their senses, touch, taste, smell, and especially sight, as well as hearing. . . .Wherever human beings exist they have a language, and *in every instance a language that exists basically as spoken and heard, in the world of sound*."[34]

These seemingly innumerable languages—nearly 7000 as of a critical accounting in 2004[35]—do not have nearly the staying power or historical tenacity as those committed to writing, which draws most critical attention. Summarized from the proceedings of a conference held at Keble College, Oxford: "[F]ewer than 100 major scripts have appeared during the 5 millennia since writing first emerged on the same Mesopotamian plain as the legendary Tower of Babel."[36] 100 out of 7000 languages known today are manifest and available for critical, textual study. Even as "[t]he basic orality of language is permanent,"[37] so also Ong claims: the focus and study of human consciousness through textual forms represents only a minute portion of human awareness, communication and expression. The implications of this claim are far-reaching for reconsidering interrelationships of perception, understanding, knowledge, and more. Ong's essay on the "sense analogues for intellect," for example, makes explicit connections with Bernard Lonergan's methodological work toward a more comprehensive awareness of humanity's interiority made possible within this concept of orality and its broadened horizons through sound and sensation.[38]

---

34. Ong, *Orality and Literacy*, 7. Emphasis added.
35. Lawler, "Slow Deaths of Writing," 30.
36. Ibid., 30.
37. Ong, *Orality and Literacy*, 7.
38. Ong, "I See What You Say," *Interfaces of the Word*, 121–44.

The symbiotic relationship between writing and study further qualifies this irony significant to our question of integrating performative mode into critical discourse. Scholars must awaken to orality and its distinctive habits of mind because writing invites study which then invites more writing. Scholars are trained as scholars by other scholars to master textually-oriented traditions reflecting upon the human condition (among other things). In contrast,

> [h]uman beings in primary oral cultures, those untouched by writing in any form, learn a great deal and possess and practice great wisdom, but they do not 'study.' They learn by apprenticeship. . .by discipleship. . .by listening, by repeating what they hear, by mastering proverbs. . .by assimilating other formulary materials, by participation in a kind of corporate retrospection—not by study in the strict sense.[39]

Scholars *have* to rediscover orality because study so closely relies upon writing and tends to veer away from modes of thinking-being distinct from writing and study. Ong begins to pursue the implications for embodiment and context in his essay, "The Writer's Audience is Always a Fiction." He reminds us that the abstraction entailed in writing means an *absence*, not presence, of any living audience, truly known and knowable, which then impacts the kind of thinking possible shaped by *absence*.[40] Orality does not correlate with literate assumptions about it either. Oral cultures have been presumed within modern purview to be primitive, un-analytic or inferior. Ong clarifies: "All thought, including that in primary oral cultures, is to some degree analytic: it breaks its materials into various components."[41] Literate habits of mind within writing and critical inquiry (narrowly conceived) simply rely on certain ways of understanding that veil other awarenesses more readily available in *oral* habits of mind and. Literacy flows within communication and knowledge of abstraction, sequential or linear understanding, classification, and explanatory examination of phenomena and propositional truths. Orality's contributions are quite different, though difficult for literate minds to conceive.

---

39. Ong, *Orality and Literacy*, 8–9.
40. Ong, "Writer's Audience is Always a Fiction," 57ff.
41. Ong, *Orality and Literacy*, 8.

To illustrate this conceptual difficulty, Ong describes literate minds thinking of *horses* as *automobiles without wheels*.⁴² "Instead of wheels," he writes, "the wheel-less automobiles have enlarged toenails called hooves; . . . instead of a coat of lacquer, something called hair; instead of gasoline for fuel, hay, and so on." Anyone who has ever been in the presence of horses begins to feel a dissonance in this image. "In the end," Ong concludes, "horses are only what they are not."⁴³ He criticizes the literate willingness to conceive of "oral literature," as another example. Such pairing neglects an obvious incongruity that prefigures critical inquiry, and therefore its validity, into terms incongruent with oral phenomena. "You cannot without serious and disabling distortion describe a primary phenomenon by starting with a subsequent secondary phenomenon and paring away the differences. Indeed, starting backwards in this way. . .you can never become aware of the real differences at all."⁴⁴

In contrast, congruent with Gordon's theoretical origins, Ong stakes his claim for orality in proximate relation to but radical⁴⁵ distinction from literacy. He defines *orality* as the first and broad state of human cultural development surrounding a human communicative consciousness (primary orality). The development and evolution of literacy interweaves into primarily oral cultures, resulting in new forms of human consciousness corresponding to the characteristics of script, writing, and historical record. Both primary orality and literacy have since interfaced amidst the development of digital communications, resulting in a secondary orality, with similarities and differences from oral and literate integration.⁴⁶ With the rise of digital media, contrasts between literacy and orality become apparent both in modes of expression and in the concurrent transformations of human consciousness. Given these antecedents, Ong's work articulates aspects and particularly psychodynamic characteristics through which the full force of orality has yet to be felt, at least within a musicological sense.

---

42. Ibid., 12ff.
43. Ibid., 12.
44. Ibid., 13.
45. Radical, meaning "at the root."
46. Ong, *Presence of the Word*, 17ff.

Orality: Aspects and Psychodynamics

Ong highlights orality's distinctiveness for literate minds through its rootedness in sound, or a prioritizing of the audible, and its characteristic accomplishment of memory without written record. Primary orality, unavailable for observation today, refers to human communication and consciousness untouched by any actions or artifacts of writing. Words in orality are therefore primarily sounds or voicings, *not* the visual signs or abstracted significations you are reading right now. Oral-aural communication fully nests in sound and hearing that is offered and received within human interaction, not in sight, seeing, or assigned significance made available within written prose. Yet literate consciousness wrestles to conceive of orality in sound-based forms. No one 'looks up' anything in an orality, for instance, because sound cannot be written, only represented through abstracted notation. Likewise, sounds have no focus or trace, which are both visual terms. They are evanescent events, which then give them more sensate-impact or effect than often realized.[47] As early as 1923, Ong notes that literarcy critic Malinowski argued for oral cultures, "language is a mode of action and not simply a countersign of thought,"[48] a distinction difficult to parse until Ong's ground-breaking work. To literate awareness, oral cultures seem to ascribe near magical-power or action to words out of an ascribed primitivistic, mental capacity. But words have power in orality not because of inferior mental capacity but because soundings have an event-character, which, to be remembered for posterity, must take on easily memorable form. Ong notes, "Deeply typographic folks forget to think of words as primarily oral, as events, and hence as necessarily powered: for them, words tend rather to be assimilated to things, 'out there' on a flat surface."[49] Orality has no such assimilating records or print/script-based realities.[50]

This rootedness in sound also prefigures orality's distinctive relationship to time and memory, a connection with Begbie's work to be developed below. All information, narratives, and gleaned wisdom are to be remembered through personally embodied transmissions, from person to person, older generations to younger ones. Time is therefore

---

47. Ong, *Orality and Literacy*, 31.
48. Ibid.
49. Ibid., 32–33.
50. Ibid., 95ff.

referenced internal to a community, not to some abstracted historical timeline of written record. Said another way, oral cultures often rely on social, internally referenced time—event or *kairos* time—while less oral or literate cultures have timepieces measuring *chronos* time, external to a community and abstracted to all at once.[51] Orality still has memory, of course, though it cannot be as historically tenacious as written record. As Ong reminds us, one only knows what one can recall, in oral cultures. Without any visually available record, other habits of mind, like mnemonic devices and repetition, are necessary to cull information, stories, and wisdom of communities. The confinement of orality to sound heightens human awareness not only to the making and receiving of sounds, but also to the kinds of thought processes that must be developed in relation to such communication. Skills of communication in this fashion ultimately have a primarily relational, psychodynamic character, which become significant when considering music as a primarily aural-oral phenomenon with unique integrity.

Psychodynamics of Orality as a Primarily Relational Mode

Ong's summary of orality's psychodynamic characteristics takes particularly analytic or literary shape as it attempts to describe human communication that is rooted in sound and steeped within the unavoidable complexities of contextualized embodiment and human relationality. Consider the list of his literary-communicative descriptors. The psychodynamic characteristics of orality are:[52]

1. Additive rather than subordinative
2. Aggregative rather than analytic
3. Redundant or copious
4. Conservative or traditionalist
5. Close to the human lifeworld
6. Agonistically toned
7. Empathetic and participatory rather than objectively distanced
8. Homeostatic

---

51. Levine, *Geography of Time*.
52. Ong, *Orality and Literacy*, 37–57.

9. Situational rather than abstract

All these descriptors meld literary-communicative elements with those that describe contexts of communication and human interaction that are primarily relational and embodied. The first three are most clearly observable in textual sources steeped in ancient, oral cultures. Pointing to Genesis 1:1–5, Ong notes orality demonstrates addition and aggregation over subordination and analytical distinctions. This text shows "oral residues" because the ancient Hebrew has nine introductory *and*'s but contemporary English translations, within highly literate conventions, show prose with only two *and*'s and condensed, compound sentences.[53] The orally-steeped, original Hebrew becomes literate prose in which some elements are more significant, others are less significant, and some may even be completely omitted. Literate minds, therefore, in contrast to oral addition and aggregation, manifest subordinative and analytic habits. Without written historical record, orality also demonstrates habits of redundant and copious communication. Communication and shared understanding, regardless of oral or literate habits, requires the establishment of some sense of continuity. Writing accomplishes this with texts outside of the mind, but oral discourse must rely upon "repetition of the just-said" if speaker and listener are to be in communication with one another.[54]

The remaining psychodynamic characteristics given in Ong's perspective are more readily conceivable within embodied, situational, and primarily relational terms, usually abstracted away from sensate awareness by literate habits. Orality requires a more conservative or traditionalist orientation of mind because "conceptualized knowledge that is not repeated aloud soon vanishes [and] oral societies must invest great energy in saying over and over again what has been learned."[55] Knowledge in orality and literacy is treasured, but in distinctly two directions. Wise elders' abilities to recall are more highly valued in orality for sustaining communal memory, while literate cultures may de-value their elders as repetitive in face of new discoveries of the young. Print makes storage of memory more independent of a society's elders. On the other hand, orality views intellectual experimentation with great

---

53. Ibid., 37.
54. Ibid., 40.
55. Ibid., 41.

suspicion, while literate habits can store information and abstractions enabling new connections previously inconceivable without such speculative freedom.

Oral cultures must also remain close to the human lifeworld for communication and shared understanding, which means "assimilating the alien, objective world to the more immediate, familiar action of human beings."[56] A more implicitly human-bias may result, even as knowledge stays relevant to primarily personal and relational concerns. Significant for educational considerations, this also means that oral cultures "tradition" knowledge in empathetic and participatory ways rather than objectively distanced methods. "Writing separates the knower from the known and thus sets up conditions for 'objectivity,' in the sense of personal disengagement or distancing."[57] Orality, in contrast, remains close to the human lifeworld, with knowledge traditioned from elders who model and foster as much as they might verbalize. An example Ong offers is that oral cultures can have no equivalent to any "how-to" manuals or tradesbooks. "Trades were learned by apprenticeship, which means from observation and practice with only minimal verbalized explanation."[58] Given these characteristics, orality demonstrates a clear preference for the *present*, which Ong names its homeostatic character. Oral cultures maintain their equilibrium by focusing on the present and conserving memories only for the knowledge relevant to the present.

The prevalent tone of oral communication Ong describes, at least as experienced by the literate mind, as *agonistic*. He explains, "By keeping knowledge embedded in the human lifeworld, orality situates knowledge within a context of struggle. Proverbs and riddles are not used simply to store knowledge but to engage others in verbal and intellectual combat."[59] Not only does such vibrant interaction keep knowledge memorable within more oral communities, it does so in both verbal (sound-based) and physical (embodied) fashion. Orality reveals itself in a "portrayal of gross physical violence," which steadily decreases in later literary narrative. As Ong summarizes it, "When all

56. Ibid., 42.
57. Ibid., 45.
58. Ibid., 43.
59. Ibid., 44.

verbal communication must be by direct word of mouth, involved in the give-and-take dynamics of sound, interpersonal relations are kept high—both attractions and, even more, antagonisms."[60]

Ong spends a bit more time on the final psychodynamic characteristic of orality, which is its situational rather than abstract aspect. He acknowledges that all conceptual thinking is abstract, in a sense, but certain ways of thinking or kinds of associations suggest a more situated habit of mind, close to lifeworld realities. A most helpful illustration that Ong uses here comes from A.R. Luria's *Cognitive Development: Its Cultural and Social Foundations*, a study of illiterate persons (whom Ong names *oral*) and somewhat literate persons in Uzbekistan and Kirghizia during 1931–32.[61] Just as one example, oral subjects without connection to reading or writing identified geometrical objects by assigning them names of situational things, not the abstractions expected, such as "circles" or "squares." Instead, oral subjects identified the shapes using terms of things they knew: "a circle would be called a plate, sieve, bucket, watch, or moon; a square would be called a mirror, door, house, apricot drying-board."[62] Situational, not abstract. The exercise of categorical thinking also differs between those who are literate and those who are illiterate, or oral, in habits of mind. Categorical thinking was deemed unimportant, uninteresting, even trivializing by oral subjects. Literate ways of classifying or categorizing—tools with like tools, distinct from other objects without direct relation, etc.—are not valued nor therefore engaged in the same fashion.[63]

Much more could be said—or written—in this brief overview of orality, its origins, definition, and psychodynamics, but Ong concludes his summary in a vein appropriate to our musical-theological interests. He observes the power of orality to connect humans in intimate and communal fashion, with a particular relation to the sacral or the "ultimate concerns of existence."[64] Rooted in the physicality of sound—offered *and* received—orality relates the interior, sensate-experience of individuals to others in outwardly expressive

60. Ibid., 45.
61. Luria, *Cognitive Development*, cited by Ong, *Orality and Literacy*, 49ff.
62. Ong, *Orality and Literacy*, 50.
63. Ibid., 52.
64. Ibid., 73–74. See also Ong, "Orality-Literacy Studies and the Unity of the Human Race," *Faith and Contexts*, 209–18.

and relationally-configured ways: additive and aggregative, close to the lifeworld, empathetic and participatory, highly situational and physically embodied. Awareness of orality, distinct from but in relation to literacy, extends human consciousness in primarily relational and unifying ways—self-awareness in relation to the self, and self-awareness in relation to the other. "Knowing the effects of writing on ourselves," Ong observes, "knowing how much what we consider simply human is due to the appropriation of writing, we can enter into the state of consciousness of oral peoples—never directly, but reflectively."[65] Not only does orality connect bodies with the physical world and aural-dimensions of communication, it aids deeper self-awareness of the other, intimately connected with one's own interiority, one's sense of being human. "Entering oral consciousness reflectively, we can experience the people there as our brothers and sisters. We can feel what we are like without the support of writing technology."[66] Ong then argues that the cross-cultural understanding possible within this expansion and transformation of consciousness—orality to literacy back into a reflective orality—cannot but enrich the human spirit and open possibilities for greater understanding and love between diverse peoples.[67] The enacted connection between human interiority, communicative expression, and diverse communities leads Ong to claim an oral force to the holy, what he calls the sacral, the ultimate concerns of human existence.[68] At the very least, Ong's ground-breaking work in orality offers highly literate habits of mind opportunity to see new things, or hear new words with a more sensate impact. Literate perspectives become potentially more generative when awakened to a sound-based, primarily relational mode of awareness, distinct from but in relation to linguistic thought.

The music learning theory of Edwin Gordon stakes its claim for a distinct mode or world of musical understanding, a *world of audiation* distinguishable in observable, human behavior. All learning of music "begins with the ear, not the eye,"[69] he argues. The world of audiation requires a primacy of the auditory, the audible. "Music 'hears' us," he

---

65. Ong, "Orality-Literacy Studies and the Unity of the Human Race," 213.
66. Ibid.
67. Ibid., 217–18.
68. Ong, *Orality and Literacy*, 73–74.
69. Gordon, *Learning Sequences in Music*, 27.

writes, "we do not hear music. We *give* meaning to music, and music in return sensitively guides us to a better understanding of our total selves and our environment."[70] Musical understanding requires the offering and receiving of sound, a giving-over and received guidance available only within an immediate lifeworld. Gordon identifies the communicative aspects of music that urge continued rationalizations about music as a universal language, but *audiation* ultimately breaks with the categories and abstractions within literate habits of mind, choosing instead the embodied, immediate, and relational mode of learning within music's own terms, its unique integrity as intelligible, ordered sound enacted in embodied, integrative fashion. Ong's orality suggests a distinct but related mode of human communication-in-relationality, similarly recognizable in the primacy of the auditory or aural. Ong shares Gordon's methodological presupposition as well. Just as musical understanding cannot be accurately conceived within a more narrow or linguistic cognition, neither can orality be conceived easily within literate habits of mind.

In this context, Ong's work potentially awakens literate awareness to the transformation of human consciousness in encounter with music as a primarily aural-oral phenomenon. Communication fully nested in sound invites a reconsideration, even a willingness to encounter music, with or without words, in primarily sensate ways. Music becomes intimately connected with both its orally-located, *event*-time in performative mode, and its literacy-oriented *chronological* time through a substantial, literate tradition of notation and study. A renewed appreciation of music in this way also explains its contributions to shared understanding across cultural "musics." Remember David Byrne, who argues that music mysteriously opens human beings to one another, even when culture commodifies it as "world music."[71] Orality allows a renewed appreciation of musical traditions outside one's own, connected through interiority, primary relationality, and a sense of shared human awareness. Most significantly, however, orality's role for connectionalism or primacy of relationality[72] expands consciousness to a

70. Ibid., 33.

71. Byrne, "I Hate World Music," *New York Times*, 3 October 1999.

72. *Relationality* is admittedly more cumbersome than *relationship*, but it better signifies the broadest web of relationships conceivable. Relationality therefore becomes more appropriate when entering into theological discourse, especially if

more relationally-centered mode of thought-being. New resolutions to abstracted dichotomies emerge in the most unexpected places.

Orality's intimate location within sound, not sight, offers opportunity to reconcile opposites or discordant populations, potentially without violence and through the human voice. Awareness of power may be shared within orality because of the relationship between producer of sound and receiver of sound. "Sound unites groups of living beings as nothing else does," Ong writes, "[because] sound reciprocates."[73] In its evanescent form, sound creates a momentary performative mode of production and reception. The human voice also has a particular place in this reciprocal character of sound. Ong again: "Voice has a kind of primacy in the formation of true communities of persons, groups of individuals constituted by shared awarenesses."[74] Orality's shared immediacy and awareness have the realistic potential to unite people in ways quite different from those of the literate mind. In orality, there may be extreme disagreement, but the mode of orality lives a "rule of relation"[75] into human community that is unavailable to written discourse or habits of mind shaped unreflectively by systems of writing.

Jeremy Begbie's sense of music's distinct mode—a *performative mode*, which has originated this entire study—offers contributions in terms both resonant and incongruent with Gordon and Ong's aural-oral mode. We may now turn our attention to a critical theological appropriation of Gordon's *audiation world*, Ong's *orality*, and Begbie's performative mode, ultimately to be defined as a distinct but related mode of human communication-in-relationality, recognizable in 1) the primacy of the auditory or aural, which makes it congruent with Gordon's theory; and 2) its identifiable, psychodynamic characteristics, which attest to a primary relationality enacted in a participatory,

---

trinitarian in intention.

73. Ong, *Presence of the Word*, 122–23.

74. Ibid., 124. William Benzon argues that this shared awarenesses can be observed in improvisational jazz, where minds are linked within a shared musical consciousness. He calls this "coupling" within the active verb of 'musicking.' His argument is more persuasive than Ong's statement, but more complex than space/time permits. See Benzon, *Beethoven's Anvil*, 23ff.

75. Ochs, "Introduction" to Ochs and Levene, *Textual Reasonings*, 10–11. Ochs introduces the "rule of relation" in his introduction of textual reasoning, a form of scriptural reasoning originating from within Jewish philosophical-exegetical scholarship, which lives textual inquiry in more overtly *oral*-communicative fashion.

oral-aural phenomenon such as music. Brief attention will be given to the marks of a performative mode, for further extrapolation into theological method in chapter 5.

Begbie's Performative Mode, in Encounter with Music as Oral-Aural Phenomenon

Begbie's *performative mode* originates in Christian theological discourse that has been shaped in multiple ways by Greek philosophical traditions—especially the Aristotelian concepts of *phronēsis* (practical wisdom) and practice—but also in an uninterrupted line with traditions of the Greek *logos*, or the Word. Begbie's work undergirds this study *because* he insists upon encountering music in its distinctive way of working in the world, as opposed to subordinating it to the traditional theological categories or classifications. This study also requires music to be conceived in its unique integrity, so as to encounter and indwell it, not subordinate it. Begbie stresses that music will only advance theological scholarship if considered in this way, as "first and foremost *enacting* theological wisdom."[76] Confronting habits of conceiving music in its pure form or as an objectivistic phenomenon, Begbie charts music as a pathway of set practices for enacting wisdom. Music is "best construed primarily as a set of practices, actions involving the integration of many facets of our make-up."[77] By using this language—wisdom and practices—Begbie associates his sense of performative mode with a long-established Aristotelian tradition in Christian theological discourse, that of *phronēsis* or practical wisdom.[78] He also innovates beyond this tradition, however, in a manner more congruent with Gordon and Ong's work, even though his perspective remains captive to highly literate habits of mind. The remainder of this chapter therefore draws out the compelling themes and careful distinctions necessary to conceive music's performative mode within primarily aural-oral and embodied-relational ways.

Much (practical) theological work attempts to locate a space of practice, praxis, or even performance and action, within the Aristotelian

---

76. Begbie, *Theology, Music, and Time*, 5.
77. Ibid., 5.
78. Browning, *Fundamental Practical Theology*.

frames of *phronēsis* and its concurrent terms, particularly *practice* as it has evolved more recently through moral theory. Not only does this legitimate the disciplinary tradition of (practical) theology in today's governing scientific rationalities, it establishes a lengthy, critical tradition in continuity with such philosophical heritage. No one can argue against Greek philosophy's intimate shaping of Christian theology for very long, though more narrowly-oriented rhetoricians are regularly motivated to try.[79] Philosophy professor, Alasdair MacIntyre, reclaimed the term *practice* to mean

> any coherent and complex form of socially established cooperative human activity through which goods internal to that form of activity are realized in the course of trying to achieve those standards of excellence which are appropriate to, and partially definitive of, that form of activity, with the result that human powers to achieve excellence, and human conceptions of the ends and good involved, are systematically extended.[80]

Many contributions have evolved from this concept, most significantly for this study the work begun by Dorothy C. Bass and Craig Dykstra in the conceptualization of Christian practices of faith. Bass, Dykstra, and their colleagues have refined MacIntyre's work for ways of living the Christian life toward abundance, reconceiving *practice* to emphasize the hidden epistemological and largely somatic implications neglected within much critical theory.[81] A now sizeable literature articulates practices for communities, variously defined, from cultural anthropologists such as Pierre Bourdieu[82] to theologians Kathryn Tanner, Miroslav Volf, and Reinhar Hütter.[83] Stewards of this discussion, Bass and Dykstra,

---

79. Allen and Springstead, *Philosophy for Understanding Theology*. By narrowly-oriented rhetoricians, I am trying to name those with more fundamentalist habits of discourse without using a term like fundamentalist, so heavily laden with polarized and antagonistic hues in (post-)modern academic circles.

80. MacIntyre, *After Virtue*, 187.

81. Dykstra, "Reconceiving Practice."

82. Bourdieu, *Outline of a Theory of Practice*.

83. Kathryn Tanner, "Theological Reflection and Christian Practices"; Volf, "Theology for a Way of Life"; and Hütter, *Suffering Divine Things*. See also Stubbs, "Practices, Core Practices, and the Work of the Holy Spirit."

frame their own contributions to this discourse with practices as a *way of life for a searching people*.[84]

Bass and Dykstra define Christian practices most succinctly as "the things Christian people do together over time to address fundamental human needs, in response to and in the light of God's active presence for the life of the world."[85] These include honoring the body, hospitality, household economics, saying yes and saying no, keeping Sabbath, testimony, discernment, shaping communities, forgiveness, healing, dying well, and singing our lives. This last practice description, singing our lives, argues *music* as a human practice and therefore as a *primary means for enacting a living faith together within community*. Others have drawn distinctions in definition and nuance in the ongoing, critical-theological discourse. Drawing a necessary distinction between a *life-style* and the *way of life* toward abundance taught/learned within Christian discipleship, Bass and Dykstra emphasize several facets of a practice, shared by all.[86] They address fundamental human needs and conditions. They involve us in God's activities in the world. They involve a deep kind of knowing or holy awareness. They are social and historical, therefore crafted in various ways and forms over centuries of Christian community. They pursue the good, defined in this context as those life patterns that reflect God's grace and love. Yet they are also difficult and rarely transparent; a practice considered unto itself can be twisted to destructive purposes even as it can be shaped within holy agency for the common good. Inherent to these aspects is the shaping agency of all practices: they shape people in particular ways, with particular "habits, virtues and capacities of mind and spirit." Ultimately, Bass and Dykstra argue, "all of the practices of daily life come to a focus in worship." In this end, each practice renders the presence of God "more visible, more articulate, more pure." An important distinction arises here too: sacraments within Christian tradition are *not* considered practices, but gifts. Practices are those human creations for daily participation in an overarching way of life, not the gifts of instituted sacraments, "greater than our

---

84. Bass, *Practicing Our Faith*, 5.
85. Bass and Dykstra, "Christian Practices and Congregational Education in Faith," 1.
86. Ibid., 4ff.

own power to conceive."[87] (Practical) theology has spent considerable disciplinary time on practices, which makes its depth of engagement a suitable lens for viewing Begbie's innovation and contributions toward conceiving music in a performative mode.

The interconnections between Begbie's work on music as a complex set of practices for the making and receiving of sounds and the practical theological school of thought on music as a human practice become clear quickly. Both works are aiming for the lived realm of action with awareness in which dynamic learning and transformation occur. Both are deeply rooted in the Aristotelian philosophical heritage attempting to name this mode or agency of practical wisdom within that learning and transformation. Begbie leaves the precise configuration of practice implicit, however, making little overt reference to the extensive practical theological discourse of less interest in his systematic theological circles. Practice is a term to enflesh the path toward wisdom, but unimportant for his main interest, which is the temporal dimension(s) of music-making and music-hearing. Practical theologians naturally focus much more energy upon the conceptualization and implementation of practices as a theoretical-praxis construct to engage more people in an integrative way of life below and beyond static notions of skills or techniques of abundant living. For our purposes here, practical theologians have given critical distinction to human practice, though with a side-effect of reifying into analytical concepts the very way of life they are attempting to retrieve from analysis. The Aristotelian heritage also demonstrates the fundamentally dialectical habits of mind, shaped as it was within the evolution of writing and literate formulations of human thought. Begbie's approach, in contrast, names an overarching space or mode for this way of life for enacting theological wisdom, for awakening into a deeper knowing. Begbie and the practices literature complement each other nicely, urging us to refine critical understanding of this performative mode as a comprehensive frame within which practices take place.

Begbie's work moves our attentions beyond (practical) theological *phronēsis* by conceiving music's practices attuned primarily to its own sound-based, relational constitution, instead of with reference to Aristotelian categories of human making, doing, and being. Some

---

87. Ibid., 7.

terms remain, of course, but they do not distinguish music from human agency or vice versa. For instance, "Music," Begbie argues, "is fundamentally about making and receiving sounds, and this book is designed to show some of the theological fruit which can emerge from examining carefully what is involved in this making and reception."[88] *Poesis*, human action of "making," remains in Begbie's definition, but its use is generative, ongoing, not one action but a participation in making, connected relationally to receiving. As he clarifies in the next chapter, "there are two interlocking and mutually informative procedures [for speaking of music as a multiplicity of practices]: those which engender music—music-making, and those of perception—music-hearing, and under 'hearing' I mean to include all the faculties associated with musical reception, not only the ears."[89] Music's performative mode, as a result, is not defined around a human action toward a separate end, as analytically specified within Aristotelian philosophical, then theological, precision. Music's performative mode signifies an essentially reciprocal, relational, participatory space made palpable in both a primary relationality and a sensate embodiment able to feel or hear sound. Here we may find the first two seeds of a performative mode with theological nuance: primarily relational and explicitly embodied.

Begbie also distinguishes music's performative mode with reference to music's interconnectedness *and* its distinctiveness. He names the extrinsic and intrinsic theories of music developed from its multidimensionality and therefore intimate connection with particular facets of human experience, consciousness. He observes the social and cultural embeddedness of musical practices: "Music always, to some extent, embodies social and cultural reality . . ."[90] Embodiment figures high in music's performative mode, according to Begbie. Music-making and music-hearing involve "an engagement with the distinctive configurations of the physical world we inhabit."[91] Musics are different across the world because the geography, the natural world, and the distinctive cultures all converge to make diverse materials available for sound production and shape human perception in diverse ways to receive

---

88. Begbie, *Theology, Music, and Time*, 5.
89. Ibid., 9.
90. Ibid., 13.
91. Ibid., 13.

their culture's sense of musical sound. Yet a performative mode is essential in each environment for this making and receiving of sounds. Performative mode also highlights the embodied and emotional aspects of music-making and music-hearing. The enactment of wisdom places persons in unavoidable interaction with their environment and others such that bodies and the accompanying psychological dimensions of being in relationship become intertwined.

Significant in this context is Begbie's clear articulation of music in its performative mode from any misunderstanding of music as a textually-conceived musical work. Bringing in the historical-philosophical essay of Nicholas Wolterstorff, "The Work of Making a Work of Music," Begbie challenges the easy assumption within musically-literate circles of music as a text or primarily literate phenomenon. A "musical work," Wolterstorff writes, "entails a complex interplay between a 'performance-kind' (types of performance); a set of correctness and completeness rules (rules of correctness specify what constitutes a correct playing or singing); a set of sounds and (usually) ways of making sounds such that the rules specify those as the ones to be exemplified."[92] The literate phenomenon of music, within a particular aesthetic and set of sociocultural norms, does not encompass the manner in which Begbie articulates music in its performative mode. Performative, within the primarily literate sense of a musical "work," is contained within the abstracted conception or ideal form of a piece of music. Begbie's sense of music, and its associated performative mode, contrasts with literate presumption and makes possible a different kind of encounter with music in its unique integrity. We therefore receive the sense of another mark of performative mode: an irreducible multidimensionality.

This is the final point that Begbie makes with respect to music's distinct mode, necessary for advancing theological scholarship. For all of music's embeddedness and interconnectedness, Begbie argues that music is also "marked by a unique and irreducible integrity, its own ways of working."[93] As such, "music has an *irreducible* role to play in coming to terms with the world, in exploring and negotiating the constraints of our environment and the networks of relationships with others, and

---

92. Wolterstorff, "Work of Making a Work of Music," cited in Begbie, *Theology, Music, and Time*, 10.

93. Begbie, *Theology, Music, and Time*, 19.

thus in forming human identity."[94] Making and receiving sounds, in Begbie's overview, instigates complex webs of interaction between local context, geography, the natural world, human selves-in-relation, and symbolic-narrative significance. Music interconnects human beings and their world in multiple dimensions. Even so, it enacts its own life or "way of working," irreducible to any one of these dimensions. It is marked by a unique integrity through which it invites participants to come to terms with themselves and their world. Music therefore has a unique role and potential power for advancing theological scholarship and, for our purposes, transformative learning.

Begbie's later work continues to develop the contributions begun in *Theology, Music, and Time*, aimed for a more general readership and broader introduction to Christian theological history in encounter with music. As such, deeper theological investigations into music's performative mode—its traditions, referents, intentions, future directions—are not directly pursued in disciplinary terms. Nonetheless, this later work demonstrates repeatedly the primarily aural-oral and relational marks of music's distinct mode. First of all, the entire work attests to the unique integrity of music, within which Christian wisdom is enacted, in which it may become comprehensible. The world of music, at least within God's ecology,[95] is more expansive than the literate and enacted traditions of Christian theological wisdom, which are also more expansive than the world of critical theological discourse. Begbie continues to honor the irreducible, performative phenomenality of music as the making and receiving of sounds. He offers further instructive detail through historical encounters with music in this performative mode—music in action in biblical times, through its articulations and understandings shaped by Greek philosophical currents, theological reformers, three musical theologians and two theological musicians. A marvelous overview of Bach in theological reflection intimates the classical theological yearning for a "wisdom beyond words"[96] so often communicated within music. Begbie even entitles the chapter "Wise Beyond Words," carefully arguing for a "theology in sound" and a specifically

---

94. Ibid., 20.

95. Begbie, *Resounding Truth*, 185. He intends it in a twofold manner: as a guiding framework, but also with reference to the created world distinct from the human sphere alone, i.e., attentive to a theological doctrine of creation.

96. Ibid., chapter 6.

theological power in music *without texts*.⁹⁷ Here, Begbie argues in exquisite detail his legitimate confidence in Bach's trust of God's wisdom *beyond words*. Music, "insofar as it shares in the world's harmony—a harmony that testifies to its Maker—. . . can glorify God in its own way, *even without texts*.⁹⁸ Begbie's sense of performative mode, rooted within the extensive philosophical traditions of Aristotelian *phronēsis* and even more complex traditions surrounding the Greek *logos*, the Word, moves theological discourse toward an encounter with music in its unique integrity, in distinction from but relation to language.

Ultimately, we receive a critically-appropriated sense of what *performative mode* means with respect to *music*. Gordon's music learning theory articulates the types, stages, and world of audiation as a pre-rationative, unconscious, and conscious model for hearing and comprehending music, a deep understanding of music in relation to self and world. Distinct from but in relation to literate habits of mind, this musical understanding becomes newly conceivable within the conceptual-reality of orality, also distinct from but in relation to literacy. Begbie's performative mode originates out of theological traditions radically incongruent with Gordon's methodological presuppositions. His immersion within music's primarily sound-based phenomena—both in piano performance and in his philosophical project on music's essentially temporal character—shape his contributions in ways suggestive of congruent themes and trajectory of thought. Regardless of whether he would follow me into the framework of orality for music's advancement of theological scholarship, his work moves in the direction of a methodologically congruent, theologically-suggestive way to conceive music's performative mode beyond the confines of contemporary practical theology. Performative mode, in this study, becomes defined by its 1) primacy of the auditory or aural, which makes it congruent with Gordon's theory; and 2) its psychodynamic characteristics, which attest to a primary relationality enacted in a participatory, oral-aural phenomenon. At least three marks of performative mode become explicit in conversation with Gordon, Ong and Begbie. The primacy of sound-based phenomena as human communication result in a particular mode of communication that is primarily relational,

---

97. Ibid., 130.
98. Ibid., 134.

explicitly embodied, and irreducibly multidimensional. What has been overt within human experience—before written, historical record—becomes available for renewed disciplinary investigations. What Begbie called music's performative mode, previously constrained within (practical) theological and linguistic habits of mind, becomes the radically critical proposition: music contributes most to disciplinary inquiry when conceived, encountered, and indwelt as a primarily aural-oral phenomenon with an irreducibly embodied-relational integrity. The next chapter provides the disciplinary seeds for a multidimensional theological method of indwelt encounter, inherited in the transformational logic of James E. Loder.

4

Religious Education and the Challenges of Learning in Music

One Discipline's Attempts to Bridge Learning from Music and Learning in Music Resolved in a Transformational Logic

AN OVERVIEW OF RELIGIOUS EDUCATION WITH RESPECT TO MUSIC throughout the twentieth century shows one discipline's struggle to articulate and implement music's educational presence in teaching and learning. Several strands of discourse could have been selected, of course, but a couple facets of religious education make it stand out for our purposes. It is both a young and well-established discipline in historical-theological settings. With over one hundred years of history, it also claims an origin with educational interest in the arts. Critical reflection on the role of music for a variety of religious educational purposes began as early as 1926. Religious education connects fairly easily across perceived religious-secular divides. Not only does secular educational theory contribute to religious educational concerns, but religious communities of all kinds—Jewish, Muslim, Hindu, Christian, Buddhist (by those who do not consider it purely philosophically)—benefit from the interdisciplinary and secular contributions to religious education. Earlier versions of this study even argued educational ministries as a subdiscipline of practical theology, thereby staking claims within theology. Religious education, as a discipline, offers a diverse but historical, potentially theological examination of the importance of music in educational settings. It also demonstrates the difficulties entertained in learning from music in Enlightenment and (post-)modern discourse, only recently resolved in the transformative-learning work of theological educator, James E. Loder.

The substantial difficulty redressed in this study is also confirmed in the literature. The objectivist captivity of music—that music is a thing to be taught in and for itself —appears in full force, reminding once again the disciplinary challenges for learning from music in performative mode. Just like theological and musicological scholarship, educational theory has been imprisoned within its various theory/practice dialectics, preventing a clear understanding of music as a primarily oral-aural phenomenon with integrative potential for transformative learning. As such, this chapter offers a more constructive model for what learning from music in performative mode entails. A primarily embodied theory of transformative learning, rooted in the theological-educational work of James E. Loder, suggests that transformative learning in music not only originates in a performative mode but operates with a particular logic, pattern, and destination: insight. We begin to see learning in music can become *learning in a musical key*, beyond a focus on the music itself to the unanticipated, multidimensional learning that occurs in music in performative mode. This disciplinary move into a critical theory, rooted in performative mode, requires theologians to awaken to the deepening sensation of oral-aural phenomena, organize unruly sensation according to a transformational logic, and endure long enough to articulate unforeseen contributions to critical theological discourse in tune with their horizon of ultimate value. The significance of a fourth mark of performative mode—insight amidst indwelt multidimensionality—becomes a clear link between learning in music, through its primary gift, and learning that is multidimensional beyond anticipated objectives and educational theory.

Religious Education—One Discipline's Attempts to Conceive Learning in Music

The emergence of progressive education at the start of the twentieth century began a focused interest in the role of art, music, literature, and dramatics *for educational purpose*. A purely chronological approach appeals for understanding the context of religious education as a discipline, as it developed from its earliest traditional forms through the rise of professionalism into its (post-)modern contributions today. A more comprehensive lens offered within curriculum theory illustrates more in less space. In *Conflicting Conceptions of Curriculum*, educational theorists Eisner and Vallance argue for five orientations to curriculum in twentieth century educational discourse. These orientations, for our purposes, serve as a fivefold lens for understanding how music in religious education has been understood, engaged, and directed over time. Each brings out a different facet of music. An overview of all of them offers a historical survey of religious educational praxis with respect to music, significant in its literate inability to allow music its own integrity and transformative potential for learning across human intention(s). The orientations include the *development of cognitive processes, technology, consummatory experience (sometimes called self-actualization), social reconstruction-relevance,* and *academic rationalism.* Each will be defined before the thematic understandings and uses of music are examined within twentieth century religious education.

Development of Cognitive Processes

One facet of curriculum addresses *the development of cognitive processes.* Instead of a primary focus on the actual content of what is being learned, this orientation focuses heavily on the processes of learning. "This approach is process oriented in two senses: it identifies the goals of schooling as providing a repertoire of essentially content-independent cognitive skills applicable to a variety of situations, and it is concerned with understanding the processes by which learning occurs in the classroom."[1] In this sense, any curriculum planning of this orientation focuses on the intellectual maturation or development of intelligence within the learner.

Twentieth century religious educators, by and large, struggled to demonstrate music's role in the development of cognitive processes. The use of music within early traditional settings—i.e. Sunday School movement combining literacy education with basic biblical teachings—made no explicit connection between the songs children sang

1. Eisner and Vallance, *Conflicting Conceptions of Curriculum,* 6.

together and the development of intellectual reasoning. In contrast, the early professional education movement organized religious education's initial impulses within education circles to consider the development of intelligence through the use of music and other arts. *Creative Expression: the Development of Children in Art, Music, Literature and Dramatics* was published by the Progressive Education Association in 1926 as an edited compilation for guiding the education of children through development of their natural artistic potential, in opposition to more traditional foci on literacy and transmission of content.

In the music section, Thomas Whitney Surette offers a general view of music education for children that begins in the home and invites the whole child into self-expression and communal creation. Instead of the specialized sense of music for music education in which the practical and theoretical elements of music are taught through technique and training, Surette suggests a wholeness in music both in itself and in its relation to human beings. Creative expression in its best sense involves heart and mind in the educational process. In his view, music allows a child to feel vividly, to hear accurately, and to think the music. Intellectual development here is part and parcel of a wholeness in relation—child and music. Similarly, Calvin B. Cady argued professional assessments of musical capacity in children have failed because they do not reach the intuitional power of mind crucial to experience and learning through music. He even suggests a potential for music in general education through a biblical image—the kingdom of God—understood and engaged by means of the (then) current, evolutionary psychological concept of intelligence. Education in its broadest sense here is a process through which a child is led by an intuitional spring to discover and organize herself. Music allows access to that intuitional spring, and intelligence—the cognitive processes of knowing, understanding, and expressing—orders experience into discovery and expression, informed by generations of genetic heritage. In the decades that followed, intellectual development as a primary curricular purpose for music within religious education appears intermittently but regularly. Sue Ellen Page's *Hearts and Hands and Voices: Growing in Faith through Choral Music* offers a recent effort to incorporate various ways in which music develops intellectual comprehension through music education and choral programming.[2]

A more contemporary perspective on the role of music in the development of cognitive processes, congruent with both liturgical and postmodern impulses in educational theory today, arises with the work of Don E. Saliers, first in a small article in the *Christian Spirituality Bulletin* and ultimately in a recent volume, *Music and Theology*. The liturgical and postmodern framework pushes first and foremost against narrow understandings of cognitive processes, for one thing. In "Music and Spirituality: Listening for God's Voice," Saliers suggests that music has an uncanny way of opening awareness by awakening emotional life. His question centers on why music might be called 'religious' but he describes three dimensions in which music facilitates a holistic intellectual, emotional, and social formation of human beings. First, music elicits in human beings a state of receptive awareness to existence and to the world.[3] Second, human beings receive the fundamental form of their emotional, (pre-rationative)[4] lives in music; therefore music presents a means to explore humanly sensual, emotional, and the not-cognitive-but-not-irrational experience.[5] The third dimension in which music fosters human development is the extensive traditional expressions of music in religious communities over long periods of time. In other words, the social, historical-cultural strands of human experience that intertwine musical and human community life offer abundant treasure stores for further comprehension and interpretation of music's impact on human being.

Technology

Another lens through which to view religious education with respect to music is Eisner and Vallance's identification of curriculum as *technology*. This approach is also focused upon process, but not with the processes of knowing or learning themselves. Curriculum as technology attends to *the means through which* knowledge is gained and learning

---

2. Page, *Hearts and Hands and Voices*, xii.
3. Saliers, "Music and Spirituality," 10.
4. Langer, *Philosophy in a New Key*, 38–39.
5. Saliers, "Music and Spirituality," 10.

occurs. "[Curriculum as technology] is concerned . . . with the technology by which knowledge is communicated and 'learning' is facilitated. Making little or no reference to content, it is concerned with developing a technology of instruction."[6] Curriculum in this sense articulates a means-end, dynamic instrumentality established for its products: communication of knowledge and facilitation of learning.

Creative Expression, the Progressive Education volume, shows a particular emphasis upon this curricular view of music within educational praxis. Though several authors insisted upon the wholeness of music, the entire volume hinges on the use of music as a technology of instruction, whether that be music's constituent elements learned within musical theory or its experiential dimensions that encouraged group cooperation, creative thinking, and leadership development. Harriet Ayer Seymour and Norval Church, progressive educators in New York City in the 1920's, were intent upon linking the creative spirit of children with the overall educational aims of an institution through music, vocal or instrumental.[7] Each argued for music as a primary tool for the general education of children, and by doing so, each challenged a specialized sense of music. They reached similar conclusions in their work. Seymour emphasized the natural link between music and a child's creative spirit, representative of the one Creative Power or Creator, and the central role such a link plays in developing a creative and full life. Norval Church argued for the central role music plays in accomplishing the aims of modern education—group cooperation, creative thinking, and leadership. Music, in this view, is a method of instruction that must be harnessed for children to learn to lead developed, fully creative lives.

Elizabeth McEwen Shields encourages a practical approach to music as instruction method, with a slightly different nuance than the earlier resources.[8] In its most basic use, musical selections create the learning environment by either introducing a topic and preparing children to engage it, or by summarizing or concluding an educational unit of some kind. Theme songs can model a lesson's moral in both inductive and deductive fashion. Shields also points to music's use for lending variety to classroom activities and for motivating good conduct as stu-

6. Eisner and Vallance, *Conflicting Conceptions*, 7.

7. Seymour, "Creative Expression in Music," 81ff.; Norval Church, "Teaching Instrumental Music through Music," 103ff.

8. Shields, *Music in the Religious Growth of Children*.

dents work together toward some common goal. She describes music's capacity to enrich a playful spirit and to aid the further development of listening skills. For her Christian context, she observes music's ability to help children to an intimate experience of 'what the Bible teaches.'

Other voices develop this view of music in religious education too. A classic of church music or liturgical thought in the mid-20th century, *Music and Worship in the Church* offers music as a technology of instruction that moves church educational life through moments of exploration, interpretation, participation, and evaluation.[9] Jerry W. McCant explores stimulus-response and Gestalt Field Theory to describe music as, itself, a teaching method because it stimulates and provokes response as well as involves the whole person in the learning process.[10] *Music Worth Talking About: a Guide for Youth Leaders* provides resources for church-oriented, programmatic approaches to youth ministry. Music here is a technology of instruction to help groups of young and older people "practice the art of listening to the music bombarding...existence in North American culture."[11] Intent upon engaging popular songs with interested youth, Tim and Patty Atkins hope to foster popular music's positive messages and counteract its negative ones.[12] They open each chapter with a popular song, an opening story, a list of related topical questions, and then related biblical passages that engage the message and topics discussed. "Crank It Up," "Talk It Up," and "Look It Up" refer to this musical method of instruction. Theological educator Roberta King observes music to be a tool for powerful ministry, though she fails to specify much concrete detail.[13] Singer Bob Stromberg offers a touching view of music in this sense too: "Get Kids to Sing."[14] Music is the technology best suited, in his view, to developing faith, building togetherness, having fun, worshipping God, and expressing God's creation and creativity within us. He spells outs specific ways to appease the anxiety of youth about singing in public,

---

9. Lovelace and Rice, *Music and Worship in the Church*, 5.
10. McCant, "Music and Christian Education," 65–67.
11. Atkins and Atkins, *Music Worth Talking About*, 6.
12. Ibid., 7.
13. King, "Role of Music in Theological Education," 35–37.
14. Stromberg, "Get Kids to Sing!," videocassette.

together. Music in each of these religious education approaches serves as a particular tool or technology for various educational objectives.

Consummatory Experience (Self-Actualization)

A third curricular orientation through which to understand music within religious education is that of *consummatory experience*, often called *self-actualization*. In this lens, the value and meaning of human experience, personal purpose, and personal development constitute the primary emphasis. "Strongly and deliberately value saturated, this approach refers to personal purpose and to the need for personal integration, and it views the function of the curriculum as providing personally satisfying consummatory experiences for each individual learner."[15] It focuses upon the value of the experience to communicate most personally the values inherent in the particular educational practices and social community within which the individual is learning. Eisner and Vallance further describe curriculum as consummatory experience to be focused sharply on content, to be child centered and autonomy and growth oriented. Education in this curricular frame is an enabling process that provides the means to personal liberation and healthy development.

The endless human fascination with music and the regular intersection of music with religion or transcendence give ample evidence of consummatory experience as a curricular lens for religious education. One of the major pedagogical purposes of the entire progressive education movement, manifest in *Creative Expression*, was *pure experience* for learner-centered, imaginative, and collaborative education. Ruth Doing reflects on musical experience in educational settings and argues in "Rhythmics" that the bodily experience of rhythm is the crucial element in that it reveals the self in all its organic, evolutionary, and conscious elements.[16] Unless the musical experience is fostered in whole and for itself, such self-revelation becomes in danger of being disrupted by others' aims and agendas. Even as she offered practical tips for music's instructional method, Elizabeth McEwen Shields also understood music for the religious growth of children to

---

15. Eisner and Vallance, *Conflicting Conceptions*, 9.
16. Doing, "Rhythmics," 98–99.

be of two types. The first type is "songs that lead to worship experiences" and the second, "songs that express previous worship experiences." Theological ethicist Max Stackhouse offers a view of this kind of event from within his Triune vision as well. In a threefold structure of ethics, theology, and socio-cultural analysis, all areas align with a similarly threefold aesthetics—art (how things are expressed), beauty (how things ought to be), aesthetic transcendence (how things will be, experienced in the ecstatic moment of aesthetic insight). He argues for a cooperation between aesthetics, religion and ethics that will bring the power of the ecstatic moment, feeding further artistic pursuits into an ethical vision so that all may participate in the deeper logic behind all that is.[17] Consummatory experience of some kind is fundamental, in this view, for music's educational power.

Social Reconstruction-Relevance

Eisner and Vallance identify a fourth orientation within curricular theory as *social reconstruction-relevance*. Focus here rests on the larger social context and education's role and content for meeting societal needs and expectations, over and sometimes against individual needs. "An approach in which social values, and often political positions, are clearly stated, social reconstructionism demands that schools recognize and respond to their role as a bridge between what is and what might be, between the real and the ideal. It is the traditional view of schooling as the bootstrap by which society can change itself."[18] They identify two basic dimensions within this one orientation as well: a present and a future orientation, an adaptive and a reformist interpretation of social relevance.[19] Curriculum as social reconstructionism or social relevance suggests educational focus upon the dialectic of the real and ideal in human daily living: who we are and know as well as whom we could become, could know. Curricular orientation here identifies education's role in adapting its learners to the realities of individual experience in socialized contexts—adaptive, present orientation. It also demonstrates education's role in reconstructing

---

17. Stackhouse, "Ethical Vision and Musical Imagination," 149.
18. Eisner and Vallance, *Conflicting Conceptions*, 11.
19. Ibid., 11.

awareness and actions toward new possibilities within uncertain social contexts—a future and reforming orientation.

Music in 20th century educational praxis finds ready example of this curricular orientation, particularly within the 1960's and 1970's. An original source of social reconstructionism, however, comes in Archibald T. Davison's *Music Education in America*. Davison was an associate professor of music at Harvard University and conductor of the Harvard Glee Club in the 1920's. He offers insights into American music education that disregarded explicitly 'religious' ideals in musical educational settings.[20] 'Music' for him refers to the largely European, ultimately non-church, non-religious sound, organized and taught as an object of study in its own field of inquiry, seen especially in his choices for suggested requirements in specific music to be learned and appreciated.[21] Although not an indictment and certainly within his era, the musical tradition 'required' neglects the music of the majority of people in the United States, let alone from other non-European settings. His understanding of music is a highly specialized, budding professional one for study in the European university tradition. Accordingly, his understanding of education is a nation-based one, aiming for 'national character' and a reformation of America's youth, boastful confidence, reverence for efficiency, and mechanical-mindedness through a traditional European re-evaluation and renewal. Davison also stresses a necessary division between church and state in educational institutions, with a bit of derision about 'church music' instead of the preferred, more 'community-based' singing groups. Music in the highest professional guise would reform young American society. I find myself wondering whether he survived to see the 1950's and Elvis Presley.

A tried-and-true approach to social relevance, even an approach to social reconstruction within the religious ideals of the Christian tradition, was the identification of music as somehow an essential part of religion, by shared universality or as a religious language. Shields relates music to progressive educational praxis through a "shared universality." Both music and religion fill an instinctive need in humankind. As a unifying medium of expression independent of words, music "speaks a universal language that transcends racial and national barriers. Because

---

20. Davison, *Music Education in America*, 193.
21. Ibid., 199–203.

true religion is also universal in its appeal, there is a bond between the two." Social development is aided by music, a socializing medium of expression. Religion has clearly shown use of "an art that has not only the power to draw one nearer to God but, at the same time, the power to draw people nearer to each other."[22] Finally, the presence of music that conveys information and that appeals to the emotions finds much resonance with religion in its interpretations of life and world woven into the very felt depths of human experience.

Vivian Morsch aimed for social relevance in religious education praxis via music by arguing music to be a language of religion, integral to worship, historically rooted in hymnody, and known creatively from the progressive educational reform of the church school. First, Morsch argues that a human being, in all its relational splendor, is a cultural, intelligent, spiritual being who is subject to powers of communication. Music, proved time and again in its association with human religious activities, speaks of spiritual experience.[23] The second quality for music as a language of religion is its near universal, historical transmission. "The fact that music has continued, down through history, to speak to [humanity] of God and to be the language through which [humanity] has tried to express his religious thoughts and feelings is evidence enough that music is a very important religious expression."[24] The third character of music that gives it status as a language of religion involves its aesthetic effect and corresponding appreciation in human culture. Morsch here relates the wide appreciation of music in human culture with the similarly wide appreciation of beauty that so often results in religious response. The Psalter, Christian hymnody, and choral music dominate Morsch's descriptions of music in the church, although instrumental and creative music (in the progressive sense) gain some attention. As a language of religion, and one observable in Christianity, music is Christian education. It must therefore be taught through the best insights music education has to offer.

The 1960's and 70's offer a sampling of musical praxis in religious education, directed toward social reconstructionism and relevance in the face of popular music (rock'n'roll) and the need for strategies of

22. Shields, *Music in the Religious Growth of Children*, 21, 22.
23. Morsch, *Use of Music in Christian Education*, 11.
24. Ibid., 13.

confrontation and change. B. Lee Cooper spends particular effort in her "Rock Music and Religious Education: a Proposed Synthesis," which offers a practical approach to rock music in and for the church school that 1) assumes the need for its presence and 2) prepares a response for its expected opponents.[25] She suggests that religious education itself will occur if controversial music is placed in educational settings aiming for institutional change. Four goals are offered, complemented by the manner in which to select themes and lyrics in tandem with those goals. First, participants must identify socially relevant Biblical ideas that connect the scriptural text with contemporary events. Second, indigenous personal and social concerns within the church must be defined. Leadership and discussion members must then foster active debate, investigation, and cooperation among young people and adults in the church discussing significant problems. Finally, church members should be urged to undertake an introspective analysis of their own personal value structures.[26] In this way, rock music—or popular music of surprise to the older generations of church membership—embodies a technology of instruction but more importantly, shows educational praxis in which social reconstructionism is at the heart. Cooper offers another essay with similar intent, "Christmas Songs: Audio Barometers of Tradition and Social Change in America, 1950–1987," which is to explore how Christmas songs may be used as illustrations of historical information, cultural borrowing, and social change.[27] Related resources illustrate this curricular orientation with respect to music in educational praxis as well.[28]

The work of theologian Edward Farley on music within human existence and what he calls "the web of life" resonates with a curricular lens of reconstructionism, of a sort. His essay, "Music and Human Existence," raises the question whether music's communicational quality—i.e., music as a language of religiousness or transcendence—offers the best metaphor through which to understand the role of music in the religious life. Instead, he pushes for a relation between music and

25. Cooper, "Rock Music and Religious Education," 290–94.
26. Ibid., 290–92.
27. Cooper, "Christmas Songs," 278–80.
28. Lawhead, *Rock Reconsidered*; Atkins and Atkins, *Music Worth Talking About*; Cluck, George, and McCann, *Facing the Music*.

human existence within an alternative metaphor of transformation.[29] "Music (and the other arts) are aspects of human transformation insofar as transformation unavoidably takes place in connection with three elements in the web of existence:" the messy mysterious reality of human relationships, the human orientation to beauty, and the human attraction to the sphere of the Thou.[30] Well versed in the development of aesthetics in relation to theological concerns, Farley argues compellingly for important distinctions to be kept about the power of music, the limited capacity of music itself apart from the sphere of the Thou, and the unavoidable influence of human will in cultural specificity. For our purposes here, music contributes to the transformation of human existence and shared reality.

Academic Rationalism

The final curricular orientation that Eisner and Vallance describe is curriculum as *academic rationalism*. Curriculum here refers to a tradition-bound education primarily concerned with transmitting the wisdom and cultural tools of previous generations in order to enable the young to participate in a particular culture.

> Those embracing this orientation tend to hold that since schools cannot try to teach everything or even everything deemed worth knowing, their legitimate function is that of cultural transmission in the most specific sense: to cultivate the child's intellect by providing him with opportunities to acquire the most powerful products of [humanity's] intelligence. These products are found, for the most part, in the established disciplines.[31]

Their choice of descriptor, *academic rationalism*, brings a marvelous dissonance when considered specifically within religious education. Often, those who create and participate in "tradition-bound education" and who are "primarily concerned with transmitting the wisdom and cultural tools of previous generations" within religious education are considered anything but "academic"! Nonetheless, the proponents of religious education that are specifically interested in creating future

---

29. Farley, "Music and Human Existence," 178.
30. Ibid., 178–80.
31. Eisner and Vallance, *Conflicting Conceptions*, 12.

generations within an historical tradition of faith fit the spirit of the curricular lens here described by Eisner and Vallance. Perhaps an additional nuance of *ecclesial rationalism* will extend critical purview of this curricular orientation defined by living theological traditions. Regardless, this orientation presupposes that education must be rooted in the heritage of past traditions even as this teaching/learning contributes to the future. Education is the functional transmission of that heritage. Focus is upon knowledge as conceived in terms of the classical or ecclesial ideas, tools, and skills developed over many, many years in that tradition, as well as upon what constitutes knowledge, determined by those in the established ecclesial communities or academic disciplines of thought.

Not surprisingly, musical praxis within 20th century religious education finds ready example of an academic and ecclesial rationalism. *Education in Church Music* offers an illustrative approach to music and religious education in this fashion.[32] Written by Karl Pomeroy Harrington in 1931, it attempts to synthesize the traditional understandings of church music, 'music education,' and congregational education toward an integration of music into *ecclesiastical religious education*. Harrington assumes a specialized understanding of church music and proposes a specialized, music education approach to music for the church. As such, he does not argue so much for education with religious affective or intellectual import for which music can be employed as he does for the education of congregations specifically about musical theory, practice, and performance training. His hope is that the role of music in Christian worship will gain credible footing and increased congregational understanding and involvement through professional guidance from music education. *Education in Church Music*, though well intended, illustrates an early and obviously ineffective attempt to synthesize the newly developing progressive education movement, the rising professionalism in both music and religious education and the traditions of music in the church. Music is specifically "church music" here, and music education is redirected into the church for continued life within the church.

Similarly, though with a neo-orthodox, theological flavor suited to 1953, Edith Lovell Thomas offered a biblically grounded understanding

---

32. Harrington, *Education in Church Music*.

of music in church education. She conceives it as a ministry of song shared among the members of a Christian community of faith for the purpose of education in worship and habits of devotion.[33] The intention, however coherent within her Christian tradition, is clearly a "tradition-bound education" with "primary concern in transmitting the wisdom and cultural tools" of that tradition—in this case, via a sacramental logic. First, Thomas defines music in terms quite specific to her tradition: the song of the church sung by rejoicing Christians all over the world. Music is that which "rejoicing Christians" expressed, testifying to their Christian conviction and irrepressible joy in the gospel of Jesus Christ. Thomas describes music in reference to two phrases of Colossians 3:16: "the inspiration of Christ" and "train one another with the music of psalms."[34] The inspiration of Christ is a threefold sacrament enacted at the Last Supper: a humble act of service to daily physical need, a supper of bread and wine in the fellowship of friends, and finally a singing of hymns. She asks, "Have we underestimated the significance of the sacrament of song?"[35] In these biblical, educational, and historical terms, Thomas establishes her understanding of music for Christian education as a sacramental ministry that declares confidence in the One who will not fail the faithful in any test. The ultimate aim of sacramental song in Thomas's work is to lead the entire family of God to true worship, which will lead people to the maturity of faith through growth in love of God and neighbor. Thomas demonstrates well an ecclesial rationalism curricular orientation, in that her hopes for musical praxis within Christian educational settings are all defined in terms of that faith tradition and its historical theological terminology.

Various voices speak a similar message within religious education tinged with a liturgical focus. In the aforementioned *Music and Worship in the Church*, Lovelace and Rice offer their treatment of Christian education in music informed by their own professional experience, a Commission on Education of the First Methodist Church in Evanston, Illinois, and Vivian Morsch's *The Use of Music in Christian Education*. They present worship to be the primary task of Christian education and argue music's crucial ability in this task to impress and express the

---

33. Thomas, *Music in Christian Education*.
34. Ibid., 9.
35. Ibid., 14.

Spirit and Truth of God in Christian community.[36] Hymns and spiritual songs impress values into the mind as noted in the words of Paul to the Colossians, and music expresses in form and substance that which often cannot be communicated in words alone. These forms of music are considered a liturgical offering that educates participants' cognitive development through information and exploration, interpretation, participation, and evaluation. The end point, however, is an ecclesiastically centered rationalism for Christian worship and the Spirit and Truth of God in Christian community. Frank Gaebelein offered a short piece of similar substance, "Music in Christian Education," which placed any truth in music to be created only by God, revealed in the Incarnation.[37] Such conviction resonates clearly within the Christian tradition as it uses resources to further that tradition's heritage.

Another sampling of musical praxis rooted in a ecclesial rationalism can be found in "Hymns in Religious Education: Three Perspectives," by Ronald A. Nelson, William B. Rogers, and Don E. Saliers, which offers a tri-part perspective on hymns in a choir program, church school, and catechesis, respectively. Nelson offered the solid view of hymnody in his day as the 'hymn bank' for adult theology, quoting the oft-heard phrase, "I know that my theology was shaped more by the hymns I sang than by the Bible itself!" Rogers compiled a concise summary of music in Christian education guided by the then-contemporary resources.[38] Saliers, however, proposes an original look at music in educational praxis with his section entitled, "A Crucial Catechesis: Hymns and the Church Year." He draws attention to a relationship between spiritual formation, education, and music, argued from a simple premise: over time, Christian worship both forms and expresses the Christian faith experience, making the Gospel visible and audible through its faithful congregants. "There is therefore a necessary relationship," he writes, "between education for worship and the formative/expressive power of the texts we sing and prayer."[39] He then urges Christian educators to further understandings and appreciation of congregational hymn singing within the context of the church year and the Word of God read,

---

36. Lovelace and Rice, *Music and Worship*, 169.

37. Gaebelein, "Music in Christian Education," 30–32.

38. Nelson et al., "Hymns in Religious Education," 80. See also Lynn and Wright, *Big Little School* and Lovelace and Rice, *Music and Worship in the Church*.

39. Nelson et al., "Hymns in Religious Education," 80, 83.

prayed, and proclaimed. In that 'crucial catechesis,' Saliers claims the experiential validity and theological substance of congregational song can be recovered. Again, the focus of musical praxis is tradition-bound and clearly defined for Christian traditional transmission and/or evolution. Other samples give similar attention to the ecclesial rationalism embodied in some musical praxis within religious education.[40]

This survey of religious education's contributions to and challenges in understanding music's role in learning gives specific answers to our original questions, at least as gleaned over the past one hundred years, in this disciplinary strand of thought. Learning from and in music develops and extends cognitive understanding. It functions as a technology or means to all kinds of educational purposes. A favorite aim within human community is music used for consummatory experience or self-actualization, amidst awareness of something larger or greater than the self. As a result, music has been directed toward religious or spiritual experience for longer than we can account in historical record. Music's immediacy and diversity of form also encourages social reform, sometimes empowering peaceful ways for social reconstruction. It just as easily conforms traditional or conservative social values and expression, however, seen in its use for rationalisms of both academic and ecclesial forms. Music as a cultural curriculum, in the aforementioned sense, suggests an embodied and widely diverse path to learning of all kinds.

Confronting Music's Multidimensionality: the Transformative Logic of James Loder

Endemic to the competent religious education enterprise, however, is music's irrepressible multidimensionality amidst the required clarity of educational purpose and implementation. Educational theory manifests the latter in articulate attention to the goals, specific objectives, pedagogical strategies, educational environment and more. It does less well with multifaceted phenomena like music in performative mode.

---

40. Swaggart with Lamb, *Religious Rock'n'Roll*; Wimberly, "Church Family Sings"; Westerhoff, "Children: Faith, Formation, and Worship," 13–14; Pfatteicher, *School of the Church*; Blice-Baum, "Of Saints and Song." See also Brink, "Introducing *Songs for LIFE*" and Engle, "Teaching Children the Songs of the Church."

The well-established "Tyler Rationale" offers a rigorous paradigm for accomplishing a clarity of mission and implementation, yet it also hides significant dimensions of teaching/learning in controlling fashion. In 1949, Ralph Tyler articulated what he called a "rationale" through which any educational curriculum could be constructed. He was insistent upon this rationale or paradigm as a "way of 'viewing, analyzing, and interpreting' the program of an educational institution,"[41] and not to become a manual of any sort. But Tyler's rationale has been, more often than not, a step-by-step guide to curricular writing, and, less often than desired, the only approach to educational expertise. Necessarily accountable to the relationship between intentions and outcomes, educators today get penalized within the larger educational ecology when they divert energies away from Tyler's way of viewing, analyzing, and interpreting educational praxis.

The rationale centers around four basic questions:

1. What educational purposes should the institution seek to attain?
2. What educational experiences can be provided that are likely to attain these purposes?
3. How can these educational experiences be effectively organized?
4. How can we determine whether these purposes are being attained?[42]

These questions structure nearly every educational rationale offered within the ecology of primary, secondary, and post-secondary education today. And well they should. The rationale, at least when deeply engaged, provides a compelling, pragmatic, and effective means within which to consider all of the logistical-concrete details involved in any educational process toward responsibly articulate purpose(s). It offers vehicles of accountability for schools today, assuring parents and citizens alike that schools are attempting to meet high standards of performance and transparency in the education of younger generations.

For our purposes of discerning what learning from music in its performative mode requires, however, Tyler's Rationale obscures the multidimensionality of learning that occurs within participatory musical events within previous categories of human conceptualization. We

---

41. Walker and Soltis, *Curriculum and Aims*, 55.
42. Ibid., 56.

have so divided and dissected this musical multidimensionality that we have two apparent options within literatures assessed here: *learning from music* and *learning in music*. But music in its performative mode educates in ways impossible to anticipate within critical educational discourse. Music may be used as a method of instruction for religious educational ends, given careful consideration as a pedagogical strategy. Unintended by teacher or learner alike, this music engaged in *performative* mode may instigate consummatory experiences that disrupt the learning environment and distract everyone from the identified educational objectives. It may lead to a deep connection with what is sacred and needs to be spoken. An educator with intended objectives for community bonding and group building may invite students into musical participation toward that end, only to discover that for some unknown reason, the music did not serve that purpose at all. It may have even created a space in its performance that *divided* the group instead. Seasoned educators learn to anticipate the unexpected, of course, which (ironically) can *always* be anticipated with music in a performative mode. So how might we better open to learning in music, critically interpreted, such that we honor its multidimensionality and harness its unique way of working within human community? How may we conceive of learning from music in its performative mode rooted in its integrity and multidimensionality, made available in a primarily oral-aural mode? Theological educator, James E. Loder, offers a transformational logic with real potential for learning primarily in performative mode, independent of Tyler-Rationale habits of mind and promising for critically assessing the learning within multidimensional phenomena like music.

Developed in response to convictional spiritual experience and rooted in psychological and theological science, Loder's work suggests a constructive model for understanding learning in music as an embodied, deeply sensate yet imaginative awakening to music's gift, insight. Framed as a methodological practice, it may even suggest new ways of advancing theological scholarship by means of music in its performative mode. When encountered in performative mode, music offers regular but unpredictable opportunities for (un)intended learning become conscious or self-aware within a perceivable logic or pattern. Given the traditioned habits of literate mind specific to disciplinary theological formation, learning in this fashion may invite scholars to awaken to deepening sensation of oral-aural phenomena previously inaccessible to them. The logic offers *one* way for organizing unruly sensation and encourages a duration long enough such that unforeseen connections and contributions may result.

Embodied Epistemology: Tacit Dimension, Indwelling, and Interpretation

The first step in Loder's work, urged here by Gordon's musical learning theory, is a post-critical but realist, embodied epistemology. He relies upon Michael Polanyi here, who highlights the primacy of the body in human knowing in the *tacit dimension* whereby we become newly aware of the body's apprehension of sensation. Polanyi names the necessary role of *indwelling* as entrance into a performative mode. The transformational logic itself then gives specific contour to learning in music, one facet of which is insight. The chapter concludes with two examples—one historical, one contemporary—to illustrate a musical event in which all human participants, regardless of role and expectation, were shaped and invited into the kind of multidimensional learning possible with music in *performative* mode.

There has been a huge resurgence of interest in the role of the human body in the construction of human knowledge. Interconnected with deep contextualization of scholarship in some circles and with gender and ethnicity in other circles, the body can no longer be denied as an epistemological center. It *is* regularly denied, of course, for reasons as varied as rhetorical resistance and philosophical purity. This model for learning from music in performative mode aims simply to offer a plausible route into embodied learning for those unaware of or unaccustomed to it. The work of Michael Polanyi—a precursor to the work of James Loder to follow—gives as good an orientation as many, centering on the character of knowledge as somatic, the function of the tacit dimension in this knowledge, and the methodological role of indwelling for embodied learning.

The first pin of Polanyi's post-critical, realist work gives details for largely *somatic* knowledge in and through human action. Theological educator Craig Dykstra concurs, if with some caveat. "Some of this knowledge [in practices] may be almost entirely somatic in nature . . . It is possible that without such somatic knowledge, other forms of cognition for which this is a prerequisite become impossible."[43] Polanyi makes the point more strongly. The human body, traditionally eclipsed in cognitive developmental thought, is the primary instrument through which all investigation, experimentation, and discovery occurs. Polanyi writes,

> Our body is the ultimate instrument of all our external knowledge, whether intellectual or practical. In all our waking moments we are relying on our awareness of contacts of our body with things outside for attending to these things. Our own body is the only thing in the world which we normally never experience as an object, but experience always in terms of the world to which we are attending from our body. It is by making this intelligent use of our body that we feel it to be our body, and not a thing outside.[44]

Regardless of the level of awareness, humans rely on the body as context and container for all knowledge and learning. We do not normally experience our body in this way, unless perhaps we focus on it for organic maintenance, care, and intimate interaction (i.e., showering, hygiene, food that's too spicy, pain of a hot stove, danger implied in a situation that requires body movement, sexual intercourse, etc). Nonetheless, all human interaction presupposes a somatic beginning. Scientist-become-philosopher, Michael Polanyi, presents an accessible but nuanced description of knowing through the body reliant upon a *tacit* dimension. Awareness of this dimension is important for human knowledge of the outside world and comes from attending to outside things mirrored within human sensation.[45]

Awareness of the tacit dimension begins with Polanyi's obvious phrase, "We know more than we can tell."[46] Within a reflective orality, we remember that humans know more than momentary sensation and language could ever articulate. In terms resonant with musical understanding that somehow connects the figural with the formal, the "knowing that" and the "knowing how," Polanyi's contribution was articulating an analytical-relational *gestalt* able to conceptualize elements of the outside world as both outside of and within bodily sensate-awareness.

43. Dykstra, "Reconceiving Practice," 45.
44. Polanyi, *Tacit Dimension*, 15–16.
45. *Mimesis* is sometimes the term more familiar, with a literary denotation.
46. Polanyi, *Tacit Dimension*, 4.

Any act of knowing, regardless of the knower's awareness or admission of it, interweaves "knowing that" and "knowing how." Polanyi's sense of knowledge offers theoretical and practical integration without any presuppositional dialectics. "[I]n an act of tacit knowing," he observes, "we *attend from* something for *attending to* something else; namely *from* the first term *to* the second term of the tacit relation. In many ways, the first term of this relation will prove to be nearer to us, the second further away from us."[47] He describes this gestalt in terms of the *proximal* and the *distal*, the *subsidiary* and the *focal*. These two terms-in-relation constitute a way of knowing reliant upon embodied awareness without requiring dissections or dialectics that then need to be unified. The tacit dimension never becomes "tacit" versus "explicit" knowledge, which suggests a more negative or limited meaning in "we know but cannot say." Polanyi's tacit dimension highlights that all personal knowledge is fundamentally embodied or *interiorized*, only sometimes conceivable within literate habits of mind or articulated within shared expressions or communication.[48] In sum, Polanyi argues for the body in its entirety as the primary instrument of any knowing, conceivable in the *tacit dimension* as an analytical-relational gestalt.

The more methodological phrase for engaging in knowing that is relationally-embodied or interiorized is *indwelling the phenomenon of inquiry*. For his sense of *indwelling*, Polanyi draws upon the substantial German hermeneutical tradition of Dilthey and Lipps that articulated knowing through empathy.[49] Beyond their sense of 'empathy,' however, Polanyi argues for full embodied-awareness, not simply an affective or feelings' sense of the term. "Indwelling, as derived from the structure of tacit knowing, underlies all observations, including all those described previously as indwelling . . . It brings home to us that it is not by looking at things, but by dwelling in them, that we understand their . . . meaning."[50] Indwelling in Polanyi's 'post-critical' philosophy identifies the absolute centrality of the body to all human awarenesses, and

---

47. Ibid., 10.

48. Polanyi, *Personal Knowledge*. Connections and contrasts with Mary Frohlich's sense of *critical interiority* would be a fruitful avenue of development here, though Polanyi and Frohlich come from drastically different fields of inquiry.

49. Polanyi, *Tacit Dimension*, 16. Polanyi cites Dilthey, *Gesammelte Schriften*, 213–16 and for translation, Hodges, *Wilhelm Dilthey*, 121–24.

50. Polanyi, *Tacit Dimension*, 17–18.

therefore, to all human knowing of both narrowly cognitive and social construction. He emphasizes this comprehensive sense in indwelling by relating it to the *interiorization* of social teachings and the resulting twofold interpretation required for internal and external, private and public comprehension.

Polanyi defines *interiorization* to be an individual's identification of self with moral teachings or observations under examination. He writes, "To interiorize is to identify ourselves with the teachings in question, by making them function as the proximal term of a tacit moral knowledge, as applied in practice. This establishes the tacit framework for our moral acts and judgments."[51] Indwelling in this case, involves a process of self-identification, which necessarily entails a felt-sense of connection or commitment, whether conscious of it or not. Indwelling, which leads to interiorized knowledge, also requires two complementary, interrelated variations of interpretation, *congruence* and *correlation*. The former refers to the sense-making engaged within an individual's inquiry, and the latter, correlation, defines the sense-making required to make interiorized knowledge comprehensible within broader human groups and sociocultural settings.

This review of Polanyi's contribution to an embodied epistemology emphasizes the crucial role played by the human body in its entirety in critical knowledge, regardless of the limitation of the literate mind. The tacit dimension provides an analytical-relational gestalt through which we may conceive of and observe learning from music in its performative mode. It offers a plausible mechanism whereby we can appreciate the body's apprehension of sensation, the reception of sound, in the case of music. The function of indwelling further elucidates the integration of embodied sensation and the concurrent assignment of meaning amidst interiorized knowledge and communal settings of interpretation. Developed from Polanyi's work and articulated by James E. Loder, a transformational logic developed from Polanyi's *tacit dimension*, methodological *indwelling*, and communications of knowledge through *congruent* and *corresponding* interpretations gives conceptual contours for learning from and in music responsive to its multidimensionality through encounter and insight.

51. Ibid., 17.

A Transformational Logic

The work of James E. Loder spans the concerns of classical Christian theology, physical science, developmental psychology, educational ministries, and the reclamation of the Spirit within Christian congregational life. A renegade, academic traditionalist, he extended the discipline of Christian practical theology into Chalcedonian theological method and human development in theological perspective. His teaching relied upon intensely intimate encounters with his students, demonstrating both pedagogical strength and disadvantage. Deep commitments to relationality have resulted, which are so necessary for reclamation of Trinitarian impulses in Christian practical theology, funded by spiritual growth unto maturity. No less common, however, are the patterns of prolonged recovery, seen in the struggles for differentiation of scholarly voice in his students. Powerful intimacy often results in an unintended, pedagogical imperialism difficult to transcend. Amidst this complex, contextual reality lies the heart of Loder's research and teaching: a transformational logic or pattern of critical knowing observable within the performative mode of holy-encounter between, in his words, the Holy Spirit of God made known in Jesus Christ and the human spirit, "the uninvited guest" to every knowing event.[52] The logic involves five facets or elements that offer this study into learning in music a palpable pattern, transcendent of educational ministries usually held captive to Tyler Rationale thinking and objectivistic models of learning.

Loder's transformational logic articulates a pathway for what he calls *convictional knowing*, and what I would describe as "knowing in your very bones," or embodied knowledge. Five facets constitute the logic presented here in a linear fashion but by no means experienced in that order: *conflict-in-context*, an *interlude for scanning*, *insight* or a *constructive act of the imagination*, a *release of energy and openness of the knower*, and *interpretation* that operates both backwards for *congruence* and forward for *correspondence* with a consensual, communicative view of the world.

He observes a *conflict-in-context* as a crucial phase in any transformation of experience into convictional knowing. For clarity's sake, he describes this phase first in his exposition. "The first step [in the transformational logic] begins when there is an apparent rupture in the

---

52. Loder, *Transforming Moment*, 12.

knowing context. Conflict initiates the knowing response, and the more one cares about the conflict the more powerful will be the knowing event."[53] An *interlude for scanning* then ensues toward the collection of information to resolve the conflict. Loder describes it as temporary bafflement (of either instantaneous or many years' length) that draws the knower both consciously and unconsciously into a more familiar process of searching for solutions, assessing errors, and sorting helpful from unhelpful information.[54] He also specifies that this scanning is not only for outside information, but also for the refinement and possible redefinition of the problem within the original knowing context.

The third step of Loder's transformational logic is an a-ha moment. He describes it as a constructive and imaginative act of human knowing that conveys the essence of the conflict's resolution. In his own words, it is "a constructive act of the imagination; an insight, intuition, or vision that appears on the border between the conscious and unconscious, usually with convincing force, and conveys in a form readily available to consciousness the essence of the resolution."[55] He further describes it in terms of Arthur Koestler's "bisociation" and Einstein's intuitive understandings that eventually resulted in special relativity.[56] Ultimately, however, Loder describes this moment as a transformation of the elements in the context of human knowing from which the conflict emerged. This transformation bestows new perception, perspective and perhaps even a new world view, depending upon how major or minor the conflict-knowing event is to the person.

The fourth step follows with a *release of energy* that had been required to sustain the conflict and with an *opening of the knower* to both herself and the contextual situation. As the elements previously conceptualized are transformed through the constructive act of the imagination, the human knower experiences a release of energy. Loder writes, "The release of energy is a response of the unconscious to the resolution and the evidence that one's personal investment in the event has reached a conclusion; the conflict is over."[57] This release also manifests itself in

53. Ibid., 37.
54. Ibid.
55. Ibid., 38.
56. Ibid. See also Polanyi, *Personal Knowledge*.
57. Loder, *Transforming Moment*, 39.

an openness of the knower to him/herself and the contextual situation. Loder reasons, "The opening of the knower to his or her context is the response of consciousness to being freed from an engrossing conflict and for a measure of self-transcendence."[58] This release of energy and openness to self and environment signals the resolution of the conflict, if not the final and necessary process of interpretation.

The fifth step follows logically as an *interpretation* of the imaginative solution both into the behavioral and/or culturally constructed world of the original context and into the established assumptive world of the knower's larger community(ies). The knower's conflict has been resolved but the new knowledge has yet to translate into personal or communal contexts with any *congruence* and *correspondence*. The original, socio-cultural knowing context requires an interpretation of the new associations and world view that is congruent with original parameters. In other words, without any backward-moving interpretation, the knower cannot integrate the new perceptions or associations into his/her new and intelligible world-view. At the same time, this apparent congruence must also be aligned with a public, consensual view of the world, or correspondence. The resolution of the conflict in transformed terms must not only show congruence with the previous context, but be interpreted in a manner that corresponds to a public consensus and communally organized view. Without forward-moving interpretation, the new associations or world-view is intelligible only to the knower—a situation that threatens the individual's ability to function in an established worldview with divergent assumptions.[59]

Fleshing Out the Model

Two illustrations, one historical and one contemporary, enflesh the open-ended and multidimensional learning that music in its performative mode makes palpable for critical reflection. Instead of narrowing focus to music itself as the object of inquiry, or even focusing upon the

---

58. Ibid.

59. Important to note is Loder's distinction of congruent and correspondent interpretation from conformity. He argues that the creation of new knowledge in the constructive act of the imagination can never be restated fully into the old settings, so must be translated or interpreted backwards and forwards into previous and public world-views. See ibid., 39–40.

role music may play toward educational objectives articulated within a curricular program, i.e. learning *from* music, music in its performative mode invites—nay, requires—a willingness to enter into primarily embodied-relational and oral-aural space in which all participants may learn what they did not expect, may even be transformed in relational ways that make previous life and understandings difficult.

Both situations described here highlight music in its performative mode, but the first one shows musical participation to be the impetus to unexpected transformation and new insight. It is a historical illustration of a vocal orchestra in a prisoner-of-war camp during WWII. The second situation, much more contemporary, illustrates the primacy of the performative mode in which encounter and transformation may occur, only concluding with musical participation elicited by such oral-aural multidimensionality. This is for the express purpose of illustrating the virtue of *performative mode*, apart from the music itself. The hope is to suggest what music in its performative mode taught a historical community fraught with the violence of WWII, and then to see that the difference is the *performative mode*, not the sound-structure or music itself. Primarily oral-aural phenomenality, made palpable within musical experience but powerful regardless of organized sound, creates contexts for multidimensional learning, which are comprehensible within a transformational logic, when indwelt and interpreted. I will describe both situations before sculpting their contribution to learning from music in its performative mode, which embodies this multidimensionality of learning.

Historical: Song of Survival and Paradise Road

During WWII, thousands of men, women, and children who had lived in peace in the Dutch East Indies attempted to flee oncoming Japanese troops as the war came to the islands. One particular camp of women, interned as prisoners-of-war on what we would now call Sumatra, kept themselves alive as human beings by forming a women's vocal orchestra. Their story is told in a book and documentary called *Song of Survival: Women Interned*, written by one of the women, Helen Colijn.[60] Presbyterian missionary, Margaret Dryburgh, and her fellow prisoner,

---

60. Colijn, *Song of Survival*.

Norah Chambers, gleaned and taught from memory scores of classical music—Dvorak to Haydn to Bach to Tchaikovsky, even Percy Grainger and Maurice Ravel. Although camp martial law prevented women from gathering for any reason, let alone something like a rehearsal, the vocal orchestra met in unconspicuous learning groups until it bravely gathered as a whole for its first performance on December 27, 1943.

The head guard approached, companioned by his armed cohort, with visible attempt to enforce martial law. He was stunned into inaction by the music. Faced with an unexpected conflict-in-context, he and his cohort, one by one, sat down, laying their weapons on the ground beside them. For the duration of a vocal performance, a POW camp became a peaceful community of music produced and heard, offered and received. For the next three long years, this unusual event was repeated again and again, with the commandant and guards dressing up in their finery to attend vocal orchestra performances offered by the imprisoned women and children. Helen Colijn gives her first-person account of these years. *Paradise Road* tells the story of the vocal orchestra, with a message about the power of vocal music to bring people of diverse experience together, even in the most antagonistic of settings such as a POW camp.

Here is music in performative mode versus how music is intentionally used for human purposes. This historical situation, recorded in written and human memory, was not planned to teach the Japanese something, nor was it to teach prisoners of war how to survive. Its educational import for us here cannot become legible or audible within that frame of reference. Music as a tool or as an object of influence is not the right conceptual avenue for examining what happened, and what appears to have been learned, despite human intentions on either side (prisoners or guards). Yet unspeakable transformation and human reconciliation unfolded, both of which are worthy of critical reflection and theological interpretation. Even with the limitations of the example—peace was not achieved, nor did participants become ultimately reconciled—it still challenges a critical assessment of what music in its performative mode accomplishes beyond current theoretical lenses available within educational theory. The second illustration is both more contemporary, and more suggestive for the direction of this work for theology in performative mode in the years to come. It is not evidence for any argument in this

Christian spirituality study—what Schneiders disavows as "methodological narcissism"[61]—but it does illustrate the multidimensional force within performative mode, which only secondarily becomes a musical mode. For now, the description relates narrative events when two Presbyterian ministers met for refreshments after the synagogue service in a modern Orthodox Jewish community.

CONTEMPORARY ILLUSTRATION

A wholly secular Israeli and his family, including their daughter of quiet inquiry, welcomed others into their home—several Orthodox Jews, men and women both, a couple Presbyterian ministers. Among the group included doctors, writers, lawyers, a financier, and, of course, a rabbi. The rabbi had brought this crew together, for conversation, for learning, for whatever holy fireworks might unfold. Religious identity spawned the first rounds of conversation—variations of Christian denominational experience, strands of Jewish identity and observance. Friendly antagonisms welcomed a spirit of play, honoring both the horrific wounds of times past and the tentative hopes for a more generative life to come. Each found a role to play, sparring in diverse display.

Volleys of exchange began in earnest after entry questions like "How do Presbyterians and Methodists differ?" were safe to become the more pointed, "What about the role of women in Christian history?" Realities were named too—"If we were in Israel now, we would be killing each other!" and "All my teachers were *survivors*. . .do you understand? All my teachers are survivors *of your kind*." This Jew then invited one of the Christians to offer his own "conceptual grenade" into the fray, "as we have thrown many already." A young voice tendered her question, "Why does the Torah only seem to speak to men?" and her rabbi offered a glimpse of his own mishna, nearly formed, only becoming fully manifest. The Presbyterian minister, with her own scars for redemption, reached out to the young woman, then to receive from a Jewish companion, "You see?! Proselytizing! I knew it would happen!" Unexpectedly, laughter rose as incense at the gift and ready release of one more fear, alongside those feared, each and all. It was a Kiddush Club, alongside the lives and home of the honestly-secular, the

---

61. Schneiders, "Study of Christian Spirituality," 18–20.

faithfully-observant and the occasionally-invited. Then, one fellow had to depart for other responsibilities, but before he left, the group agreed to breathe into the possibility of sharing a family blessing in song. They sang, paused a little, then sang some more, "so we can really learn it." One Shabbat morning in May, a couple Presbyterians, a secular Israeli Jew and his family, Orthodox Jews who were doctors, lawyers, writers, and a rabbi shared a sung blessing, upon their satiation from and thanksgiving for shared rest, table fellowship and Torah-learning. They had listened and then they sang.

> Be with us at this table Lord
> Be here and everywhere adored
> Thy people bless, and grant that we
> May dwell in Paradise with Thee.

Here is the primarily embodied-relational *performative mode* of encounter and transformation, learning amidst multidimensional questions and answers, concluded and sanctified by musical form but not dependent upon the music itself.

The logic of transformation may be understood in a variety of ways between these two complex narratives, but each sustained *conflicts-in-context*—systemically and individually conceivable. *Paradise Road* describes a socio-political conflict steeped in war and armed conflict. Each prisoner would have her own conflict to resolve, too: innocent bystanding in men's violence, injustice of captivity, ignorance of country and family about her captivity. Often forgotten, each guard would have had just as intense of conflicts to resolve in some fashion: dehumanizing women and children, eating while others starved, inflicting injury to enforce military domination. The "kiddush club" suggests its own conflicts-in-context as well: post-Holocaust recovery between Jews and Christians, religious difference and centuries of intolerance, gender challenges and more. Amidst these systemic realities, each participant had his/her own conflicts sustained in the encounter: loving, learning from, even losing those who had survived Auschwitz; being silenced in a text perceived to be for men alone; attempts to redeem past suffering met with accusation, on both sides. Conflicts unbearable in human awareness often spur extraordinary human attempts to resolve them: a vocal orchestra, learning musical parts for compositions each may or may not have known, laying down one's arms when confronted by music offered; or sitting down at table for healthy debate and honest difference, sharing Orthodox practice with outsiders, singing a previously Protestant Christian table blessing within a gathering able to honor a "rule of relation"[62] more essentially than the retained, doctrinal-divisions and irreconcilable differences of the past.

Each narrative offered interludes for taking in information and indwelling the context. Paradise Road happened both in a moment—when the guards laid down their weapons—and over three long years—when the commandant and guards would dress up in their finery for vocal orchestra performances. The same could be said for the kiddush club—a momentary meal shared within hours, alongside decades of interactions in the face of the unspeakable horror of genocide. Both narratives demonstrate remarkable energies released amongst unexpected interactions and new ways of interacting within the context. Prisoners, who had little food and should not have had energies to sing, sang rehearsal after rehearsal, year after year, for three long years. Guards and captors made performances occasions of splendor and formality. The energies of the kiddush club expressed in the playful but aggressive debates, the extremes of volume and silence, the breathing in and out of loss and hope.

Most intimate and universal, most complex for articulation, each narrative also resolves its conflicts-in-context through shared insight in unexpectedly reconciliatory ways, transforming participants within and beyond their immediate contexts. An overly cognitive and linguistic focus on knowledge often emphasizes insight as the most important *product* of learning instead of its embodied-relational means to learning. In this case, however, the transformative logic presses us to see dynamic elements that flow and converge to affect new learnings observable in transformed *settings*, relations, actions. Insights of all kinds occurred because for these three years, the POW camp peacefully conspired, through music's own way of working, to be transformed into an intermittent but regular community of performance, not war. All involved entered into this mutually created, completely unimaginable new frame of human action. All participants learned, were shaped into, new patterns of interaction. In sum, *Paradise Road* illustrates the kind of systemic, multidimensional learning, centered around intimately received,

---

62. Ochs, "Introduction," in Ochs and Levene, *Textual Reasonings*, 10.

multidimensional insight, which is possible when music is encountered in performative mode. The kiddush club illustrates an explicit movement into multidimensional insights, divergent amongst participants but coalescing together in the communal breathing into old and new song, willingly shared across persistently felt-conflicts. "Be with us at this table Lord" begins a Christian hymn and table blessing sung for generations by Anabaptist Protestants, the Brethren in Christ denomination, centered at Messiah College in Grantham, Pennsylvania. In mutual trust and transformed relation, Orthodox Jews and Presbyterians sang it together. The shared musical activity attests to the primacy of an embodied-relational performative mode for multidimensional learning, given final expression in a musical form.

Regardless of whether the logic aids interpretation and understanding that proves transformative learning, music within its performative mode demonstrates a greater multidimensionality in learning beyond the conceptualization of disciplinary education, which yet remains significant for critical consideration of transformative learning in its dimensions and complexities. We see learning in this fashion requires a willingness for repeated awakening, what some might call an epistemological humility but which is much more complex than merely epistemological. It is embodied-ontological, connected with action and surrounding context through a constructive act of the imagination or receiving of insight, what may now be called the fourth mark of a performative mode. As such, music in performative mode urges a disciplinary vulnerability to contexts, to conflicting literatures outside one's expectation or expertise, to the unpredictable but necessary arrival of insight upon the constructive acts of the imagination.

This kind of learning also requires an openness to deepened and heightened sensation, whether pleasurable or not. Edwin Gordon and Michael Polanyi speak mysteriously about the significance of the entire body for learning in performative mode, at least with respect to operation. Not only empirically through the senses, or internally via biochemical pathways of an objectivistic materialism, but learning in an integrative fashion courses through one's entire body—sensations, mental habits, and more. As such, a mental and relational acuity for recognizing and organizing such sensation as part of learning beyond today's rationales must be developed. Conditioned into scientific and educational methods that prioritize the narrowly cognitive and intellectually interpretive, learning that is *not* multidimensional must somehow become so, open to new practices of recognition and trained abilities to organize unexpected sensation. Critical inquiry must move outside its texts and communities of affiliation toward an embodied indwelling of the phenomena being examined.

Multidimensional learning also requires a tenacity prolonged enough to sustain cognitive-dissonance or emotional-discomfort. Lengthy periods of scanning may be required, up to years, while presenting problems force waiting for resolution and clarity of insight, toward release of energies and activities of interpretation to follow. Perhaps the most difficult in today's fast-paced, over-achieving educational ecologies, learning that is ironically "performance-driven" for demonstrable achievement must somehow enter into the differently timed and spaced performative mode, which operates according to body-pace and body-time, not that of narrowly cognitive, intellectual prowess apparent in learning and scholarship for consumption today.

Conclusion

Learning in performative mode, what we may now call *learning in a musical key*, confronts historical and theological disciplines with numerous practical and methodological challenges well outside the confines of this study. When performative mode is reconceptualized by means of the dimensions and psychodynamics of orality, as done here, multiple categories of critical analysis become necessary for reconsideration: event-time/chronological time, mind/body problems (consciousness, perception), social constructions of identity (within literate or more oral norms), historical legitimation (historical-critical method and more orally-oriented narrative methods), and more. Performative mode is certainly a disciplinary Pandora's Box, with uncertain gains and visible, critical losses. Even so, theological methods are becoming increasingly conceivable for organizing some semblance of order amidst Pandora's confusions in the immediacy of performative mode. The rest of this study offers the fruits of one sustained encounter with music in performative mode, resulting in what David Tracy might call a *non-correlational* approach to theology. The primary marks of performative mode take on specific shape toward a redefined aim of theological inquiry: an expressive theological delight able to companion suffering of self and others. Such an approach relies upon the contributions of previous critical-correlational modes of thought, but resists their interpretive captivity in primarily two ways: first, a methodological commitment to an embodied epistemology in relational context; and second, multidimensional learning shaped toward a shared delight as the horizon of ultimate value.

5

Learning in a Musical Key

A Contemplative Empiricism in an Artisanal Way for Integrating a Performative Mode into Theology

PREVIOUS CHAPTERS HAVE FOCUSED UPON WHAT LEARNING FROM MUsic in a performative mode requires, guided by historical-theological and music-educational resourcing. Within the bulk of musical-theological literatures, the study has moved from learning *from* music—examinations of musical events from a more objectivist distance—to learning *in* music—explorations of the challenges and processes for learning within musical participation itself. The multidimensionality of music encourages a similar multidimensionality of learning, newly conceived with an inherited pattern or logic of transformation centered around insight. Musical phenomena have the potential, in other words, to open willing participants to new insights and levels of awareness, unhinged from previous anticipations or intended objectives in a teaching/learning environment. This chapter, ironic as it may be in light of the progression to performative mode, builds upon received insights to offer a theology in performative mode, what may now be called *learning in a musical key*, or that which is *relationally-formed, explicitly embodied, multidimensional* and *centered around insight*.

This *performative-mode theology*, gleaned from a sustained encounter with music in its primarily aural-oral phenomenality, is a *non-correlational* theological method that has all the marks of performative mode. It is relationally-formed through a methodological commitment to compassionate companionship(s), lived within practiced rhythms of life-giving, covenantal relationship. It is explicitly embodied in indwelt operations of contemplative inquiry with heightened attention to sensation toward awakening in new insight. Critical-correlational habits of mind inform the method's interpretive practices, but it becomes explicitly multidimensional in an *erotic* rationality and an extension of tasks beyond interpretation toward the fullness of human living through *contemplative wondering, impassioned gentle conviction, intimacies of difference,* and *joyful celebration that yet knows sorrow.* Named here a *contemplative empiricism* within an *artisanal way,* this non-correlational method for theology in performative mode articulates a horizon of ultimate value reliant upon Christian theological heritage but transcendent of its tradition's particularity: an *expressive theological delight able to companion the suffering of self and others.*

Making all this comprehensible within contemporary methodological discourse is no mean feat, and I suspect what follows will instigate more questions than easy understanding or replication. Much like Ong's literate conceptualization of a horse as a wheelless automobile, contemporary theological methods have conceived horizons and tasks with critical-correlational habits of mind, built upon the very dichotomies theological understanding (*theologia*) is argued to unify.[1] Even within a neo-Aristotelian *practical reason* and *habitus,* however, theological understanding will not be sufficient for performative-mode theology. This chapter addresses the challenge of disciplinary theologians preparing to integrate a performative mode into critical discourse first by offering the methodological fruits of this seventeen-year, critically-engaged encounter with music in performative mode—a *contemplative empiricism* within an *artisanal way.* The theological antecedents to this work will then be reviewed, not only for due attribution but for felt-comparisons and limitations. Stewarding a performative mode within critical theological discourse, in the end, requires not only greater facility with personal and communal life integration so well-articulated in the academic study of Christian spirituality. It requires a fundamental reorientation of mind and body and literate/oral dimensions of consciousness. Theology in performative mode, with all its complexities and risks, promises generative and ultimately integrative contributions to the fullness of

---

1. Farley, *Theologia*.

human life. One might say it offers new ways of non-being in companionable delight amidst the world's suffering toward renewal.

A final preliminary word. Far from being a systematic recommendation within historical-theological disciplines, this approach aims in singular fashion for what Gerald May calls the "crucible of personal transformation," the internal transformation of individuals, one at a time.[2] A contemplative psychologist, May recognized and resisted an observation of the Dalai Lama: that the internal transformation of individuals is difficult, yet it is the *only* way toward peace and justice. May cannot deny that systemic methods for what human beings want to know have failed. He cannot ignore that systemic approaches to the challenges of human suffering, violence, and oppression have fallen short. "They have not saved us from ourselves," he writes. "In this sense, they have not worked."[3]

In a similar though much more circumspect fashion, a non-correlational theological method does not presume any systemic response to the problematic of the performative in critical theological discourse. It simply articulates a long-discerned theological interpretation of what music in performative mode offers toward the advancement of theological scholarship aimed at the fullness of human life. The fundamental reorientation of mind and body, of literate and oral dimensions of consciousness, comes not through any correlational integration, but a willing surrender to the marks or seeds of performative mode—methodological relationality, embodied epistemologies, unending multidimensionality, and tenacity toward insight. Far from releasing its critical acumen for theological understanding, theology in performative mode enacts it one context at a time. It thereby receives a more deeply rooted invitation to generative discourse and collective wisdom within an erotic rationality toward an expressive theological delight intended for all.

Methodological Fruits: A Contemplative Empiricism within an Artisanal Way

Engaged and critically examined for over seventeen years, music in performative mode suggests a *contemplative empiricism* as theological

---

2. May, "From Cruelty to Compassion," 165.
3. Ibid., 166.

method. This jolting juxtaposition of terms describes a receptive, listening posture of theological inquiry governed primarily by a *contemplative turn*, guided toward what James Heisig calls *orthoaesthesis*, or a *recovery of the senses*. Within his comparative-religious frame of inquiry, Heisig advocates for a critical surrender to sensate insight that releases the scholar from previous attachment to ordinary (i.e. previous, well-established) ideas *and* from previously embodied (or lack of embodied) ways of engaging theological discipline.

> In the same way that consistency with received tradition is taken as a measure of religious truth, or *orthodoxy*, the embodiment of a tradition in the moral choices of life is understood to be a measure of religious action, or *orthopraxis*. But these two—right thinking and right action—are incomplete without some measure of the true liberation of the senses, an *orthoaesthesis*.[4]

He argues for a critical surrender to embodiment, discernment of sensation, release of previous mentality into contemplative inquiry indwelt over time. In similar fashion, a contemplative empiricism is entirely rooted and apprehended in what philosopher-theologian Jean-Luc Marion calls *love without being*, or explicitly theologically, *God without Being*, made known in desire and heightened sensation toward received insight.[5] This methodological reorientation describes a radically sensate approach to *theo*logical knowledge[6] received, released, and renewed within covenantal inquiry and graced awareness.

For clarity's sake, a review of terms. *Empiricism* historically, philosophically, describes the view of experience, especially of the senses, as the only source of knowledge. John Locke allowed room for things like logic and mathematics to describe experience, however, citing the mathematical cathedrals of the mind sustained with logic of inestimable or inarticulate beauty.[7] Immanuel Kant went whole hog into an idealism, returning the empiricism of sense-perceptions to a neglected backyard phenomenology has been attempting to clean up ever since.[8] The "radi-

---

4. Heisig, "Recovery of the Senses," 74.
5. Marion, *Erotic Phenomenon*; *God Without Being*, respectively.
6. See Marion, *God Without Being*, with his symbolic representation of more apophatically-oriented *theo*logy and the highly kataphatic, disciplinary theo*logy*.
7. Woolhouse, "Locke's Theory of Knowledge," 146–71.
8. Parsons, "Transcendental Aesthetic," 62–100.

cal" or "all-encompassing" empiricism of William James re-opened the door to sense-perceptions and more. He pursued knowledge with a supple, inquisitive openness to all experience, not only that identified with clear-cut sensory data, passively received or free of theory-content.[9] In the throes of these realistic-idealistic currents, contemporary practical theologians have balanced between contributions emphasizing right thinking and those urging more attention to right action. For instance, the empirical theology van der Ven investigates experience as the "here-and-now actualization of religious attitudes, which consist of cognitive, affective and volitive components."[10] Cognitive, affective, and volitive—a good blend of orthodox habits of mind and feeling, alongside corresponding orthopraxis of will, volition, agency.

Rarely juxtaposed with empiricism, *contemplative* refers to a mindful practice of non-conceptuality and companionable delight, even erotic union. Counter-intuitively, when one enters into sustained contemplative inquiry, the limitations of the mind can open into non-conceptual space and heightened awareness of unforeseen interconnections, even previously unperceivable interdependence. Observation and connection arise, with greater critical acumen. Even so, the role of sensation still plays an ambivalent melody. Depending upon tradition, contemplative practice promises wildly contradictory ends. At one end, we see a submission and detachment from all sense experience for legitimated knowledge. At the other end, we see an exploration and potential renewal of sense experience, deepened and broadened before potentially released and revived—made more vibrant and exquisite. This contemplation resembles mystical experience described in sensate or even erotic language.

The contemplative empiricism intended here offers a sensate and thematically empirical method, quite distinct from Johannes van der Ven's sense of empiricism. The recovery of the senses paradoxically stabilizes and repeatedly renews the balance between orthodoxy-orthopraxis debates so prevalent within theological disciplines today. With a true liberation of the senses, not neglected or denied but heightened, deeper critical awareness of unforeseen interconnections arises. Webs of relationships—between ideas and objects and between communities

---

9. van der Ven, *Practical Theology*, 10.
10. Ibid.

of discourse—become explicit. Critical inquiry deepens with a more expansive generativity that has unexpectedly relational implications.

Not only does learning become reoriented within embodied insight, it becomes *methodologically relational*, by which I mean self-aware of specific communities of discourse and the practices of relationship sustained (or neglected) within them. One often enters into indwelt contemplative inquiry with one objective in mind, in other words, only to receive insight into other dimensions of critical inquiry. Much of Christian theological heritage presumes a communal framework within which discourse occurred. Rooted in agricultural even early industrial settings, much of the human past depended upon communal living as locally-proximate, interdependent persons who needed each other in order to survive. Not so today. Or at least not as directly perceivable today.[11] Yet rarely is it made explicit that communal affiliation, lived experience, and the resulting rooted identity in today's increasingly narrow, often ideological communities have shaped even critical thinking into increasingly narrow habits of mind, unhinged from conceptualizations of expansive life-giving relationship toward the fullness of human life within and beyond theological-religious-secular affiliation. Here is where the operations of a contemplative empiricism rest within an *artisanal way*.

An Artisanal Way

The use of *artisanal* here derives largely from the world of bread-baking, but other nuances combine to describe a classical, traditionally rooted, yet reasonably (post-)modern frame for theological method that is *relationally-formed* in lived methodological commitment. *Artisanal* in bread-baking refers to historical-classical ways of baking bread by hand in one's own kitchen, or even a small bakery. Another description in contemporary use includes ten defining characteristics for everything *artisanal*: human scale, handmade, relatively raw and untransformed, unbranded, personalized, transparent, authentic, local, preference for a new connoisseurship (tasty but without pretence), and simplified.[12] The term here signifies a methodological commitment to lived

---

11. Myers, "Joy May End in Grief."
12. Online: http://www.cultureby.com/trilogy/2006/11/the_artisanal_m.html.

relationship(s) as primary context(s) of learning, a context that has been presumed historically but is largely neglected in today's specialized theological disciplines. It refers to that kind of exquisitely empirical, local and personalized thinking, offered by theologians who fully indwell relational contexts of discourse while refusing to release the primacy of the interpersonal beyond previously-cognitive categories. The result in the bread-baking world is a living tradition of relational artistry, living wisdom that invites experimentation, and of course, uniquely crafted and reasonably efficient loaves of bread around which communities of celebration gather. All this originates not from technological precision or expertise, but from centuries of apprenticed methods and continuing artistry with lived experimentation.

An artisanal way for theological discipline makes explicit the awareness (or not) of communities of affiliation out of which disciplinary contributions emerge. With a *methodological* commitment, it actively shapes its critical discourse through the practiced rhythms of *compassionate companionship(s)*. *Companionship* names the public expression of human community and social civility today. Covenantal companionships refers to those partnerships and groups who share a common religious affiliation, who relatively easily identify the communal commitment and perspective of one another, or who advocate within tolerant alliances of shared understandings of value, ideology, class etc. *Compassionate* companionship, what has been previously called *radically covenantal companionship*, refers to those claimed and claiming relationships across community affiliation within which a more deeply rooted covenant or rule of relation becomes determinative.[13] Compassionate companionships grow from within both unidentified and covenantal companionship to press the life-giving force and integrity of human-other relationship beyond the internally normative boundaries of social, political, or religious affiliation. They embody an intimate interdependence of all sentient beings in the lively web of creation. They enliven and challenge, wound and heal, discomfort and nourish those within them. Centuries of historical precedent across religious traditions confirm their existence and the need for broader

---

Cited by Mary Mullino Moore, Forward to *Artisanal Theology*, ix.

13. See Hess, *Artisanal Theology: Intentional Formation in Radically Covenantal Companionship*.

covenantal companioning within which to live into them.[14] Various theological disciplines today demonstrate their validity as well.[15]

Within this primarily relational, methodological commitment, the specific operations of a contemplative empiricism may be more fully drawn out for those preparing to integrate a performative mode into critical discourse. Bernard Lonergan's classical, theological methodological work, conveniently named *Method in Theology* but developed from a preceding work called *Insight*, established the primary function of method to be the ordering of inquiry and discovery of knowledge, aligned with the "conspicuously successful science" of the time. "Science" refers here, of course, to the successful disciplines of inquiry and investigation available in a particular age.[16] Lonergan's approach requires a look to the successful sciences for at least a preliminary notion of method, which he defines as "a normative pattern of recurrent and related operations yielding cumulative and progressive results."[17] The next move is, in his view, to go behind those procedures to the procedures of the human mind. He argues such a *transcendental* method as a basic pattern of operations employed in every cognitional enterprise. By operations, he intends the following: seeing, hearing, touching, smelling, tasting, inquiring, imagining, understanding, conceiving, formulating, reflecting, marshalling and weighing the evidence, judging, deliberating, evaluating, deciding, speaking, writing.[18] Within these operations, Lonergan also identifies different levels of consciousness and intentionality within the procedures of the human mind, where the divine-human drama plays out in human awareness.[19] One of Lonergan's

---

14. See Aelred of Rievaulx, *Spiritual Friendship*; Addison and Breitman, *Jewish Spiritual Direction*; Jelaluddin Rumi, *Glance*; Subhuti, *Buddhism and Friendship*; and Weaver and Messer, *Connected Spirits*.

15. Scriptural Reasoning, the broader term for Textual Reasoning, Comparative Theology, Theologies of Religious Pluralism, for example.

16. Lonergan, *Method in Theology*, 3.

17. Ibid., 4.

18. Ibid., 6–7.

19. The *empirical* names that "on which we sense, perceive, imagine, feel, speak, move." *Intellectual* describes the level "on which we inquire, come to understand, express what we have understood, work out the presuppositions and implications of our expression." The *rational* level names where "we reflect, marshal the evidence, pass judgment on the truth or falsity, certainty or probability, of a statement." And finally, *responsible* describes that "level on which we are concerned with ourselves, our own

contributions, among many, was to go behind articulated scientific procedures to these procedures of the human mind. Contemplative empiricism simply completes the circle toward a comprehensive sense of embodied or sensate mind, released and renewed in covenantal, contemplative inquiry. The empirically oriented operations remain, as do the various levels of consciousness and intentionality within the procedures of the human mind. Yet both, all, are held within sustained contemplative inquiry that indwells phenomena of interest with the body in its entirety, within explicitly relational frames of affiliation.

This move arises out of the epistemological humility required by music in performative mode, a phenomenon that is never the same twice because of its fundamental relationship with (linear) time. Humility does not mean, as Roberta Bondi observes, "a continuous cringing, cultivating a low self-image and taking a perverse pleasure in being always forgotten, unnoticed, or taken for granted."[20] In its ancient sense, and as it is intended here, humility is primarily a relational term, motivated by an order in service of love. It is "an attitude of heart," in the ancient sense of one's whole person. It is counter-intuitive and calls for the renunciation of much that the contemporary world holds dear: material prosperity, advancement, satisfaction of desires at the expense of others, right to dominate.[21] Humility, therefore, cannot be humanly achieved, though it can be received in an active openness to "the other," to the sacred, to the secular. Being open to knowledge rooted in the love of others requires a chosen, risked vulnerability, healthily chosen with a curious willingness. It means indwelling multiple environments and conflicting textual resources for unexpectedly multidimensional contribution.

This disciplinary vulnerability is not a virtue in itself, but a venue to deepened awareness, life-giving relationship, and critical encounter in intimate difference. It offers avenue to relationships that sustain self and others. Vulnerability also entails risk of injury, of course,

---

operations, our goals, and so deliberate about possible courses of action, evaluate them, decide and carry out our decisions." See *Method in Theology*, p. 9. Particularly helpful is the observed distinction between intellectual and rational, the former expressed as a particular inquiry and the latter manifest in mutually enforcing, communal norms of public reason.

20. Bondi, *To Love as God Loves*, 18.
21. Ibid., 54.

but injuries that can be stewarded wisely for greater understanding and unexpected compassion. The problem in theological disciplinary thought, of course, is that no one can teach humility, nor are theologians encouraged within it. One receives it, models it, lives it. Even so, skills and practices—deep listening, covenantal belonging, spiritual practices centered in silence engaged in multiple, conflicting contexts—can create intentionally, healthily vulnerable space within which receptivity grows, within which humility emerges, within which new insight arrives.

Ultimately, the operations of a contemplative empiricism within an artisanal way for theology in performative mode demonstrate a radically sensate approach to theological knowledge rooted in practices of receptivity in multiple contexts toward heightened sensation, compassionate advance, and risked innovation upon behalf of the other. Hermeneutic, strategic, empirical, even fundamental models of theological research contribute their methods to particular investigations of phenomena and praxis toward interpretation and right action. These methods offer potential significance and meaning correlated between verifiable observation and received understandings. But a contemplative empiricism within an artisanal way fundamentally reorients critical-correlational habits of mind toward a non-correlational approach within an erotic rationality only recently conceivable within today's theological disciplines.

The Move into Non-Correlational Theology

Correlation within contemporary theological method can refer to many things, depending upon discourse and scholarly inclination. It is generally understood as "a causal, complementary, parallel, or reciprocal relationship, especially a structural, functional, or qualitative correspondence between comparable entities."[22] The stated need for conceivable relationship between two entities—a conformation, correspondence, even an agreement—brings a tension or need to bridge them toward articulation, understanding, interpretation. An imprecise but efficient focus of correlation named by David Tracy is the negotiated tension between reason and revelation. Reason often refers to the patterned

---

22. *American Heritage Dictionary of the English Language.*

or ordered methods of a public rationality, unusually reliant upon empirical or material reality. Revelation often refers to the inconveniently intimate, even incomprehensible, claims of the unknown, usually reserved for realities become known in religious faith but also indicative of unknowns encountered in human-other interactions. How may the independent and publicly verifiable claims of rationality be correlated or bridged with the intimately convicting claims of the other?

Tracy's voice resounds within the (post-)modern, pluralist conversation on theological method, amplified outward into the public and the scientific from the University of Chicago. He describes a contemporary, fundamental theology as "philosophical reflection upon the meanings present in common human experience and language, and upon the meanings present in the Christian fact."[23] Theological discourse offers the critically-correlated interpretation or analytical relationship within and between these foci. His five organizing theses in *Blessed Rage for Order* identify a theological approach to human knowledge intent upon two principal sources for theology (Christian texts and common human experience/language) and proper methods of investigation for each of these sources: for the texts, a historical-hermeneutical investigation; for human experience and language, a phenomenology of the religious dimension present in everyday and scientific experience and language. Truth-status of all results or convictions is determined by a critical correlation of the investigations' results determined with a transcendental or metaphysical mode of reflection. Tracy's work has been fundamental for the formation of theological scholars around the globe, and I count myself as one of his students, if from a distance. He articulates well the theological tasks of his day, and moves his early work into later and later view with an analysis of these tasks as determined by a theologian's social location—in the church, the academy, and the public.[24] A persistent aim for him has been to craft a theological method that non-believing or non-confessional theologians could engage, with verifiable results.[25]

The gift of revised, critical correlation today in a (post-)modern academy is the clarity of relationship between the sources of revelation—scripture and tradition—and the well-tested tools of reason.

23. Tracy, *Blessed Rage for Order*, 43. This summary comes specifically from chapter 3, 43–63.
24. Tracy, *Analogical Imagination*, 1–46.
25. Tracy, *Blessed Rage for Order*, 57 n. 3.

Tracy's commitment to public discourse with theological integrity has brought him to the apex of correlational approaches to the theological enterprise, a place where the claims of reason are correlated to those of revelation, and vice versa. A difficulty, of course, is that one of the stated principal sources, "the major expressions and texts of the Christian tradition," is articulated as "the Christian fact" while self-limited to "texts, not events."[26] The primarily oral frame of a performative mode argued within this study disallows such absolute distinction. With "Christian fact," Tracy insures his characterization of the theological task(s) independent of whether the theologian is a believing member of the Christian community. [27] A sole focus on texts, however, offers a conceptual clarity at too high a cost for a faith tradition(s) posited on incarnation, crucifixion, and resurrection—all of which are events of embodiment, not text. True to his environment and training, his use of "the Christian tradition" also de-emphasizes in dangerous fashion the unavoidable realities of difference and the political hierarchy of his own tradition. Christian communities are intimately particular and widely diverse across cultures and histories, yet Roman Catholic polity is such that those few in political power overly determine what "the Christian tradition" means, in limited and silencing voice. Nonetheless, Tracy's revised critical correlational method has established theological discourse in university settings—nationally and internationally—with clear and compassionate attention to the mysterious theological task claimed by the Christian fact and tradition(s)'s contributions to public scholarly discourse.

Tracy's work is significant here because he also opens the door to legitimately conceiving theological method as *non-correlational*. In his introduction to an early text of French philosopher-theologian, Jean-Luc Marion, Tracy observes that Marion has crafted a model of theology that "does not partake of *any* form of…the more familiar correlational stance of most modern Christian theologies. Therein lies its great interest and provocation," he admits, "even for basically correlational theologians like myself."[28] The authorship of Jean-Luc Marion extends too deeply into both disciplinary philosophy and theology for adequate

---

26. Ibid., 15 n. 5
27. Ibid., 57 n. 3.
28. Tracy, "Foreword," in Marion, *God Without Being*, xi.

introduction here. Others have offered excellent critical introductions anyway. What the following small glimpse into Marion's thought offers is much more circumspect and appropriate to this study's aim.

Marion demonstrates that a *non-correlational* theological approach is not only conceivable beyond correlational habits of mind, but it is also recognized and legitimated by a leading critical-correlational voice. Marion has already cleared a path, in other words, for what I have learned from music in performative mode and begun to articulate in this study. Marion's articulation of *love without being*, or for theological scholarship, *God with Being*, also gives confirmation to a primarily relational frame, distinct from but related to the one I have articulated here. This explicitly embodied and primarily relational method deepens in significance through Marion's argument for a specifically erotic rationality within which the seeds of performative mode may find some beginning internal congruence and external correspondence. His entire authorship has continued to deepen my encounter with music, consequently theology in performative mode, which is also a debt that requires due acknowledgement, perchance further studies beyond this one. For now, however, two themes in Marion's work demonstrate the necessary transition from critical-correlational habits of mind toward a non-correlational theological method.

Marion introduces a fundamental methodological shift away from objective-subjective, epistemological-ontological rationalities toward an *erotic rationality* more coherent than critical-correlation for the primarily relational and embodied seeds of performative-mode theology. Complementing the traditionally epistemic and ontological dimensions, Marion names an erotic dimension that opens up a more multidimensional and primarily relational rationality, well-suited to performative-mode theology. Second, Marion posits a *quest for assurance* instead of *certainty*, which is significant for entering into a primarily relational theological method embodied in indwelling and contemplative inquiry. The horizon of ultimate value within contemplative inquiry is rarely certainty, after all, but terms more like awakening, awareness, intimacy, union, and the like. What results is an erotic rationality within its proper horizon of a love without being, or theologically, God without Being, whose final divine name is self-giving love.

Ultimately, Jean-Luc Marion's authorship aims to speak *love* for modern philosophy, *caritas* for modern theology, both of which have largely silenced or at least betrayed and mistreated it, in his view.²⁹ Contemporary theological knowledge questionably witnesses to *caritas*, Marion argues, *except* in its proper horizon of God without Being, a God who sacrificed being out of deeper self-giving love, in God's excessive self-revelation as Love. All the strategies of correlation—of knowing-being-doing, reason-revelation, theology-praxis, etc.—become secondary in the givenness of love's gifts, or theologically, in the iconic *theo*logical focus on God's excessive self-revelation as the ultimate Divine name, *caritas*. The challenge, the non-correlational way of heightened sensation and insight, is to enter into or indwell love *in order to* know; to surrender to the subjectivity of the other in order to *know* beyond what correlational presuppositions will allow.³⁰

Erotic Phenomenon: Rationality, Assurance, Reduced Reciprocity, and Insufficient Reason

In philosophical terms, Marion charts a path into an erotic rationality that honors the traditional epistemic and ontological dimensions of shared reason, but then he moves beyond them into primarily relational mode engaged by an *erotic phenomenon*. Marion acknowledges the *epistemic*, or "that which keeps in a thing only that which stays repeatable, permanent, and as if permanently under the mind's regard or gaze."³¹ This philosophical move establishes the centrality of the thinker and the useful ability to certify material, even conceptual objects, for public scrutiny. Marion also nods to the *ontological* dimension, or "that which only keeps in a thing its status as being in order to lead it back to its being, or indeed eventually, to track it to the point of catching a glimpse of being itself."³² Here he engages the established traditions of thought centered in metaphysics—being, Being, character, essence and more. Both philosophical dimensions—the epistemic and the ontological—promise certainty of a sort, a clarity of thought and communication about phenomena of mutual interest and public complexity. Neither dimension can satisfy the certainty of the thinker,

---

29. Marion, *Erotic Phenomenon*, 1.
30. Ibid., 2. See also Olthuis, "Love/Knowledge," and "Crossing the Threshold."
31. Marion, *Erotic Phenomenon*, 21.
32. Ibid.

however, the "me" each of us knows for him/herself. Therefore, Marion pursues a third dimension, the *erotic*, identified by a *quest for assurance* determined by two primarily relational questions: "Does anyone love me?" and "Can I love first?" In the erotic phenomenon, Marion states, "I must discover myself as a given (and gifted) phenomenon, assured as a given that is free from vanity."[33]

The drive for certainty, in Marion's view, expends its energies toward certainty of objects and sustenance of being in the world, all the while neglecting its embodied-relational center of thinking. This transference of existential uncertainty can be illustrated in the forever penultimate conclusions of all critical theory, leading to skepticism, even nihilism, eventually to the question, "What's the use?" This question signals postmodernity's doubt of certainty that has embroiled so much classical and contemporary thought in various expressions of what Marion here calls "vanity." "Vanity," he observes, "disqualifies every certainty, whether it bears upon the world or upon myself. ... Nothing resists vanity, since it can still skirt and annul all evidence, all certainty, all resistance."[34] In contrast, the erotic phenomenon opens the door to radically different resolutions of uncertainty with a quest for assurance. This resolution, in Marion's view is "thus opposed to the cogitant...[it] renders destitute the quest for certainty and replaces it with a quest for assurance."[35] Here, notions of being, conditioned by correlational habits of mind, are abandoned. Way opens for a primarily relational-embodied, rational, and ultimately non-correlational way of engaging inquiry in the world.

The *quest for assurance* differs radically from the quest for certainty not only in its reorienting questions. Its relational-embodied rationality also reverses the expected reciprocity and economy of correlational habits of mind. When constitutional notions of *knowing* and *being* are abandoned, the correlational logics of reciprocity and economy also disappear, revealing a counter-intuitive logic to an erotic rationality and its paradoxical phenomenon of a love within a proper horizon: *God without Being*, who sacrifices being out of self-giving love and receives assurance beyond expectation. This methodological shift is recognizable

33. Ibid., 22.
34. Ibid., 19.
35. Ibid., 28.

in what Marion describes as a reduced reciprocity. A thinking being, an *ego cogito*, faces the invitation of doubt and the quest for certainty with repeated attempts to certify the objects and important subjects in one's world, to create one's world in a recognizable, familiar fashion where one can be certain of love, resources, survival. Yet, these epistemic and ontological moves mean that love enters in only indirectly, with the ego's attempts to certify its existence and neutralize the felt threat of uncertainty and vanity. "Love here plays only the hypothetical and nearly unattainable correlate to my lack of assurance when confronting the question, "What's the use?"...Love only appears by default."[36] The epistemic and ontological dimensions result in the objectification of both objects and subjects, distanced and then related again in various dialectical moves of consciousness. "The *ego*, from the outset, expects from love only a more or less honest exchange, a negotiated *reciprocity*, an acceptable compromise."[37]

In contrast, when engaged in a quest for assurance, the willing lover enters into love's distinct rationality, recognized in a *reduced reciprocity* and a principle of *insufficient reason*. "Precisely when . . . I suspend reciprocity, and no longer economize, engaging myself without any guarantee . . . The lover appears . . . and loves without requiring to be loved, and thus, in the figure of the gift, abolishes economy."[38] In so doing, the lover contradicts economy's sufficient reason. Here, the

> issue is not an inability of the lover to find reasons, or a lack of reasons in or of good sense, but rather the failure of reason itself to give reasons for the initiative to love. . . . Love does not reject reason, but reason refuses to go where the lover goes. . . . When loving is at issue, reason is not sufficient: reason appears from this point forward as a principle of *insufficient reason*.[39]

Paradoxically, this insufficient reason is also the basis of pure assurance. Reducing reciprocity and finding oneself within a pure assurance, the conflict between reason and love within the erotic reduction reverses the logic of correlation based upon sufficient reason, nudging the lover into the phenomenon of pure assurance and compassionate

36. Ibid., 68.
37. Ibid., 69.
38. Ibid., 78.
39. Ibid., 79.

advance into strength in weakness. Asking and answering the primarily relational questions, ""Does anyone love me?" and "Can I love first?", engages the *ego cogito* in the methodological moves toward knowledge's horizon. Answering the second question in the affirmative distinguishes love in its own horizon, a love without being that reduces reciprocity, that introduces a chosen surrender at the heart of all revelatory knowledge—scientifically in the surrender to incontrovertible, sensate evidence and theologically in the surrender to human limitation and the giftedness of love.

In Marion's radically *theo*logical sense, this kind of love or *caritas* is no longer something to be *made* or a secondary objective that thoughtful understanding will inspire. Love already is. Love knows. Love bears all things. Love believes everything. Love loves without seeing. "Nothing can triumph over [love] because [its] very weakness makes [its] strength."[40] Here come the missing pieces for philosophy's (and much contemporary theology's) failure to integrate knowledge, being, and doing in a coherent way. The promise here (for our purpose, especially) is a radically constructive and rigorously *theo*logical method in which dialectic lessens as enacted love grows. Correlation becomes more obsolete as an erotic rationality increasingly assures an ego from elsewhere. "Assurance still comes to me," Marion writes,

> but no longer from an ontic elsewhere that would conserve me in my beingness; rather it comes from an elsewhere that is more inward to me than myself: the elsewhere that comes upon me in the very gesture in which I give up what I have (my gift) and what I am, in order to assure myself only of what I truly make in this instant—love."[41]

Paradoxically within correlational habits of mind, but completely coherent within an erotic rationality, understanding and interpretation become secondary to bringing shared awareness into a sensate present, continuously received and not achieved. Love without being harnesses traditionally representational knowledge in the painful and painstaking immediacy of knowing *what is* as it becomes drawn out and into what could be.

40. Ibid., 89.
41. Ibid., 75.

Theologically, Marion argues that modern Christianity has misunderstood the most esteemed theological virtue, *caritas*, which is also the last of the divine names for God. Accordingly, his authorship redresses this omission and fearful rigor by rooting *caritas* in its own rationality lived in the quest for assurance found only within a primary relationality and proposition of receiving what love knows. "In short," Marion writes, "in order to produce a conceptual determination of love, it is not sufficient to qualify as love the access to rationality by representation."[42] Distinctions and dichotomies of love—eros/agape, self-love/disinterested love, et al—illustrate the dialectical, correlational manner of mind, which, regardless of intention and desire, wound love's rationality. In Marion's words, "One can easily see that these dichotomies risk bringing us back . . . to the dichotomy . . . we have just sketched, and that every border traced upon the heart of love, rather than being of service, wounds it definitively."[43] *Caritas* promises a rational and startlingly non-correlational approach to performative-mode theology, rooted in a quest for assurance, a willingness to love first, and the reduced reciprocity and assurance that follow within the horizon of a love without being. *Theo*logical knowledge results and becomes radically redefined within its horizon of God without Being, appropriate to a non-correlational *theo*logical method.

In sum, these two themes within Marion's authorship have confirmed several aspects of performative-mode theology legitimated within critical theological discourse. A sustained encounter with music in performative mode, theologically examined, has led to a *non-correlational* theological method that has all the marks of a performative mode. A contemplative empiricism within an artisanal way is primarily relational as traditioned within a methodological commitment to compassionate companionships, lived within practiced rhythms of lifegiving, covenantal relationship. Its operations of indwelt, contemplative inquiry build upon previous theological methodological discourse, leading concerted attention back to sensate embodiment as a whole with heightened attention to sensation toward awakening and new insight. Critical-correlational methods inform its interpretive practices, in other words, but a contemplative empiricism urges a greater

---

42. Marion, *Prolegomena to Charity*, 159–60.

43. Ibid., 160.

multidimensionality in an *erotic* rationality more suited to its primarily relational commitments. One implication of this multidimensionality lies in the necessary extension of disciplinary tasks beyond interpretation and right action toward the fullness of human life amidst transformation and self-transcendence.

Extended Disciplinary Tasks

Variously conceived, these tasks can be described as *contemplative wondering, impassioned conviction, intimacies of difference*, and *joyful celebration that yet knows sorrow*.[44] Much theology, particularly practical theology as a discipline, has focused on the interpretive tasks of lived faith: how do we *understand* God's work in this time, this event, this place? What does this *mean* for what should be *done*? This highly literate and overly narrow emphasis upon interpretation and responsive action has overshadowed the multidimensional way of life that theology is within the emancipatory praxis of God. The burgeoning literature on Christian practices makes the same move as I argue for here, most recently in *For Life Abundant: Practical Theology, Theological Education, and Christian Ministry*.[45] Interpretive precision often hides broader horizons of ultimate value, particularly ones that evolve more easily from primarily relational methods of inquiry. Inclusive of interpretation but not confined by it, a contemplative empiricism within an artisanal way urges four other learning tasks crucial to theology in a performative mode, as guided by the lived events of music.

The first such learning task, *contemplative wondering*, is a life-giving, grace-filled exploration of the goodness, beauty, and truth within creation. This exploration is less and less available within theological learning communities governed by internalized dualisms, now apparent in forms of "in vs. out," "us vs. them" communal norms. Only when communities remember the natural world in which they live and serve, only when we learn to value the other as much as we value ourselves, will the true blessing of life infuse theological learning communities within and beyond the periphery of communal affiliation. Theological

---

44. These tasks continue the work begun by James Loder, who never fully pursued them before his death in 2001. See Loder, "Transformation in Christian Education," 13–15.

45. Bass and Dykstra, *For Life Abundant*.

discipline, often divided by ideological church disputes and increasingly pressured into new financial straits by a competitive market, regularly neglects the embodied, epistemological humility of contemplative wondering, a root of innovation and unexpected contributions.

Impassioned but gentle conviction describes a second learning task, much misunderstood in critical inquiry and debate within theological learning communities. This humble, self-effacing "assurance of things hoped for yet not seen," this thirst for knowledge egged on by irresistible grace, has been replaced by increasingly rigid positions that claim a sure knowledge of God, scripture, and tradition. Truly convictional experience, however, is that which disrupts our own certainties first, often in extreme discomfort. A gentle conviction replaces human, individual centrality—of certainty, of self, of absolutes—with relational interconnection, new awareness of one's precious limitation, and regularly resonant insights therefore held gently, with care. *This* kind of learning, in contrast to professional expertise, leads into intimately assured but irreconcilable truths held in gently relational connection. It is the root of the next learning task, which has been called *learning to face and embrace constructive conflict*, but is better framed as intimacies of difference.

Intimacy of difference names the primarily relational way of holding to one's absolute particularity in action or belief while equally honoring the particularity of another whose beliefs or actions may be diametrically opposed to your own.[46] It names a necessary part of any critical inquiry that integrates a self-implicating method into communal discourse, aiming toward transformation of self, other and world. Intimacy here describes the phenomenon that arises in a counter-intuitive way when particularity or difference is sustained within a methodological commitment to relationship. Deeper connection often (but not always) results, when relational rupture or division is expected.

A fourth learning task relates all the others, thereby leading into the horizon of ultimate value for a contemplative empiricism in an artisanal way. *Joyful celebration that yet knows sorrow* refers to the two-dimensional learning task that addresses the depth dimensions of the human condition—indescribable joy and meaningless suffering. Within this task, that which is considered completely distinct or

---

46. Hess, "Toward an Intimacy of Difference."

separate becomes somehow paradoxically connected, though in multidimensional ways. Hildegard named the purpose of music within her community to be that of scriptural command: the mandated praise of God. This conviction is often diffused today between practices of communal worship and a pleasurable but private sentimentality. But one depth dimension within the human condition that theological discipline aims to interpret is this phenomenon of utter joy. The other depth dimension with which theology wrestles, perhaps with more regularity, is that of suffering. Distinct from pain, suffering creates the problematic of theodicy—the meaning of suffering against the witness to a gracious, mercifully loving God. This final learning task witnesses to a conviction that joy is not joy unless it is interconnected with its counterpart, suffering. Music in a performative mode illustrates this quite clearly, from its presence in times of great celebration and joy, to its power in prophetic advocacy against oppression and suffering. Think of music's regular facilitation of transcendent experience, a felt-sense of being connected to something or someone larger than oneself. Think of its unexpected power in the Civil Rights' movement or in the eventual, mostly peaceful conclusion of apartheid in South Africa. Performative mode suggests much is yet to be learned about the participation in joyful celebration and the companionable advocacy against human suffering.

Analytically focused yet contextually inter-related, these four tasks extend beyond interpretive purposes, even discernments of right action, for several reasons rooted in the inarticulate complexities of compassion, received and offered. With the primary methodological commitment to compassionate companionship(s), interpretation and understanding are no longer the primary means for bridging differences. Living into the rule of relation embodies the bridge, making shared understanding secondary and more broadly shared interpretation even further removed. Skills for entering into intimacies of difference root in the willingness to enter into contemplative wondering, receiving gently impassioned convictions, which then further attention and awareness of differences to be sustained, each amongst (not against) the other. Coherent only within the horizon of a love without being, with its erotic rationality, the need for shared understanding actually recedes in importance as the assurance within compassionate companionship grows. One can even begin to imagine the possibility of loving without theological understanding at all. Critical-correlational habits of mind serve the fullness of human life with their aims for interpretation and strategic guidance toward moral action, but life's fullness could never be contained within those tasks.

Within an integrated view, these additional tasks beyond interpretation all suggest a more robust horizon of ultimate value, suitably complex for Christian theological perspective, but intentionally articulated in non-sectarian language appropriate to music's irrepressible multidimensionality. Sitting at the metaphorical feet of music in its performative mode, I discovered that one can easily get overwhelmed at the innumerable values expressed as ultimate within the traditions, practices, styles, and interpretations of musical phenomena. As George Steiner argued earlier, "Music is at once cerebral in the highest degree . . . and it is at the same time somatic, carnal and a searching out of resonances in our bodies at levels deeper than will or consciousness."[47] How does one focus the irreducibly multidimensional? The horizon of ultimate value within a critical spirituality study offers both context and direction, coherence of investigation and correspondence in all its complexity. Therefore, music in performative mode urges a horizon for theology in performative mode, appropriate to such an expanse of interconnection amidst all facets, all depth dimensions in the human condition.

Horizon of Ultimate Value: An Expressive Theological Delight

The heart of a contemplative empiricism within an artisanal way for performative-mode theology is *an expressive theological delight able to companion the suffering of self and others.* This kind of delight is not a willed happiness in the face of pain, nor is it a Pollyanna preference for a beautiful or cheerful sentimentality. Delight is intimately related to a capacity for wonder, not self-deception; risked trust, not assured clarity. It balances an attentive discipline of wonder with accurate seeing that may discomfort. It empowers a willing participation in suffering—one's own and that of others—with a strength and gratitude for what life already is, as fullness of life. Not the companionship of suffering fueled by a rage—no matter how righteous—or a wound received and left untended. Not the willed sacrifice of time

---

47. Steiner, *Real Presences*, 217.

and personhood based in communal morality or work ethic. A theological delight originates from compassion unexpectedly received, hidden wounds healed, undeserved love erupting into situations of injustice or poverty. This kind of delight is a gift, what Marion calls "a given (and gifted) phenomenon, assured as a given," which cannot be grasped or produced, imposed or taught.

It can be received, however, through a quiet discipline and receptive practices of compassionate companionship. It is received through critical inquiry amidst facing the pain of fears, wounds, limitations held in relation with an other. It comes amidst a tenacity to learn things undesirable and unexpected from as many conflicting legitimate sources as feasible. Delight arrives unexpectedly after accepting these prickly realities of human life. It comes amidst the hard work of contemplative inquiry, or what Roberta Bondi describes as prayer: not discarding damaged parts of ourselves, but gathering and reclaiming them for daily healing in heightened awareness and sacred presence.[48]

Unexpectedly, undeservedly, in proportion to one's self-knowledge of non-being, delight arrives, overflowing with an irrepressible joy. This is an observable paradox and felt-sensation of divinely intimate nobody-ness. It is received in the touch of a hand, or the brush of a breeze in a meadow. Amidst bustling populations of passers-by on a street corner in Kentucky,[49] or in a field full of sunflowers. With the aroma of freshly baked bread before a friend arrives, or the sacred heaviness of incense offered in glorious praise and prayer. It arrives in secular truths shared openly and held with an impassioned devotion to another. An expressive delight arrives, and then it cannot be contained. Even the most arid theological prose can witness to it and create within the believer's heart the seed that then blossoms in due season.

In sum, the methodological fruits given expression here have been gleaned from a sustained engagement with music in performative mode, *complemented by* a sustained critical inquiry into the phenomena, habits of mind, and intentions of critical investigation amidst music's irreducible multidimensionality, explicit embodiment and primary relationality. Many more voices than those represented here have contributed to this non-correlational method for theology in performative

---

48. Bondi, *Memories of God*, 33–5.
49. Merton, *Thomas Merton: Spiritual Master*, 144.

mode. What remains for the chapter to serve its aim, however, is due attribution, with critique, of the practical theological discourse within which a contemplative empiricism in an artisanal way emerges. The methodological fruits ultimately become simply one way of integrating a performative mode into critical theological discourse.

Theological Antecedents to a Contemplative Empiricism in an Artisanal Way

A recent *Handboek Praktische Theologie* or "manual for practical theology" by Gerben Heitink gives crisp historical and analytical edges to practical theology as a discipline today, though the "inherited problematic of practical theology" has been conceived and addressed in diverse fashion for decades.[50] The direct antecedents to a contemplative empiricism may be traced to Richard R. Osmer, James E. Loder, and Mary Elizabeth Mullino Moore, though the significant departures required stem from the integrity and demand of music's performative teaching, not critical flaws or lack of contribution in their work(s). Heitink's work will craft a frame within which the other theological voices may be engaged before concluding the chapter with attribution and critique.

Practical Theological Overview—Heitink's Handboek Praktische Theologie

Gerben Heitink defines practical theology "as a theory of action . . . *empirically oriented theological theory of the mediation of the Christian faith in the praxis of modern society.*"[51] Correlation looms large here as the theoretical assumption: the Christian faith is to be mediated in the realities of modern society, and vice versa. The unique object and theological character of the discipline are located in praxis dealing with "God's activity through the ministry of human beings."[52] Two distinct concepts of praxis also interact here—praxis 1, the mediation of the Christian faith and praxis 2, the praxis of modern society. Again, correlates are to be drawn within the tasks of interpretation. The first

---

50. See Schweitzer and van der Ven, eds., *Practical Theology*.
51. Heitink, *Practical Theology*, 6. Emphasis in original.
52. Ibid., 8.

"indicates that the unique object of practical theology is related to intentional, more specifically, intermediary or mediative actions with a view to changing a given situation through agogics."[53] The second "emphasizes the context where these actions take place as a dynamic context in which men and women in society interact, whether or not their actions are religiously motivated while pursuing various goals."[54]

Heitink offers three governing perspectives apparent in the discipline today—the *hermeneutical*, the *strategic*, and the *empirical*. The hermeneutical offers perspective on actors and action, linked explicitly with intention and motivation as basis for actions, all of which then becomes apparent and move one from understanding into explanation, and then into change.[55] In some distinction, the strategic emphasizes actors and actions related primarily to purpose and process.[56] Instead of placing change as the result of understanding-become-explanation, this perspective aims to anticipate future developments, even steer them, through management and planning. Instead of a hermeneutic circle, one sees a 'regulative' one.[57] The third perspective, the empirical, connects actors/actions primarily to immediate context and its specifications of time, place, duration, etc.[58] In the relationship of understanding toward change, the empirical circle centers in explanation based upon distanciation, observation, and deduction from experience, relying upon the principle of causality. Given the increasingly empirical and anthropological emphases within contemporary theology today, one can see *various* types of empirical practical theology: explorative-descriptive, explorative-explanatory, testing-descriptive, or testing-explanatory.[59] A contemplative empiricism within an artisanal way would fall somewhere between the first two, distinguished from the final two.

Heitink's work illustrates well the interrelation of all these perspectives in disciplinary practical theology. He draws some parallels between the circles which may help deepen the conceptual sense of each:[60]

53. Ibid.
54. Ibid., 8.
55. Ibid., 178ff., esp. 179.
56. Ibid., 201ff., esp. 202.
57. Ibid., 235.
58. Ibid., 221.
59. Ibid., 229.
60. Ibid., 235.

Hermeneutical Circle	Regulative (Strategic) Circle	Empirical Circle
Prejudgment	Defining the problem	Observation
Observation/experience	Diagnosis	Induction/supposition
Interpretation/discourse	Plan	Deduction/prediction
Providing meaning	Intervention	Testing
Action	Evaluation	Evaluation

Each practical theological perspective interrelates with each of the others, of course. Those who find their major emphases within an empirical perspective focus their work within the dynamics of the hermeneutical circle as well, with regulative aspects toward strategic impulses. Those who are primarily interested in a strategic approach integrate empirical and hermeneutic impulses toward their ends, etc. Like any worthwhile schematic, with its advantages and limitations, Heitink's work offers newcomers and old-timers alike a frame within which to understand their distinctive work within disciplinary practical theology.

The three voices who have most affected a non-correlational contemplative empiricism have conceived the inherited practical theological problematic in quite diverse ways, nuanced by their distinct locations (embodied, geographical, economic and more), not to mention their varying intellectual passions. Richard R. Osmer[61] wrestles with practical theology in terms of the relationship between its rational orientation as a form of theology and the rational orientation of its closest dialogue partners, rooted in a scientific model of reason based on objectivity, factuality, and autonomy. His methodological treatise, "Practical Theology as Argument, Rhetoric and Conversation" addresses this problematic in terms of practical reason with a *rationality of discernment* undergirding the discipline's contributions to Christian praxis over time in 1) a performative orientation, 2) a theory of formation and transformation, and 3) a practical theological hermeneutic.

---

61. Osmer, "Practical Theology as Argument, Rhetoric, and Conversation," 113ff.

James Loder's methodological work identifies the practical theological problematic in related but distinct form. The generative problematic at the core of any discipline lies not in its practice, aim, or function, he argues, "but in *why* these, and related phenomena, are a problem."[62] As such, he conceives the issue as one of interdisciplinarity within modern research university discourse, as Osmer has. But Loder posits a self-involving, Chalcedonian method within a relational logic of the Spirit to investigate phenomena of interest—what he calls "congruent forms of action" made incongruous in the "combination of two qualitatively distinct realities," i.e. "the Divine and the human."[63] This relational-christological, theological orientation therefore shapes the field into its various dimensions: historical, ecclesial, operational, and contextual.

Mary Elizabeth Mullino Moore identifies the practical theological problematic in explicitly relational ways as well, though her method retains focus on the interaction between educational method and process theology within which each transforms the other. Standing on the interdisciplinary bridge deemed central by both Osmer and Loder, Moore moves the methodological discourse out of more narrowly focused rationalities through an organic reconsideration of goodness in theological perspective[64] into a more organic space in which "the art of teaching from the heart" happens. She reviews a mélange of educational methods in process-theological view—especially case-study, Gestalt, phenomenological, narrative, and conscientizing methods—before arguing for a more lively theology, steeped in passion and engaged with compassion.[65]

The remaining discussion presumes some familiarity with ongoing critical discourse in practical theology, both out of necessity of space and an awareness from the method enacted: a contemplative empiricism arises out of lived relationship with these practical theologians more than any limited articulations feasible within written contributions. With that caveat, specific facets of their thought significant to a contemplative empiricism will be offered below, for the attribution and

62. Loder, "Normativity and Context in Practical Theology," 359.
63. Ibid., 359.
64. Moore, "Feminist Practical Theology and the Future of the Church," 189ff.
65. Moore, *Teaching from the Heart*, 197.

critique that have led to a non-correlational method for performative mode theology.

Richard R. Osmer—Practical Theology as Argument, Rhetoric, and Conversation

Richard R. Osmer has most recently introduced practical theology as a pluralistic theological discipline of inquiry in terms of its four tasks within a Reformed perspective rooted in the threefold office of Christ—priest, king and prophet. Practical theological inquiry revolves, spiral-like, around four main tasks: first, the *descriptive-empirical* task (gathering information to discern patterns and dynamics in particular situations/contexts); the *interpretive* task (understanding and explaining patterns and dynamics by drawing upon theories of the arts and sciences), the *normative* task (using theological concepts to interpret particular episodes, situations, or contexts; constructing ethical norms to guide responses; and learning from 'good practice'); and the *pragmatic* task (determining strategies of action that will influence situations and entering into reflective conversation when they are enacted).[66] A "congregation's participation in Christ's priestly, royal, and prophetic mediation of salvation" is facilitated in this view through the descriptive-empirical task as "priestly listening…attending to others in their particularity within the presence of God;" the interpretive task as "a form of wise judgment . . . guiding others how to live within God's royal rule"; the normative task as "a form of prophetic discernment . . . helping others hear and heed God's Word in the particular circumstances of their lives and world"; and lastly, the pragmatic task as "a form of transforming leadership . . . taking risks on behalf of the congregation to help it better embody its mission as a sign and witness of God's self-giving love."[67] He offers a marvelous epilogue of recommendations for teaching practical theology in schools of theology considered in its diverse pedagogies and the state of the discipline "at the end of the theological encyclopedia." His reflections on general educational issues—i.e., the clarity of curricular

---

66. Osmer, *Practical Theology*, 4.
67. Ibid., 28–29.

end-states, teaching for understanding, and developing educational pathways—offer significant wisdom for continued consideration.

His earlier but more methodologically precise work stretches the discourse into global and Continental discussions, specifically those developing the communicative theory of Jürgen Habermas toward a rationality with integrity for a theological problematic. Osmer identifies a *rationality of discernment* for practical theology which relies upon the "rules of art" within a primarily covenantal lens or context. His theory of formation and transformation, while less developed than it might be, links the *missio Dei*, the "mission of God as active, differentiated being, whose very nature is love" with "the sort of persons and community" people are becoming "in the context of an open relationship with the relational God."[68] Here Osmer's method requires a dialectical interaction between critical and utopian thinking,[69] a recognition that all practical theological discourse needs to be "qualified and decentred as fully adequate explanations of the mystery of the triune God's saving presence in the world."[70] He even encourages the direction of a contemplative empiricism as he nears conclusion of his treatise, "This is why it is important for practical theology . . . always to operate with several perspectives simultaneously and to appropriate them in an intentionally eclectic fashion."[71]

The breadth and depth of his contributions offer a clarity to practical theological discourse in national and international purview. His recent overview of the descriptive-empirical task, for instance, not only offers multiple research lenses and a variety of strategies and corresponding methods through which to view situations for interpretation. It is steeped in narrative detail, ethnographic dimensions, and case-study illustration. Each remaining task in the introductory volume is given the same thorough consideration and clarity. He also makes an explicit connection between each practical theological task and a spirituality of some kind, which is suggestive for Christian spirituality. He connects a spirituality of *presence* with the descriptive-empirical task, *sagely wisdom* with the interpretive task, *discernment* with the

---

68. Osmer, "Practical Theology as Argument, Rhetoric, and Conversation," 129.
69. Ibid., 130
70. Osmer, "Practical Theology as Argument, Rhetoric, and Conversation," 129
71. Ibid.

normative task, and finally, a spirituality of *servant leadership* with the pragmatic task.

Osmer's practical theological work—especially its rationality and interpretive depth—has figured greatly in the development of a contemplative empiricist perspective. Both perspectives presume a penultimate reality of human action and knowledge within theology's "trinitarian turn" and both argue for the need of a distinctive theological rationality for practical theology's significant elements, suitably named by Osmer as a performative orientation, a theory of formation and transformation guiding the praxis of Christian life over time, and a practical theological hermeneutic.[72] His connective work with "spirituality" suits shared pursuits, though his definition lacks precision. It is not a primary focus of interest for his purposes. "By spirituality," he writes, "I mean leaders' openness to the guidance of the Holy Spirit as she forms and transforms them toward the image of Christ in his body and in the service of the church's mission."[73] This lacks the depth and breadth of spirituality's referent in the discipline of Christian spirituality. Attention to this other discourse might have deepened his work for new and critical interconnections.[74]

Developed within the nuances of practical reason, however, certain proclivities of a communicative rationality are unavoidable, even ultimately distracting of theology's integrative tasks toward a horizon of ultimate value well suited for today's challenges. Osmer's work remains captive to literate and interpretive presuppositions, rooted as deeply it is in the communicative work of Jürgen Habermas and the heritage of the hermeneutical tradition. With these roots, theology's "performative orientation" becomes confined within critical-correlational habits of mind to humanly matched actions in context with regularly argued communal norms: "how best to perform a particular practice or activity in a concrete set of circumstances." Osmer attempts to reframe the various thought-children of practical reason (utilitarianism, neo-Aristotelianism, neo-Kantianism) through his rationality of discernment guided by rules of art. Even with the open-ended "rules of art" that connect multiple options with reflective and fitting responses, however,

---

72. Ibid., 126.
73. Osmer, *Practical Theology*, 27.
74. Ibid., Introduction, n. 13.

his perspective over-favors issues of interpretation and shared understanding amidst all else. Practical theological tasks are conceived within the hermeneutical circle. Practical theology is a discipline of interpretation. Congregational leaders are interpretive guides.[75] Humans are interpretive beings.[76] Students are to be educated to carry out practical theological interpretation in their future ministries.[77] Yet the fullness of life, as Osmer would argue himself, stems from the relational praxis of God, made known in the *missio Dei*. Congregational leaders, students, human beings derive meaning not from interpretation, which will inevitably change over time, but from covenantal relationships lived, fractured, and reconciled amidst the frailties of the human condition redeemed within an open-ended relationship with the Triune God.

Episodes, situations, and contexts are also understood within an interpretive framework, which presupposes understanding unto interpretation as the bridge for congregations to recognize the interconnectedness of ministry. The discontinuity here, as well as in a bulk of theological scholarship, becomes explicit and increasingly untenable: shared understanding will be the bridge for theologians, religious leaders, and congregations to recognize God's relational praxis within the world. In contrast, a contemplative empiricist perspective assumes that shared understanding may grow, but it is the methodological-performative commitment to lived compassionate companionships within God's radically covenantal logic that will *be the bridge* with the relational praxis of God. Anyone who has lived in a committed, covenantal relationship for a significant duration knows well that many times, if fortunate, one loves and is loved yet neither partner can profess remotely shared understanding. In a similar fashion, while shaped by the erotic rationality within Jean-Luc Marion's work, contemplative empiricism shapes the theological problematic not primarily in terms of a governing rationality within disinterested "human sciences" but in terms of love's own horizon and principle of insufficient reason. Only a love without being, or theologically, God without Being, instigates the quest for assurance within primarily embodied-epistemological dimensions. These subsequently reduce and balance the correlational

---

75. Ibid., 18.
76. Ibid., 21.
77. Ibid., 14.

habits of mind with contemplative inquiry and Heisig's *orthoaesthesis* (recovery of the senses). Dialectic lessens as enacted love and wisdom grow. And here, understanding and interpretation become secondary to the heightened awareness of the sensate presence, the interconnection of logically irreconcilable opposites, and the need for theological discipline to extend its tasks beyond a captive rationality and interpretive method. The horizon of ultimate value, in other words, cannot be "the basis of rational communication"[78] but the *missio Dei*, lived in human particularity in the *imago Dei*, unto ends congruent with such a God. A contemplative empiricism names this lived-horizon in a God without Being who invites, for all, an expressive theological delight able to companion the suffering of self and others.

Loder—Chalcedonian Method in a Relational Logic

A theological voice similarly close to this study's origins, James E. Loder, crafted a Chalcedonian method for practical theology, enlivened by a *relational logic of the Spirit*, which represents one of his lasting contributions to theological discourse. Loder described this methodological heart as "an asymmetrical, bi-polar relational unity" that realistically and analogically reconciles logically-exclusive opposites.[79] The Other and the human encounter one another in post-critical realist fashion within a Chalcedonian formulation of christology and a pneumatologically palpable witness to Spirit-spirit intimacy in enacted wisdom. Reliant upon God's primary trinitarian relationality, this logic of the Spirit offers a powerfully theological voice resonant for contemporary challenges and potentially fruitful for theology in performative mode. In response to the interdisciplinary issue in theological discourse, Loder's response grows out of the Chalcedonian formulation in classically Christian theology. Logically exclusive opposites, modeled after divine and human natures, are unified in the *person* of Jesus Christ yet remain unconfused, inseparable, unmixable, and unchangeable. A critical review of Chalcedonian Method will demonstrate Loder's negotiation of correlational habits of mind through christological dialectic

---

78. Osmer, "Practical Theology as Argument," 131.
79. Loder and Neidhardt, *Knight's Move*.

and a palpable pneumatology. Critique then offers the warrant for a contemplative empiricism within an artisanal way.

Loder's Chalcedonian method (CM) organizes practical theological method within an inclusive divine-human action theory whereby the felt-incongruence of a discipline's generative problematic instigates critical response within a pattern or logic of transformation (examined in Chapter 4). Not only is an indeterminate space made for divine agency, alongside human action, but intelligibility is assumed, even if only at the end of time as we know it. With impending awareness of what Loder called the void,[80] that apophatic space between being and non-being, critical inquiry is driven within a relationality that constitutes each to the other. Within these overarching parameters, CM maintains an acknowledged, self-involved commitment (IV) to a nonreductionistic, mutually illuminating, and constructive relationship between disparate disciplinary fields (V), as it maintains its generative core in the human-divine relationality (VI).[81] Relationship between theological and non-theological disciplines becomes clarified in phenomena of inquiry, shared perspectives within shared assumptions and theological negation of scientifically-negated contributions. The resolution of this interdisciplinary issue is the indeterminate but trustworthy insight successively available within the *person* of the researcher, grounded theologically in the power of the Spirit within the *Person* of Christ, who is fully human and fully God, with no confusion, change, division or separation. "The Chalcedonian formulation of the relationality between the divine and the human natures in the one person of Jesus Christ," Loder argues, "provides the relationality required to address adequately the problematic in this field" (VIII). This relationality is also configured through reliance upon a logic of complementarity in which CM holds all contributions in tensive interaction, which sharpens differences toward heightened awareness of reality that is beyond current conceptualization(s). Much more could be nuanced here, of course, but the limitations of Loder's perspective urge movement beyond it.

For all its contribution, CM arises from an overly narrow and inconsistent epistemology, just as captive to correlational habits of mind within the reigning theological dualisms of his day. CM retains

80. Loder, *Transforming Moment*, 121 n. 180.

81. Loder, "Normativity and Context in Practical Theology." Roman numerals connote specific claims, as listed within the introductory paragraph.

an implicit reliance upon a modern systematics that not only belies an epistemology inadequate for today's theological milieu, but one that is actually inconsistent with a central theme in the rest of his work: determinative relationality. As argued within his other work, the primary organizing reality of authentic theological discourse is the vulnerable, cruciform love of God made known to us in the life, death, resurrection of Jesus Christ, who offered and continually offers us an advocate in the Spirit. Such relationality is to be primary and constitutive of all, with human personhood constituted in the primary relationality or triunity of God. As such, an epistemological frame centered on the question of *why* and a primacy of the systematic dimension of theology will never be suitable for organizing an intersubjective approach to theology's generative problematic.[82] He attempts to organize theology within a modern, question-answer, genetic-empiricism, consistent with Piagetian training but inconsistent with a constitutive relationality. Loder's socialized adherence to the organization of modern theology ironically makes his method inconsistent with his own relational logic of the Spirit.

Loder's CM also operates with a determined dualism of theology and the human sciences. In contemporary (post)modern thought, however, is such a distinction fruitful, or even worse, remotely viable? What is arguably non-theological in a world where materiality and nothingness are both in the redemptive power of the Spirit? What is theological when texts like John Caputo's *The Weakness of God: a Theology of Event*[83] can claim philosophy as a discipline yet argue a negative theology within postmodern communities of discourse? In related fashion, as theology has diversified into institutional expressions from the more traditional theological education for professional ministry degrees to continental philosophical theology to religious studies to cultural studies and more, does the line hold between theology and the human sciences in any meaningful way? CM's original, dialectical configuration of theology vs. the other sciences fails in the light of contemporary discourse and disciplinary diffusion.

Loder's CM enacts a conceptual, even imperialist, violence against the other seen in his configuration of a divine-human action theory

---

82. See Frankl, *Man's Search for Meaning*.
83. Caputo, *Weakness of God*.

divided into self, world, void, and divine. The performative mode so crucial for performative-mode theology is already integrated into his divine-human action theory—crucial to the development here of a contemplative-empiricist perspective—but his theory of transformation and the potentially imperialistic assignment of divine agency overshadow and limit any distinct role for the other in critical discourse. He simultaneously gives this "other" too much power within an assignment of the divine, and too little respect as an "other" who is not the "I" of the practical theologian, nor the Spirit of God in Spirit-spirit intimacy. Loder's perspective has absolutely no place, in other words, for the near-infinite human particularities alive within each human self. Here we see his version of the so-called violence of the concept,[84] the disregard of another's inviolable alterity. Such a conceptual violence and imperial prefiguration contradict the infinite valuing of the creature by a cruciform, vulnerably loving Creator. A more feasible approach would have been to lodge the generative problematic in the expression or repression of desire, which is closer to holy breath anyway. Generativity could then be understood within *relationally-formed* and *embodied* orientations of inquiry.

Needless to say, a contemplative empiricism within an artisanal way demonstrates more indebtedness to Chalcedonian method and its relational logic of the Spirit than can be articulated here. The tasks extended by this contemplative empiricist view have been developed from Loder's early work, as they were never fully integrated into his overarching theological perspective. The transformational logic, engaged within Chapter 4, served as the primary lifeline for this seventeen-year-long encounter with music in performative mode. The primary methodological commitment to compassionate companionships and the accompanying, explicitly-embodied operations of contemplative inquiry, articulated in Polanyi's indwelling, are directly attributable to the redemptive theological presence of James Loder, if not his critical work in literate forms. With all the frailties and contributions that come in the human pursuit of truth and Presence within disciplinary theology, Loder's passions and convictions created space for disciplinary confidence in theological innovation and theological conviction in disciplinary argument. His perspective, given his location

---

84. de Vries and Weber, *Violence, Identity and Self-Determination*.

and temperament, is rooted in heightened sensation toward received insight, though he offers no ready acknowledgement of operations for such a radically sensate approach to theological knowledge. There is little room within his perspective to receive from lived relationships in covenantal companionship, to be released into the expressive delights of life-giving relationship that companions suffering, or to be thereby continuously renewed in body, soul, spirit and mind.

Mary Elizabeth Mullino Moore—Goodness, Relational Power, and the Heart

A third practical theological voice shapes a contemplative empiricist perspective, both from articulation of an interactive, mutually transformative theological method and from a reconsideration of goodness demonstrative of the marks of performative mode, therefore resonant with an artisanal way. In *Teaching From the Heart: Theology and Educational Method*, Mary Elizabeth Mullino Moore argues a dynamic, multidimensional, and theological-educational method, rooted in a process-theological perspective. Built amidst five selected methods for their rooted engagement of the world, Moore's theological method resources "passion for organic theology and organic teaching for the sake of a healthy 'body.'" "The passion itself derives from God," she observes. "[T]he particular theological precepts and the particular educational methods are important, but only in relation to the whole."[85] In the breadth and its holistic depth, Moore argues method for an ultimate liveliness in theology. In a shorter, companionable piece, she addresses practical theology in its inherited problematic(s) for "a church that faces into the world."[86] She reconsiders goodness, unhinged from a contrasting definition with sinfulness, thereby crafting a new horizon for goodness as sensual relating with the Universe, as power in relationship, and as integrity. Both of these contributions to critical discourse, confirmed in her enacted wisdom espoused by this method, establish warrant for and contrast with a contemplative empiricism within an artisanal way.

Moore's voice contrasts with the previous two offered here in her willingness to rethink educational methods from a theological

---

85. Moore, *Teaching From the Heart*, 198.
86. Moore, "Feminist Practical Theology and the Church," 189ff.

perspective, and theological methods from an educational perspective. Such an approach is congruent with process-theology conviction, yet is rarely articulated with such candor in Christian theological circles, much to the detriment of their increasingly generative insight with an enacted trust in the governing reality of the divine. For example, Loder's perspective insists upon the asymmetrical ordering of theological disciplines over non-theological disciplines, a conservativism that resulted in attachment to a theological/atheological dualism ultimately untenable except within his narrowly defined communities of affiliation. Osmer's methodological perspective draws a softer line within his insistence for practical theology to operate with several perspectives simultaneously,[87] but his willingness to have theological tradition shaped by other methods remains slight. The "open relationship with a relational God" remains narrowly articulate. Beyond such polarization between classical Christian theology(ies) and process theological perspectives, however, Moore moves this methodological dispute into the entire human/divine body through the metaphor and biblical symbol of the heart—a significant move resonant with performative-theology.

Moore relies upon the image and reality of the heart to argue a formative relationship between organic theology and organic teaching, recognized in the transformation and nurture of individuals and their societies. Just as "the heart is related to the entire body, continuously giving and receiving," so it is a biblical symbol that "points beyond itself and participates in the reality to which it points."[88] The heart is part of a large circuit, though not an easily discernible one.[89] It is self-regulated by a pacemaker that controls the rhythmic pumping of the heart muscle.[90] Within this metaphor, Moore argues that "teaching from the heart" relates intimately with all other elements of theology and teaching—equanimity of education, health of educational ecologies, assessment and evaluation, etc.—even as it also nourishes and transforms that which is most alive. Most importantly, the heart as biblical symbol reminds us of the integrative complexity of human being. The heart is the center of mind, will, emotions even as it "coordinates a person's life and

---

87. Osmer, "Practical Theology as Argument, Rhetoric, and Conversation," 129.
88. Moore, *Teaching From the Heart*, 199, 203.
89. Ibid., 199.
90. Ibid.

resources all physical, intellectual, emotional, and volitional energies."[91] Even in face of human malformation, the heart guides teaching and theological method because it "embraces the fullness of human life." For Moore, *teaching from the heart* is ultimately about reverencing, a fully sensate and embodied participation in formation and transformation within the extraordinary and ordinary of God. Her reconsideration of goodness follows a similarly fruitful course.

Originating within the feminist practical theological discourse amidst its pertinent challenges, Moore's reconsideration of the sin/goodness dialectic within ecclesiastical traditions advocates for a church facing into a world where the silencing and oppression of women continue to prevail. Beyond any specifically gendered purposes, however, she writes to contribute to a new paradigm in which views of human existence within a present and future church may be repaired, as in *tikkun olam*, the repair of the world, reshaped in tune with Spirit's freedom, hope, goodness. Relevant to such a problematic, sin is reconceived beyond its traditional associations with sexuality, will to power, and chaos. Goodness, unhinged from these traditional definitions of sin, becomes comprehensible as a sensual relating with the universe, as power in relationship, and as integrity or a wholeness in which the many experiences of God and the world are woven into a full fabric in human life. "To relate sensually with the universe is to feel the tenderness and joy and hurt and outrage that relationships bring. It is to be attuned with the rhythms of one's body, with the rhythms of the earth, with the rhythms and movements of other people and other beings."[92] Though she qualifies the ease of this conviction differently for men and women, Protestants and Catholics, she ultimately urges the church of the future to be open to sensuality. "It will have to *feel*," she says, "joy and pain, peace and anger, hunger and fullness."[93] In a similar move, Moore urges goodness at its best to be "a participation in the natural power that fills creation."[94] Power here must be discerned in its contribution to life or to death, to the repair of the world . . . or not. Ultimately, goodness reconsidered demonstrates a wholeness or integrity that not only allows

---

91. Ibid., 203.
92. Moore, "Feminist Practical Theology and the Church," 201.
93. Ibid., 202.
94. Ibid., 203.

but celebrates and comes to deep appreciation of differences.[95] Teaching from the heart, resourced by the reconsideration of goodness unto the fullness of human life, confirms—even in its contrasts—the marks of a performative mode instructive for a contemplative empiricism within an artisanal way.

The contrast between Moore's interactive method, with its reorientation(s) of theological-ecclesial discourse, and this method of contemplative empiricism within an artisanal way centers not in any essential differentiation but in diverse roots of origin. A contemplative empiricism emerges primarily out of the Chalcedonian negotiation of critical-correlational habits of mind. As such, it moves—perhaps rather imperialistically—the process-theological perspective into an apophatic moment of Chalcedonian orthodoxy in the trinitarian turn of Christian theology. But the process theology perspective has transformed this Chalcedonian orthodoxy just as emphatically, from the inside, seen most fully in its articulated horizon of ultimate value. The horizon for a Christian spirituality perspective remains intact, with the horizon of ultimate value described as "the triune God revealed in Jesus Christ to whom Scripture normatively witnesses and whose life is communicated to the believer by the Holy Spirit . . . " This includes the concrete awareness of being made a child of God and living a new life celebrated communally, sacramentally, in mission in the world toward God's reign.[96] Yet the received insight with respect to this horizon is the wellspring of fullness described most accurately as an expressive theological delight able to companion the suffering of self and others. In the formative relationship between organic teaching and organic theology, given voice by Moore, lies a traditionally rooted but freely non-sectarian recognition of life's fullness claimed, within a contemplative empiricism through Chalcedonian orthodoxy yet held in relation to Moore's process-theological, interactively dynamic perspective.

Moore's theological-educational work ultimately confirms the marks of a performative mode as defined in this contemplative empiricism within an artisanal way. Her work demonstrates the primarily relational commitment within methodological discourse. She reverences the contributions of multiple perspectives, respecting the distinctions

---

95. Ibid., 204.
96. Schneiders, "Approaches to the Study of Christian Spirituality," 17.

of each, so to build an interdisciplinary bridge between organic teaching and organic theology. Her organizing principle roots deeply within an explicit embodiment—centered by the heart as metaphor and biblical symbol. Multidimensionality emerges in the concrete specifics of originating narratives, brought into theoretical play and interaction in teaching from the heart. And the reorientation of theological discipline toward the fullness of human life, repeatedly articulated in new insights, draws all this into a conceptual whole: a primacy of relationship in methodological commitment, explicitly embodied operations centered in the heart as symbol and reality, and dynamically interactive multidimensionality. Moore's language is specific to her experience and distinct from that within a contemplative empiricist perspective, but each shares in the marks of a performative mode.

Conclusion

The aim of this chapter has been to offer the methodological fruits of a sustained encounter with music in performative mode and place such a harvest in the context of critical discourse within which it arose. The fundamental reorientation of mind and body, the reorientation of literate/oral dimensions of human awareness, may or may not be truly comprehensible within such theological-methodological discourse. If it is, a newly generative way of entering into theological discipline emerges, rooted in an explicitly embodied, relationally-formed, contemplative inquiry. New ways of non-being in companionable delight amidst the world's suffering and renewal become conceivable. But perhaps such fruits cannot be easily comprehended within abstracted, literate form. A contemplative empiricism within an artisanal way lives its methodological commitment to relationally-formed, primarily embodied discipline, but it eschews any systemic intention for the integration of performative mode within historical-theological disciplines. Non-correlational theological method here simply articulates a long-discerned theological interpretation of what music in performative mode offers toward the advancement of theological scholarship aimed at the fullness of human life. Far from employing its critical acumen toward shared theological understanding, such theology in performative mode lives it one context at a time. Its fruits are deeply rooted compassionate companionships within an erotic rationality toward an expressive theological delight intended for all. Within a principle of insufficient reason, thankfully, lies a sufficiency beyond understanding.

Conclusion

AMONGST ITS EXPLICIT OBJECTIVES, THIS STUDY HAS FINALLY BEEN completed in order to articulate, model, and foster the transformative learning conceived and invited within the academic study of Christian spirituality. *Learning from music in its performative mode* requires embodied participation in musical activities with a deepening openness to music's unpredictable but assured gift, insight. One awakens to music's distinct mode as a primarily aural-oral phenomenon, which subsequently leads unsuspecting but willing participants out of objectively-distant habits of mind for learning *from* objects of inquiry into the immediately sensate, reflectively oral habits of mind for learning *in* subjective-objective phenomena of all kinds. Of course, every teaching/learning environment weaves elements of *learning from* and *learning in*, but one recognizes the latter by its four marks or seeds: primary relationality, explicit embodiment, multidimensionality, and a central role for insight. The lack of preparation for integrating a performative-mode into theological inquiry—which caused Begbie to ask his original question in the first place—must be shaped by an intentional preparation, a primarily performative inquiry, in which the aural-oral dimension of inquiry becomes a palpable and undeniable origin of new awareness shaping the critical inquiry itself. Previous habits of mind become startled into a reflectively oral, primarily relational mode in which unsolicited yet self-transcendent awareness arises, instigated by and interpreted within a horizon of ultimate value toward which human beings yearn.

Learning in a Musical Key urges Christian spirituality as a discipline to become critically articulate about how this basic human capacity for transcendence is actualized. This is a discrimen of the discipline's early formation and definition, given most substantial weight in the work of Sandra Schneiders. But how *do* historically-rooted voices of traditions or communities name the dynamics of self-transcendence? How do classical voices of a religious tradition know and love God fully yet transcend the very love and knowledge they cherish toward an even greater breadth and depth of articulate wisdom? Framing such consciousness-in-transformation(s) would be a marvelous contribution for the oft-hidden (but necessary) epistemological humility of *wise* critical inquiry. It would also provide deeper intellectual companionship in the unruly sensate experience of self-transcendence within life-integration. This study was held captive for a long time to a different disciplinary problematic, framing the inquiry in less fruitful and ultimately inarticulate ways. Here at the end, such practical theological contributions do offer substantial resources to reconsider the dynamics and dimensions of self-transcendence within life-integration toward ultimate value.

The basic human capacity for transcendence becomes actualized in an observable logic of transformation or discovery, confirmed within theological and scientific literatures.[1] The relational character of the logic—what was called a *relational logic of the Spirit*, but which has similarities with the more non-sectarian *rule of relation*—creates repeatedly new intersections between textual and living traditions in which irreconcilable difference is not only unavoidable but sought. Irreconcilable difference, held within such relation, creates both sturdy template and dissonant-energies within which self-transcendence occurs. Classical Christian tradition articulates this within a Chalcedonian formulation—two wholly other natures, human-divine, become two-in-one yet indivisible, unmixable, inseparable, unchangeable, in the personhood of Christ. The reality or phenomenon being described stands distinct from such tradition-centered articulation, however. It may be named in quite divergent language from other wisdom traditions, resulting not in "the same thing with different language," but a meeting ground for receiving the multiple ways that self-transcendence may be instigated or invited.

Regardless of traditional articulation, the performative-mode of such a relational logic holds dissonance gently—as goad to critical inquiry, as an intimacy of difference within intentional companionships, as koan for contemplative inquiry—until awakening, limitation

1. Loder, *Transforming Moment*; Loder and Neidhardt, *Knight's Move*; the contemporary classic is, of course, Kuhn, *Structure of Scientific Revolutions*.

or resolution changes the frame within which difference or dissonance created the inquiry or the lived conflict. Preparation to enter into this kind of performative-mode requires a rationality well-suited to primarily relational space, argued here within the work of Jean-Luc Marion but which could easily come from other sources yet unnamed. Questions of certainty and right at the cost of wrong become reframed within a generative assurance that grows as reciprocity reduces and reason becomes delightfully insufficient. Self-assurance grows as self-sufficiency declines and identity becomes a gift of companionship, not premeditated achievement.

The disciplinary tools that the academic study of Christian spirituality provides for *this* kind of transformative learning are too significant to be neglected. They offer a return to historical-theological roots within religious traditions, newly available as amber-like prisms of critical inquiry—invited by scholarly-communal interest, but fostered by a self-implicating method and a wealth of objective-interpretive skills modeled within the broadest scope of life-integration and articulate horizon(s) of ultimate value. Ultimately, new habits of mind become feasible in critical encounter with another's habits of mind, previously unavailable within literate presupposition but newly accessible if once-removed, seen as through a mirror darkly, for conversation about things of ultimate import within human consciousness and living communities. Problems become re-framed not solely through refined historical-critical lenses but through such lenses in conversation with a performative-mode reflective orality, attuned to life-integration and human fullness, desired by all across historical horizons.

Music in its performative mode naturally leads critical inquiry to such a conclusion, as analogously as it presents itself alongside the defined material and formal objects of spirituality. The material object of study for the discipline—spirituality as existential phenomenon—intersects with its formal object of study—spirituality as religious experience—to bring the commonly human and particularly concrete into some focus for critical inquiry. Musical inquiry, when framed beyond its traditional objectivist-subjective lenses of examination, may well be furthered in such terms—music as an existential phenomenon, and music as religious or transcendent human awareness shared within sound. At the very least, music in its unique integrity demonstrates a physical-ephemeral capacity to transform human experience in intimately singular and communally embodied ways. As ethnomusicologist David McAllester observed it in the 1970's:

> I would say that one of the most important...near-universals in music is that [it] transforms experience. . . . In all the ways it is used it seems to heighten experience. You might even say it is an actualization of the mystical experience for everybody. We are not all practicing mystics and most of us do not experience God easily. But when we hear music, something like that is happening to us. We are lifted out of ourselves.[2]

Leaving the quest for near-universals nicely back in the 1970's where it belongs, the resonance with Christian spirituality yet remains and makes music's particular contribution to the advancement of its scholarship compelling.

Christian spirituality as a discipline, aiming for deeply rooted, critical studies indicative of a shared life known by its wholeness and creative restoration, is urged here toward an expressive theological delight, "the joining of insight and compassion, wisdom and love"[3] observable and shining forth from those who engage performative-mode scholarship, in its breadth and depth. This delight is *theo*logical in the sense that it lives in a holy articulate capacity for wonder, the witnessed risk of trust, and the embodied covenant of *caritas* beyond function or expectation. It empowers a willing participation in suffering—one's own and that of others—with a vulnerable strength and joyful gratitude for what life already is. Theology in performative mode, in written discourse, signifies a material-ephemeral yet radically sensate approach to *theo*logical knowledge that becomes Love— received, released, and renewed within transformative learning and graced awareness of interconnection and interdependence, within and beyond traditional particularity.

Theology in performative mode therefore challenges contemporary disciplinary theology beyond its historical boundaries within a prose of *being* into broader communities of scholarship sustained by contemplative inquiry, named well by contemplative physicist and educator Arthur Zajonc.

---

2. McAllester, "Some Thoughts on 'Universals' in World Music," 380. Cited in Sylvan, *Traces of the Spirit*, 20–21.

3. Zajonc, *Meditation as Contemplative Inquiry*, 13.

> Systematic meditative practice and inquiry have now entered and benefit a wide range of mainstream institutions and fields, including medicine and health care, business, the law, and education, by introducing deep insights that reach beyond the reductionist, materialist conception of our world and "reality"... We require new and more embracing methods of inquiry that can accommodate the great advances of science but not be limited by the dogmatic perspective of materialism and its associated economics.[4]

Clearly, performative-mode scholarship extends beyond the anthropological-theological contribution offered here for Christian spirituality. This manner in which music advances theological scholarship therefore does not diffuse critical discourse amidst a soft, faith-based reason, manacled to previous rationalities confined and confining. The method of embodied insight articulated here joins compassionate companions across disciplines and traditions in unexpected wisdom that *sharpens* critical inquiry as it enlivens love. It draws disciplinary contributions into shared, lived purposes that empower contributions to a more public, more fully human world. In this world, which is both now and not yet, music advances theological scholarship, one theologian at a time, through any performative-mode scholarship—relationally formed, explicitly embodied, multidimensional and centered around insight—recognizable in an intimate interdependence, intelligible differences, generative humility and expressive delight.

---

4. Ibid., 15.

Bibliography

Allen, Diogenes, and Eric O. Springstead. *Philosophy for Understanding Theology*. 2nd ed. Louisville: Westminster John Knox, 2007.
Angier, Natalie. "Sonata for Humans, Birds, and Humpback Whales." *New York Times*, January 9, 2001.
Atkins, Tim and Patty. *Music Worth Talking About: A Guide for Youth Leaders*. Grand Rapids: Baker, 1995.
Austin, J. L. *How to Do Things with Words*. 2nd ed. Cambridge: Harvard University Press, 1975.
Balthasar, Hans Urs von. "Spirituality." In *Explorations in Theology I: The Word Made Flesh*, 211–26. San Francisco: Ignatius, 1989.
Bamberger, Jeanne. *Developing Musical Intuitions: A Project-Based Introduction to Making and Understanding Music*. New York: Oxford University Press, 1999.
———. *Mind Behind the Musical Ear: How Children Develop Musical Intelligence*. Cambridge: Harvard University Press, 1995.
Bass, Dorothy C. *Practicing Our Faith*. San Francisco: Jossey-Bass, 1997.
Bass, Dorothy C., and Craig Dykstra, "Christian Practices and Congregational Education in Faith." *Resources for American Christianity*. Online: http://www.resourcingchristianity.org/Essay.aspx.
———. *For Life Abundant: Practical Theology, Theological Education, and Christian Ministry*. Grand Rapids: Eerdmans, 2008.
Begbie, Jeremy S. *Resounding Truth: Christian Wisdom in the World of Music*. Grand Rapids: Baker, 2007.
———. *Theology, Music and Time*. Cambridge Studies in Christian Doctrine. Cambridge: Cambridge University Press, 2000.
———. *Voicing Creation's Praise: Towards a Theology of the Arts*. Edinburgh: T. & T. Clark, 1991.
Bell, Catherine. "Performance." In *Critical Terms for Religious Studies*, edited by Mark Taylor, 205–24. Chicago: University of Chicago, 1998.
Bell, John L. *The Singing Thing: A Case for Congregational Song*. Chicago: GIA, 2000.
———. *The Singing Thing Too: Enabling Congregations to Sing*. Chicago: GIA, 2007.
Bennett, Andy. *Popular Music and Youth Culture: Music, Identity, and Place*. New York: St. Martin's, 1999.
———. "Subcultures or Neo-Tribes? Rethinking the Relationship Between Youth, Style, and Musical Taste." *Sociology* 33:3 (1999) 599–617.
Benzon, William. *Beethoven's Anvil: Music in Mind and Culture*. New York: Basic, 2001.

Berry, J.W. "Towards a Universal Psychology of Cognitive Competence." In *Changing Conceptions of Intelligence and Intellectual Functioning*, edited by P. S. Fry. Amsterdam: North-Holland, 1984.

Blacking, John. "Expressing Human Experience through Music." In *Music, Culture, and Experience: Selected Papers of John Blacking*, edited by Reginald Byron. Chicago: University of Chicago Press, 1995.

———. *How Musical is Man?* Seattle: University of Washington, 1973.

———. "Music in Children's Cognitive and Affective Development." In *Music and Child Development: Proceedings of the 1987 Denver Conference*, edited by F. R. Wilson and R. L. Roehmann. St. Louis, 1990.

———. "The Music of Politics." In *Music, Culture, and Experience: Selected Papers of John Blacking*, edited by Reginald Byron. Chicago: University of Chicago, 1995.

Blice-Baum, Christine. "Of Saints and Song: Music Education in the Church." *Lutheran Forum* 25 (1991) 33–35.

Blumenfeld-Kosinski, Renate. *Poets, Saints, and Visionaries of the Great Schism, 1378–1417*. University Park: Pennsylvania State University Press, 2006.

Bondi, Roberta C. *Memories of God: Theological Reflections on a Life*. Nashville: Abingdon, 1995.

———. *.. To Love as God Loves: Conversations with the Early Church*. Philadelphia: Fortress, 1987.

Bourdieu, Pierre. *Outline of a Theory of Practice*. Translated by Richard Nice. Cambridge Studies in Social and Cultural Anthropology. Cambridge: Cambridge University Press, 1977.

Braun, Joachim. *Music in Ancient Israel/Palestine: Archaeological, Written, and Comparative Sources*. Grand Rapids: Eerdmans, 2002.

Brentari, Carlo. *La nascita della coscienza simbolica: l'antropologia filosofica di Susanne Langer*. Trento: Università degli studi di Trento, Dipartimento di filosofia, storia e beni culturali, 2007.

Brink, Emily R. "Introducing *Songs for Life*." *Reformed Worship* 36 (1995) 26–31.

Brody, Nathan. "History of Theories and Measurements of Intelligence." In *Handbook of Intelligence*, edited by Robert Sternberg. 2nd ed. New York: Cambridge University Press, 2000.

———. *Intelligence*. 2nd ed. New York: Harcourt Brace, 1992.

Bronfenbrenner, Urie. *The Ecology of Human Development: Experiments by Nature and Design*. Cambridge: Harvard University Press, 1979.

Browning, Don S. *A Fundamental Practical Theology: Descriptive and Strategic Proposals*. Minneapolis: Fortress, 1996.

Butler, Judith. *Excitable Speech: A Politics of the Performative*. New York: Routledge, 1997.

Byars, Ronald P. *Future of Protestant Worship: Beyond the Worship Wars*. Louisville: Westminster John Knox, 2002.

Byrne, David. "I Hate World Music." *New York Times*. October 3, 1999. Online: http://www.davidbyrne.com/news/press/articles/I_hate_world_music_1999.php.

Caputo, John D. *The Weakness of God: A Theology of the Event*. Indiana Series in the Philosophy of Religion. Indianapolis: Indiana University Press, 2006.

Carlson, Marvin, editor. *Performance: A Critical Introduction*. 2nd ed. New York: Routledge, 2004.

Casey, Michael. *An Unexciting Life: Reflections on Benedictine Spirituality*. Petersham, MA: St. Bede's, 2005.
Chittister, Joan. *Insights for the Ages*. New York: Crossroad, 1992.
———. *Wisdom Distilled from the Daily: Living the Rule of St. Benedict Today*. San Francisco: HarperSanFrancisco, 1990.
Chopp, Rebecca S. *Saving Work: Feminist Practices of Theological Education*. Louisville: Westminster John Knox, 1995.
Church, Noval. "Teaching Instrumental Music through Music." In *Creative Expression: The Development of Children in Art, Music, Literature, and Dramatics*. New York: John Day, 1926.
Clark, Linda J. *Music in Churches: Nourishing Your Congregation's Musical Life*. Herndon, VA: Alban Institute, 1994.
Colijn, Helen. *Song of Survival: Women Interned*. Ashland, OR: White Cloud, 1995.
Cooper, B. Lee. "Christmas Songs: Audio Barometers of Tradition and Social Change in America, 1950–1987." *Social Studies* 79:6 (1988) 278–80.
———. "Rock Music and Religious Education: A Proposed Synthesis." *Religious Education* 70:3 (1975) 290–92.
Cluck, Darrell W., et al. *Facing the Music: Faith and Meaning in Popular Songs*. St. Louis: Chalice, 1999.
Cole, M. *Cultural Psychology: A Once and Future Discipline*. Cambridge: Harvard University Press, 1996.
Crites, Steven. "The Narrative Quality of Experience." *Journal of the American Academy of Religion* 39:3 (1971) 291–311.
Darrow, Alice-Ann. "The Role of Music in Deaf Culture: Implications for Music Educators." *Journal of Research in Music Education* 41:2 (1993) 93–110.
Davidson, Audrey Ekdahl, editor. *Wisdom Which Encircles Circles*. Kalamazoo: Western Michigan University Press, 1996.
Davison, Archibald T. *Music Education in America*. New York: Harper, 1926.
Dawn, Marva, and Dan Taylor. *How Shall We Worship?* Vital Questions Series. Carol Stream, IL: Tyndale House, 2003.
de Vries, Hent, and Samuel Weber, editors. *Violence, Identity and Self-Determination*. Stanford: Stanford University Press, 1997.
de Waal, Esther. *Living with Contradiction: An Introduction to Benedictine Spirituality*. Harrisburg, PA: Morehouse, 1998.
de Waal, Esther, and Kathleen Norris. *Seeking God: The Way of St. Benedict*. 2nd ed. Collegeville, MN: Liturgical, 2001.
Dewey, John. *Experience and Education*. The Kappa Delta Pi Lecture Series. New York: Collier, 1963.
Dilthey, Wilhelm. *Gesammelte Schriften* VII Berlin (1936) 213–16.
Doing, Ruth. "Rhythmics." In *Creative Expression: The Development of Children in Art, Music, Literature, and Dramatics*. New York: John Day, 1926.
Dowling, W. Jay, and Dane L. Harwood. *Music Cognition*. Orlando: Academic, 1986.
Dreyer, Elizabeth A., and Mark S. Burrows, *Minding the Spirit: the Study of Christian Spirituality*. Baltimore: Johns Hopkins University Press, 2005.
Dronke, Peter. *Women Writers of the Middle Ages: A Critical Study of Texts from Perpetua to Marguerite Porete*. Cambridge: Cambridge University Press, 1984.

Dykstra, Craig. *Growing in the Life of Faith: Education and Christian Practices*. Louisville: Geneva, 1999.

———. "Reconceiving Practice." In *Shifting Boundaries: Contextual Approaches to the Structure of Theological Education*, edited by Barbara G. Wheeler and Edward Farley. Louisville: Westminster John Knox, 1991.

Eisner, Elliot W. *The Educational Imagination: On the Design and Evaluation of School Programs*. 3rd ed. New York: Macmillan College, 1994.

Eisner, Elliot W., and Elizabeth Vallance, editors. *Conflicting Conceptions of Curriculum*. National Society for the Study of Education Series on Contemporary Educational Issues. Berkeley: McCutchan, 1974.

Engle, Randall. "Teaching Children the Songs of the Church." *Reformed Worship* 36 (1995) 26–31.

Epstein, Heidi. *Melting the Venusberg: A Feminist Theology of Music*. New York: Continuum, 2004.

Erikson, Erik. *Identity and the Life Cycle*. New York: Norton, 1980.

Farley, Edward. "Music and Human Existence." *Theological Education* 31:1 (1994) 178–83.

———. *Theologia: the Fragmentation and Unity of Theological Education*. Philadelphia: Fortress, 1983.

Fassler, Margot. "Composer and Dramatist: Melodious Singing and the Freshness of Remorse." In *Voice of the Living Light: Hildegard of Bingen and Her World*, edited by Barbara Newman. Berkeley: University of California Press, 1998.

Faulkner, Gregory C. "Participation in Being Loved by God: The Christocentric Nature of Benedictine Spirituality." PhD diss., Princeton Theological Seminary, 1991.

Feuerstein, Reuven. *Instrumental Enrichment: An Intervention Program for Cognitive Modifiability*. Baltimore: University Park Press, 1980.

Flanagan, Sabina. *Hildegard of Bingen: A Visionary Life*. London: Routledge, 1989.

———. "Hildegard of Bingen—German Writers and Works of the Early Middle Ages: 800–1170." In *Dictionary of Literary Biography*. New York: Gale, 1995.

Ford-Grabowsky, Mary. "The Concept of Christian Faith in the Light of Hildegard of Bingen and C.G. Jung: A Critical Alternative to Fowler." PhD diss., Princeton Theological Seminary, 1985.

Fox, Matthew. *Illuminations of Hildegard of Bingen*. Rochester, VT: Bear, 2002.

Frankl, Viktor. *Man's Search for Meaning*. Boston: Beacon, 1963.

Fraser, Daniel. *The Music of the Spheres*. Albany: Weed, Parsons, 1887.

Frazee, Jane, and Kent Kreuter. *Discovering Orff: A Curriculum for Music Teachers*. New York: Schott, 1987.

Freeman, Cathy. "The Crystallizing Experience: A Study in Musical Precocity." *Gifted Child Quarterly* 43:2 (1999) 75–85.

Fridman, Ruth. "Proto-Rhythms: Basis for the Birth of Musical Intelligence and Language Expression." *Pre- and Peri-Natal Psychology Journal* 6:2 (1991) 181–98.

Frohlich, Mary. "Critical Interiority." *Spiritus* 7 (2007) 77–81.

———. "Under the Sign of Jonah: Studying Spirituality in a Time of Ecosystemic Crisis." Presidential address at the Annual Meeting of the Society for the Study of Christian Spirituality. Chicago, IL: November, 2008.

Gadamer, Hans-Georg. *Truth and Method*. New York: Crossroad, 1989.

Gaebelein, Frank E. "Music in Christian Education." *Christianity Today* 6 (1962) 30–32.

Gardner, Howard. "The 25th Anniversary of the Publication of Howard Gardner's *Frames of Mind: the Theory of Multiple Intelligences*." Online: http://www.howardgardner.com/Papers/papers.html.

———. *Art, Mind, and Brain: A Cognitive Approach to Creativity*. New York: Basic, Inc., 1982.

———. *Artful Scribbles*. New York: Basic, 1980.

———. *Arts and Human Development: A Psychological Study of the Artistic Process*. New York: Wiley, 1973.

———. *Art Education and Human Development*. Los Angeles: The J. Paul Getty Trust, 1990.

———. "The Borders of Intelligence." Online: http://www.theatlantic.com/past/docs/issues/99feb/intel3.htm.

———. *Frames of Mind: the Theory of Multiple Intelligences*. 10th Anniversary edition. New York: Basic, 1999.

———. "Intelligence in Seven Steps." In *Creating the Future: Perspectives on Educational Change*, edited by Dee Dickinson. Seattle: New Horizons for Learning, 1998.

———. *Intelligence Reframed: Multiple Intelligences for the 21st Century*. New York: Basic, 1999.

———. "M.I. After Twenty Years." Online: http://www.howardgardner.com/Papers/papers.html.

———. *Mind's New Science: A History of the Cognitive Revolution*. New York: Basic, 1985.

———. "Multiple Intelligences." Online: http://www.theatlantic.com/past/docs/issues/99feb/intel2.htm.

———. *Multiple Intelligences: The Theory in Practice*. New York: Basic, 1993.

———. "Reflections on Multiple Intelligences: Myths and Messages." *Phi Delta Kappan* 77:3 (1995) 200 209.

———. "A Reply to Perry D. Klein." *Canadian Journal of Education* 23:1 (1998) 96–102.

———. *Shattered Mind: The Person After Brain Damage*. New York: Knopf, 1975.

———. *UnSchooled Mind: How Children Think and how Schools Should Teach*. New York: Basic, 1991.

———. "Who Owns Intelligence?" Online: http://www.theatlantic.com/past/docs/issues/99feb/intel3.htm.

Gardner, Howard, et al. *Intelligence: Multiple Perspectives*. Fort Worth: Harcourt Brace, 1996.

Godwin, Joscelyn. *Harmonies of Heaven and Earth: Mysticism in Music from Antiquity to the Avant-Garde*. London: Thames & Hudson, 1987.

———. *Harmony of the Spheres: A Sourcebook for the Pythagorean Tradition in Music*. Rochester, NY: Inner Traditions International, 1993.

Gioia, Ted. *Work Songs*. Durham, NC: Duke University Press, 2006.

Gordon, Edwin E. "About Music Learning Theory." Online: http://www.giml.org/AboutMLT.pdf.

———. *The Advanced Measures of Music Audiation.* Chicago: G.I.A. Music, 1989.

———. "The Assessment of Music aptitudes of Very Young Children." *Gifted Child Quarterly* 24:3 (1980) 107–11.

———. "Audiation, Music Learning Theory, Music Aptitude, and Creativity." *Suncoast Music Education Forum on Creativity* (1989) 75–81.

———. *Audie.* Chicago: G.I.A. Music, 1989.

———. "First-Year Results of a Five-Year Longitudinal Study of the Musical Achievement of Culturally Disadvantaged Students." *Journal of Research in Music Education* 18:3 (1970) 195–213.

———. "Fourth-Year and Fifty-Year Final Results of a Longitudinal Study of the Musical Achievement of Culturally-Disadvantaged Students." In *Experimental Research in the Psychology of Music,* volume 10. Iowa City: University of Iowa Press, 1975.

———. "Intercorrelations Among Musical Aptitude Profile and Seashore Measures of Musical Talents Subtests." *Journal of Research in Music Education* 17:3 (1969) 263–71.

———. *Introduction to Research and the Psychology of Music.* Chicago: G.I.A., 1998.

———. *Learning Sequences in Music.* Chicago: G.I.A., 1997.

———. *A Music Learning Theory for Newborn and Young Children.* Chicago: G.I.A., 1990.

———. *Musical Aptitude Profile Manual.* Boston: Houghton Mifflin, 1965.

———. *Primary Measures of Music Audiation and Intermediate Measures of Music Audiation.* Music Aptitude Tests for Kindergarten and First, Second, Third, and Fourth Grade Children. Chicago: G.I.A., 1986.

———. *The Psychology of Music Teaching.* Englewood Cliffs, NJ: Prentice-Hall, 1971.

———. "Second-Year Results of a Five-Year Longitudinal Study of the Musical Achievement of Culturally Disadvantaged Students." In *Experimental Research in the Psychology of Music,* volume 7. Iowa City: University of Iowa, 1971.

———. "A Sound-to-Symbol Approach to Learning Music." *Music Educators Journal* 72:6 (1986) 38–41.

———. "The Source of Musical Aptitude." *Music Educators Journal* 57:8 (1971) 35–37.

———. "A Study of the Characteristics of the Instrument Timbre Preference Test." *Bulletin of the Council for Research in Music Education* 110 (1991) 33–51.

———. "Taking into Account Musical Aptitude Differences Among Beginning Instrumental Students." *Experimental Research in the Psychology of Music,* volume 6. Iowa City: University of Iowa, 1971.

———. "Third-Year Results of a Five-Year Longitudinal Study of the Musical Achievement of Culturally-Disadvantaged Students." In *Experimental Research in the Psychology of Music,* volume 8. Iowa City: University of Iowa, 1972.

———. "A Three-Year Longitudinal Predictive Validity Study of the Musical Aptitude Profile." In *Experimental Research in the Psychology of Music,* volume 5. Iowa City: University of Iowa, 1967.

Gordon, Edwin E., et al. *Songs and Chants Without Words.* The Early Childhood Music Curriculum. Book One. Chicago: G.I.A., 1993.

Gordon, Edwin E., and Lili Muhler Levinowitz. *Preschool Music Curricula: Children's Music Development Program.* Chicago: G.I.A., 1987.

Gray, Patricia M., et al. "The Music of Nature and the Nature of Music." *Science* 291 (2001) 52–54.
Greenfield, P. M. "You Can't Take it With You: Why Abilities Assessments Don't Cross Cultures." *American Psychologist* 52 (1997) 1115–24.
Groome, Thomas H. *Christian Religious Education: Sharing Our Story and Vision.* San Francisco: Harper & Row, 1980.
———. *Sharing Faith: A Comprehensive Approach to Religious Education and Pastoral Ministry, the Way of Shared Praxis.* San Francisco: HarperSanFrancisco, 1991.
Gross, Bella, and Robert H. Seashore. "Psychological Characteristics of Student and Professional Musical Composers." *Journal of Applied Psychology* 25 (1941) 159–70.
Hargreaves, David. *The Developmental Psychology of Music.* New York: Cambridge University Press, 1986.
Harrington, Karl Pomeroy. *Education in Church Music.* New York: Century, 1931.
Hart, Trevor. "Through the Arts: Hearing, Seeing and Touching the Truth." In *Beholding the Glory: Incarnation Through the Arts*, edited by Jeremy Begbie. Grand Rapids: Baker, 2000.
Hartman, Gertrude, and Ann Shumaker, editors. *Creative Expression: The Development of Children in Art, Music, Literature, and Dramatics.* New York: John Day, 1926.
Havelock, Eric A. "The Ancient Art of Oral Poetry." *Philosophy and Rhetoric* 19 (1979) 187–202.
———. *Origins of Western Literacy.* Toronto: Ontario Institute for Studies in Education, 1976.
Hawn, C. Michael. *Gather Into One: Praying and Singing Globally.* The Calvin Institute of Christian Worship Liturgical Series. Grand Rapids: Eerdmans, 2003.
Heisig, James W. "The Recovery of the Senses: Against the Asceticisms of the Age." In *Dialogues at One Inch Above the Ground: Reclamations of Belief in an Interreligious Age.* New York: Crossroad, 2003.
Heitink, Gerben. *Practical Theology: History, Theory, Action Domains.* Translated by Reinder Bruinsma. Studies in Practical Theology Series. Grand Rapids: Eerdmans, 1999.
Hermansen, Marcia "Muslims in the Performative Mode: a Reflection on Muslim-Christian Dialogue." *The Muslim World* 94 (2004) 387–96.
Hess, Lisa M. *Artisanal Theology: Intentional Formation in Radically Covenantal Companionship.* Eugene, OR: Cascade, 2009.
———. "Formation in the Worlds of Theological Education: Moving From *What* to *How.*" *Teaching Theology and Religion* 11:1 (2008) 14–23.
———. *Practices in a New Key: Human Knowing in Musical and Practical Theological Perspective.* PhD diss., Princeton Theological Seminary, 2001.
———. "Theological Interdisciplinary and Religious Leadership." *Journal of Religious Leadership* 6:1 (2007) 1–37.
———. "Toward a Full-Fledged Action Theory with a Perspective of Musical Transcendence." *Verbum et Ecclesia* 25:2 (2004) 519–33. Online: http://www.up.ac.za/dspace/bitstream/2263/8709/1/Hess_Toward(2004).pdf.
———. "Toward an *Intimacy of Difference*: Philosophical and Theological Resources for Human Connection Through Difference." In *Alienation and Connection:*

Suffering in a Global Era, edited by Lisa Withrow. Lanham, MD: Lexington, forthcoming.

Hildegard of Bingen. *Explanation of The Rule of Benedict*. Translated by Hugh Feiss, OSB. Toronto: Peregrina,1996.

———. "Letter 23." In *The Letters of Hildegard of Bingen*, volume 1. Translated by Joseph L. Baird and Radd K. Ehrman. New York: Oxford University Press, 1994.

———. *Liber Divinorum Operum Simplicis Hominis [The Book of Divine Works of a Simple Person]*. Translated by Albert Derolez and Peter Dronke. CCCM series. Turnhout, Belgium: Brepols, 1996.

———. *Liber Vitae Meritorum [The Book of the Rewards of Life]*. Translated by Bruce W. Hozeski. New York: Oxford University Press, 1994.

———. "Ordo Virtutum [Play of the Virtues]." In *Poetic Individuality in the Middle Ages*, translated by Peter Dronke. Oxford: Clarendon, 1970.

———. *Scivias*. Translated by Mother Columba Hart and Jane Bishop. Classics of Western Spirituality Series. Mahwah, NJ: Paulist, 1990.

———. *Symphonia armonie celestium revelationum [The Symphony of the Harmony of Heavenly Revelations]*. Translated by Barbara Newman. Ithaca, NY: Cornell University Press, 1988.

———. "Tenxwind von Andernach und Hildegard von Bingen: Zwei 'Weltanschauungen' in der Mitte des 12 Jahrhunderts." In *Institutionen, Kultur und Gesellschaft im Mittelalter: Festschrift für Josef Fleckenstein*, edited by Lutz Fenske et al., translated by Alfred Haverkamp, 515–48. Sigmaringen, 1984.

Hodges, H. A. *Wilhelm Dilthey*. New York: Oxford University Press, 1944.

Holder, Arthur, editor. *Blackwell Companion to Christian Spirituality*. Malden, MA: Blackwell, 2005.

———. *Christian Spirituality: The Classics*. New York: Routledge, 2010.

Holland, Dorothy, et al. *Identity and Agency in Cultural Worlds*. Cambridge: Harvard University Press, 1998.

Holsinger, Bruce W. "The Flesh of the Voice: Embodiment and the Homoerotics of Devotion in the Music of Hildegard of Bingen (1098–1179)." *Signs* 19:1 (1993) 92–125.

———. *Music, Body, and Desire in Medieval Culture: From Hildegard of Bingen to Chaucer*. Stanford: Stanford University Press, 2001.

Horner, Robyn. *Jean-Luc Marion: A Theo-Logical Introduction*. Burlington, VT: Ashgate, 2005.

Hulse, S. H., et al. "Auditory Discrimination of Chord-based Spectral Structures by European Starlings (*Sturnus vulgaris*)." *Journal of Experimental Psychology* 124 (1995) 409–23.

Hütter, Reinhard. *Suffering Divine Things: Theology as Church Practice*. Translated by Doug Stott. Grand Rapids: Eerdmans, 1997.

Innis, Robert E., editor. "Symposium on Susanne K. Langer." *Journal of Speculative Philosophy* 21:1 (2007) 1–43.

James, Jamie. *The Music of the Spheres: Music, Science and the Natural Order of the Universe*. New York: Grove, 1993.

Jaynes, Julian. *Origins of Consciousness in the Breakdown of the Bicameral Mind*. Boston: Houghton Mifflin, 1977.

Jones, Mari Riess, and Susan Holleran. *Cognitive Bases of Musical Communication.* Washington, DC: American Psychological Association, 1992.
Kegan, Robert. *In Over Our Heads: The Mental Demands of Modern Life.* Cambridge: Harvard University Press, 1994.
Kilhstrom, John F., and Nancy Cantor, "Social Intelligence." In *The Handbook of Intelligence,* edited by Robert J. Sternberg. New York: Cambridge University Press, 2000.
Kimbrough, S T Jr., editor. *Music and Mission: Toward a Theology and Practice of Global Song.* New York: General Board of Global Ministries, GBGMusik, the United Methodist Church, 2006.
Kincheloe, Joe L., et al. *Measured Lies: The Bell Curve Examined.* New York: St. Martin's, 1996.
King-Lenzmeier, Anne H. *Hildegard of Bingen: An Integrated Vision.* Collegeville, MN: Liturgical, 2001.
King, Roberta R. "The Role of Music in Theological Education." *African Journal of Evangelical Theology* 9:1 (1990) 35–37.
Klein, Perry D. "Multiplying the Problems of Intelligence by Eight." *Canadian Journal of Education* 23:1 (1998) 96–102.
Kotchetkova, Inna, Robert Evans, and Susanne Langer. "Articulating Contextualized Knowledge: Focus Groups and/as Public Participation?" *Science as Culture* 17:1 (2008) 71–84.
Kroeker, Charlotte, editor. *Music in Christian Worship: At the Service of the Liturgy.* Collegeville, MN: Liturgical, 2005.
Kuckertz, Josef. "Introduction: The Problem." In *Ethnomusicology in the Context of Other Sciences: Panel Session at the 32nd World Conference of the International Council for Traditional Music,* 1–7. Hamburg: Verlag der Musikalienhandlung K. D. Wagner, 1994.
Kuhn, Thomas S. *Structure of Scientific Revolutions.* 3rd ed. Chicago: University of Chicago, 1996.
Lamott, Anne. *Traveling Mercies: Some Thoughts on Faith.* New York: Pantheon, 1998.
Langer, Susanne K. *Feeling and Form: A Theory of Art Developed from Philosophy in a New Key.* New York: Scribner, 1953/1977.
———. *Mind: An Essay on Human Feeling.* Abridged. Foreword by Arthur C. Danto. Baltimore: Johns Hopkins University Press, 1988.
———. *Philosophy in a New Key: A Study in the Symbolism of Reason, Rite, and Art.* 3rd ed. Cambridge: Harvard University Press, 1979.
Lawhead, Steve. *Rock Reconsidered: A Christian Looks at Contemporary Music.* Downers Grove, IL: InterVarsity, 1981.
Lawler, Andrew. "The Slow Deaths of Writing." *Science* 305 (2004) 30–33.
Leaver, Robin A. "What is Liturgical Music?" In *Liturgy and Music: Lifetime Learning,* edited by Robin A. Leaver and Joyce Ann Zimmerman. Collegeville, MN: Liturgical, 1998.
LeClercq, John. "Spiritualitas." *Studi medievali* 3 (1962) 281–84.
Lescher, Bruce H., and Elizabeth Liebert, SNJM. *Exploring Christian Spirituality: Essays in Honor of Sandra M. Schneiders, IHM.* New York: Paulist, 2006.

Levine, Robert. *The Geography of Time: The Temporal Misadventures of a Social Psychologist, or How Every Culture Keeps Time Just a Little Bit Differently.* New York: Basic, 1998.

Loder, James E. *Logic of the Spirit: Human Development in Theological Perspective.* San Francisco: Jossey-Bass, 1998.

———. "Normativity and Context in Practical Theology: The Interdisciplinary Issue." In *Practical Theology: International Perspectives,* edited by Friedrich Schweitzer and Johannes A. van der Ven. New York: Peter Lang, 1999.

———. "Transformation in Christian Education." *Princeton Seminary Bulletin* 3:1 (1980) 1–15.

———. *Transforming Moment.* 2nd ed. Colorado Springs: Helmers & Howard, 1989.

Loder, James E., and W. Jim Neidhardt. *The Knight's Move: The Relational Logic of the Spirit in Theology and Science.* Colorado Springs: Helmers & Howard, 1992.

Lonergan, Bernard J. F. *Method in Theology.* New York: Seabury, 1979.

Lord, Albert B. "Perspectives on Recent Work in Oral Literature." In *Oral Literature,* edited by Joseph J. Duggan. New York: Barnes & Noble, 1975.

———. *The Singer of Tales.* Harvard Studies in Comparative Literature. Cambridge: Harvard University Press, 1960.

Lovelace, Austin C., and William C. Rice. *Music and Worship in the Church.* Nashville: Abingdon, 1976.

Luria, A. R. *Cognitive Development: Its Cultural and Social Foundations.* Translated by Martin Lopez-Morillas and Lynn Solotaroff. Edited by Michael Cole. Cambridge: Harvard University Press, 1976.

Lynn, Robert W., and Elliot Wright. *The Big Little School: Two Hundred Years of the Sunday School.* 2nd ed. Birmingham: Religious Education, 1980.

MacIntyre, Alasdair. *After Virtue: A Study in Moral Theory.* Notre Dame: University of Notre Dame, 1984.

McCant, Jerry W. "Music and Christian Education." *Journal of Christian Education* 1:2 (1981) 65–67.

McDermott, John J., editor. "Symposium on Susanne K. Langer: A Foreword." *Transactions of the Charles S. Peirce Society* 32:1 (1997) 131–200.

McDonnell, Killian, OSB. *A Benedictine Approach to Lay Spirituality.* St. Meinrad, IN: Grail, 1953.

McGinn, Bernard. "The Letter and the Spirit: Spirituality as an Academic Discipline." In *Minding the Spirit: the Study of Christian Spirituality,* edited by Elizabeth A. Dreyer and Mark S. Burrows. Baltimore: Johns Hopkins, 2005.

———. *The Presence of God: A History of Western Christian Mysticism.* 3 vols. New York: Crossroad, 1991/1994.

McKee, Kathy B., and Carol J. Pardun. "Reading the Video: a Qualitative Study of Religious Images in Music Videos." *Journal of Broadcasting & Electronic Media* 43:1 (1999) 110–22.

McKenzie, Jon. *Perform or Else: From Discipline to Performance.* New York: Routledge, 2001.

McKinnon, James. *Music in Early Christian Literature.* Cambridge Readings in the Literature of Music. Cambridge: Cambridge University Press, 1987.

McNamara, Patrick, editor. *Where God and Science Meet: How Brain and Evolutionary Studies Alter our Understanding of Religion.* Westport, CT: Praeger, 2006.

Maddock, Fiona. *Hildegard of Bingen: The Woman of Her Age*. New York: Image, 2003.
Madigan, Shawn, CSJ, editor. *Mystics, Visionaries and Prophets: A Historical Anthology of Women's Spiritual Writings*. Minneapolis: Fortress, 1998.
Marion, Jean-Luc. *Being Given: Toward a Phenomenology of Givenness*. Translated by Jeffrey L. Kosky. Cultural Memory in the Present Series. Stanford: Stanford University Press, 2002.
———. *The Erotic Phenomenon*. Translated by Stephen E. Lewis. Chicago: University of Chicago Press, 2007.
———. *God Without Being*. Translated by Thomas A. Carlson. Chicago: University of Chicago Press, 1991.
———. *Prolegomena to Charity*. Translated by Stephen E. Lewis. Perspective in Continental Philosophy Series. New York: Fordham, 2002.
Marett-Crosby, Anthony, editor. *The Benedictine Handbook*. Collegeville, MN: Liturgical, 2003.
Martin, Peter J. "The Social Construction of Musical Meaning." In *Sounds and Society: Themes in the Sociology of Music*. New York: Manchester University Press, 1995.
May, Gerald G. *From Cruelty to Compassion: The Crucible of Personal Transformation*. Deepening the American Dream series. Fetzer Institute, 2005. Online: http://www.fetzer.org/images/stories/pdf/dad_may_essay.pdf.
Merton, Thomas. *Thomas Merton Spiritual Master: Essential Writings*. Edited by Lawrence S. Cunningham. Mahweh, NJ: Paulist, 1992.
Moore, Mary Elizabeth Mullino. "Feminist Practical Theology and the Future of the Church." In *Practical Theology—International Perspectives*, edited by Friedrich Schweitzer and Johannes A. van der Ven. New York: Peter Lang, 1999.
———. *Teaching From the Heart: Theology and Educational Method*. Harrisburg, PA: Trinity Press International, 1998.
Morris, Van Cleve, and Young Pai. *Philosophy of the American School*. 2nd ed. Lanham, MD: University Press of America, 1994.
Morsch, Vivian. *The Use of Music in Christian Education*. Philadelphia: Westminster, 1956.
Myers, Ken. "Joy May End in Grief: Re-Imagining Leisure in the Face of Relentless Entertainment." Sound recording. North Cincinnati Community Church, Cincinnati, Ohio, October 3–5, 2003.
Nelson, Ronald A., et al. "Hymns in Religious Education: Three Perspectives." *The Hymn* (1983) 80–83.
Newman, Barbara. *Sister of Wisdom: St. Hildegard's Theology of the Feminine*. Berkeley: University of California Press, 1987.
Newman, Barbara, editor. *Voice of the Living Light*. Berkeley: University of California, 1998.
Ochs, Peter, and Nancy Levene, editors. *Textual Reasonings: Jewish Philosophy and Text Study at the End of the Twentieth Century*. Radical Traditions/Theology in a Postcritical Key Series. Grand Rapids: Eerdmans, 2002.
Olthuis, James H. "Crossing the Threshold: Sojourning Together in the Wild Spaces of Love." In *Knowing Other-Wise: Philosophy at the Threshold of Spirituality*. New York: Fordham University Press, 1997.

———. "Love/Knowledge: Sojourning with Others, Meeting with Differences." In *Knowing Other-Wise: Philosophy at the Threshold of Spirituality*. New York: Fordham University Press, 1997.

Ong, Walter J., S. J. *Faith and Contexts: Selected Essays, Supplementary Studies, and Further Essays—Volumes 1–3*, edited by Thomas J. Farrell and Paul A. Soukup. Atlanta: Scholars, 1992–1995.

———. *Interfaces of the Word: Studies in the Evolution of Consciousness and Culture*. Ithaca: Cornell University Press, 1977.

———. *Orality and Literacy: The Technologizing of the Word*. New York: Routledge, 1982/2002.

———. *Presence of the Word: Some Prolegomena for Cultural and Religious History*. New Haven, CT: Yale University Press, 1967.

Orff, Carl. *Music for Children*. Mainz: B. Schott's, 1960.

Orff, Carl, and Hermann Regner. *Orff-Schulwerk in der Welt von Morgen: eine Dokumentation, Symposion 1985 28 June—2 July 1985*. Salzburg: Sonderabteilung Orff-Institut, 1985.

Osmer, Richard Robert. *Practical Theology: An Introduction*. Grand Rapids: Eerdmans, 2008.

———. "Practical Theology as Argument, Rhetoric, and Conversation." In *Practical Theology—International Perspectives*, edited by Friedrich Schweitzer and Johannes A. van der Ven. New York: Peter Lang, 1999.

Osmer, Richard R., and Friedrich Schweitzer. *Religious Education between Modernization and Globalization*. Grand Rapids: Eerdmans, 2003.

Otto, Rudolph. *The Idea of the Holy*. New York: Oxford University Press, 1958.

Packalén, Elina. "In Dialogue: Response to Mary Reichling." *Philosophy of Music Education Review* 16:2 (2008) 208–12.

Page, Sue Ellen. *Hearts and Hands and Voices: Growing in Faith Through Choral Music*. Tarzana, CA: H. T. FitzSimons, 1995.

Pannenberg, Wolfhart. *Anthropology in Theological Perspective*. Translated by Matthew J. O'Connell. Philadelphia: Westminster, 1985.

Parke, Ross D., et al. *A Century of Developmental Psychology*. Washington, DC: American Psychological Association, 1994.

Parry, Adam, editor. *The Making of Homeric Verse: the Collected Papers of Milman Parry*. Oxford: Clarendon, 1971.

Parsons, Charles. "The Transcendental Aesthetic." In *Cambridge Companion to Immanuel Kant*, edited by Paul Guyer. Cambridge Companions to Philosophy Series. Cambridge: Cambridge University Press, 1992.

Peery, J. Craig, et al. *Music and Child Development*. New York: Springer-Verlag, 1987.

Peretz, I. "Processing of Local and Global Musical Information by Unilateral Brain-Damaged Patients." *Brain* 113 (1990) 1185–1205.

Pernoud, Régine. *Hildegard of Bingen: Inspired Conscience of the Twelfth Century*. Translated by Paul Duggan. New York: Marlowe, 1998.

Pfatteicher, Philip H. *The School of the Church: Worship and Christian Formation*. Valley Forge: Trinity, 1995.

Philip, Margot Leith, editor. *Ethnomusicology and the Historical Dimension: Papers Presented at the European Seminary in Ethnomusicology, London, May 20–23, 1986*. Ludwigsburg, West Germany: Philipp, 1989.

Piechowski, Michael M. "The Logical and the Empirical Form of Feeling." *Journal of Aesthetic Education* 15:1 (1981) 31–53.
Ploeger, Albert K. *Dare We Observe? The Importance of Art Works for Consciousness of Diakonia in (Post-)modern Church*. Leuven: Peeters, 2002.
Polanyi, Michael. *Personal Knowledge: Towards a Post-Critical Philosophy*. Chicago: University of Chicago, 1964.
———. *The Tacit Dimension*. London: Routledge, 1967.
Principe, Walter. "Toward Defining Spirituality." *Science Réligieuses* 12 (1983) 127–41.
Pyle, David W. *Intelligence: an Introduction*. London: Routledge & Kegan Paul, 1979.
Ramseth, Betty Ann. *Keep In Mind: Hymns for Unison Voices and Instruments with Related Prayers and Meditations*. Minneapolis: Augsburg, 1984.
Reichling, Mary. "Intersections: Form, Feeling, and Isomorphism." *Philosophy of Music Education Review* 12:1 (2004) 17–29.
Richardson, Ken. *Understanding Intelligence*. Philadelphia: Milton Keynes, 1991.
Richter, Cornelia, and Petra Bahr, editors. *Naturalisierung des Geistes und Symbolisierung des Fuhlens: Susanne K. Langer im Gesprach der Forschung*. Marburg: Tectum, 2008.
Ridley, Aaron. *The Philosophy of Music: Theme and Variations*. Edinburgh: Edinburgh University Press, 2004.
Ricoeur, Paul. *Interpretation Theory: Discourses and the Surplus of Meaning*. Fort Worth: Texas Christian University Press, 1976.
Ritson, Mark, and Richard Elliott. "The Social Uses of Advertising: An Ethnographic Study of Adolescent Advertising Audiences." *Journal of Consumer Research* 26:3 (1999) 260–77.
Roehmann, Franz L. "Making the Connection: Music and Medicine." *Music Educator's Journal* 77:5 (1991) 20–24.
Ryelandt, Idesbald. *The Quest for God: A Study in Benedictine Spirituality*. Translated by Matthew Dillon. St. Louis: Herder, 1959.
———. *Union with Christ: Benedictine and Liturgical Spirituality*. Translated by Matthew Dillon. Wilkes-Barre, PA: Dimension, 1966.
Sacks, Oliver. *Awakenings*. New York: E. P. Dutton, 1983.
———. *Musicophilia: Tales of Music and the Brain*. New York: Vintage, 2008.
Saliers, Don E. "Music and Spirituality: Listening for God's Voice." *Christian Spirituality Bulletin* (1994) 10–12.
———. *Music and Theology*. Horizons in Theology Series. Nashville: Abingdon, 2007.
———. "Singing Our Lives." In *Practicing Our Faith*, edited by Dorothy Bass. San Francisco: Jossey-Bass, 1997.
———. "Sound Spirituality: On the Formative Expressive Power of Music." In *Minding the Spirit: The Study of Christian Spirituality*, edited by Elizabeth A. Dreyer and Mark S. Burrows. Baltimore: Johns Hopkins University Press, 2005.
Saliers, Don, and Emily Saliers. *A Song to Sing, a Life to Live: Reflections on Music as Spiritual Practice*. Practices of Faith Series. San Francisco: Jossey-Bass, 2004.
Schleuter, Stanley. "An Investigation of the Interrelation of Personality Traits, Musical Aptitude, and Musical Achievement." PhD diss. University of Iowa, 1970.

Schneiders, Sandra M. "Approaches to the Study of Christian Spirituality." In *The Blackwell Companion to Christian Spirituality*, edited by Arthur Holder. Malden, MA: Blackwell, 2005.

———. "Spirituality in the Academy." *Theological Studies* 50 (1989) 676–97.

———. "The Study of Christian Spirituality: Contours and Dynamics." In *Minding the Spirit*, edited by Elizabeth A. Dreyer and Mark S. Burrows. Baltimore: Johns Hopkins University Press, 2005.

Schweitzer, Friedrich, and Johannes A. van der Ven, editors. *Practical Theology: International Perspectives*. New York: Peter Lang, 1999.

Scott, Joyce. *Tuning in to a Different Song: Using a Music Bridge to Cross Cultural Differences*. Tshwane/Pretoria: University of Pretoria/Institute for Missiological and Ecumenical Research, 2000.

Serafine, Mary Louise. *Music as Cognition: The Development of Thought In Sound*. New York: Columbia University Press, 1988.

Seymour, Harriet Ayer. "Creative Expression in Music." In *Creative Expression: The Development of Children in Art, Music, Literature, and Dramatics*. New York: The John Day, 1926.

Shields, Elizabeth McEwen. *Music in the Religious Growth of Children*. New York: Abingdon, 1943.

Sidtis, J. J., and B. T. Volpe. "Selective Loss of Complex-Pitch or Speech Discrimination after Unilateral Cerebral Lesion." *Brain Language* 34 (1988) 235–45.

Siegler, Robert S. "The Other Alfred Binet." In *A Century of Developmental Psychology*, edited by Ross D. Parke et al. Washington, DC: American Psychological Association, 1994.

Sirota, Victoria. "An Exploration of Music as Theology." *Theological Education* 31:1 (1994) 172–76.

Slobin, Mark, and Jeff Todd Titon. "The Music-Culture as a World of Music." In *Worlds of Music: An Introduction to the Music of the World's People*, 2nd ed. New York: Schirmer, 1992.

Sloboda, John A. *The Musical Mind: the Cognitive Psychology of Music*. Oxford Psychology Series 5. Oxford: Clarendon, 1985.

Slocum, Kay Brainerd. "The Harmony of Celestial Revelations: Hildegard's Theology of Music." In *Wisdom Which Encircles Circles: Papers on Hildegard of Bingen*, edited by Audrey Ekdahl Davidson. Medieval Institute Publications. Kalamazoo: Western Michigan University Press, 1996.

Small, Christopher. *Musicking: The Meanings of Performing and Listening*. Middletown, CT: Wesleyan University Press, 1998.

Squires, Paul C. "The Creative Psychology of Carl Maria von Weber." *Character and Personality* 6 (1938) 203–17.

Stackhouse, Max L. "Ethical Vision and Musical Imagination." *Theological Education* 31:1 (1994) 149–53.

Steiner, George. *Real Presences*. Chicago: University of Chicago, 1989.

Sternberg, Robert, editor. *The Handbook of Intelligence*. New York: Cambridge University Press, 2000.

Stevenson-Moessner, Jeanne. *Prelude to Practical Theology: Variations on Theory and Practice*. Nashville: Abingdon, 2008.

Stewart, Columba. *Prayer and Community: The Benedictine Tradition*. Traditions of Christian Spirituality. Maryknoll, NY: Orbis, 1998.

Stokes, Martin. *Ethnicity, Identity, and Music: The Musical Construction of Place*. Providence: Berg, 1994.

Storr, Anthony. *Music and the Mind*. New York: RandomHouse, 1992.

Stravinsky, Igor. *Poetics of Music in the Form of Six Lessons*. Cambridge: Harvard University Press, 1970.

Strunk, Oliver. *Source Readings in Music History*. New York: MacMillan, 1950.

Stubbs, David. "Practices, Core Practices, and the Work of the Holy Spirit." *Journal for Christian Theological Research* 9 (2004) 15–28.

Swan, Laura, editor. *The Benedictine Tradition: Spirituality in History*. Collegeville, MN: Liturgical, 2007.

Swaggart, Jimmy, with Robert Paul Lamb. *Religious Rock'n'Roll: A Wolf in Sheep's Clothing*. Baton Rouge: Jimmy Swaggart Ministries, 1987.

Sylvan, Robin. *Traces of the Spirit: The Religious Dimensions of Popular Music*. New York: New York University Press, 2002.

Tame, David. *The Secret Power of Music*. New York: Destiny, 1984.

Tanner, Kathryn. "Theological Reflection and Christian Practices." In *Practicing Theology: Beliefs and Practices in Christian Life*, edited by Dorothy C. Bass and Miroslav Volf. Grand Rapids: Eerdmans, 2002.

Thomas, Edith Lovell. *Music in Christian Education*. New York: Abingdon, 1953.

———. *Musical Moments in Worship: Guidance in Singing and Listening*. New York: Abingdon, 1935.

Tillich, Paul. *Systematic Theology*. Vol. 1. Chicago: University of Chicago, 1951.

Tracy, David. *The Analogical Imagination: Christian Theology and the Culture of Pluralism*. New York: Crossroad, 1981.

———. *Blessed Rage for Order: The New Pluralism in Theology*. San Francisco: Harper & Row, 1988.

———. "The Foundations of Practical Theology." In *Practical Theology: the Emerging Field in Theology, Church, and World*, edited by Don S. Browning. San Francisco: Harper & Row, 1983.

———. "Foreword." In *God Without Being*, by Jean-Luc Marion. Chicago: University of Chicago Press, 1991.

Tramo, Mark Jude. "Music of the Hemispheres." *Science* 291 (2001) 54–56.

Tucker, Mary Evelyn, and John A. Grim, editors. *Worldviews and Ecology: Religion, Philosophy, and the Environment*. Ecology and Justice Series on Global Ecology. Maryknoll, NY: Orbis, 1994.

van der Ven, Johannes A. *Practical Theology: an Empirical Approach*. Kampen: Kok Pharos, 1993.

Vernon, Philip E. "The Personality of the Composer." *Music and Letters* 11 (1930) 38–48.

Vinay, Gustavo. "'Spiritualità': Invito a una discussion." *Studia Medievali* 3a series 2 (1961).

Volf, Miroslav. "Theology for a Way of Life." In *Practicing Theology: Beliefs and Practices in Christian Life*, edited by Dorothy C. Bass and Miroslav Volf. Grand Rapids: Eerdmans, 2002.

Vygotsky, L. S. *Mind in Society: The Development of Higher Psychological Processes.* Cambridge: Harvard University Press, 1978.

Walker, Decker F., and Jonas F. Soltis. *Curriculum and Aims.* 2nd ed. Thinking About Education Series. New York: Tachers College Press, 1992.

Ward, Phyllis. *Listening with New Ears: Program Activities for Unwrapped Presence.* Louisville: Witherspoon, 1998.

Westerhoff, John H. "Children: Faith, Formation, and Worship." *Reformed Liturgy and Music* 21 (1987) 13.

Westermeyer, Paul. *Let the People Sing: Hymn Tunes in Perspective.* Chicago: GIA Music, 2005.

———. "Reflections on Music and Theology." *Theological Education* 31:1 (1994) 189–95.

———. *Te Deum: The Church and Music.* Minneapolis: Fortress, 1998.

Wiethaus, Ulrike, editor. *Maps of Flesh and Light: The Religious Experience of Medieval Women Mystics.* Syracuse, NY: Syracuse University Press, 1993.

Wimberly, Anne Streaty. *The Church Family Sings.* Nashville: Abingdon, 1996.

Winter, Miriam Therese. *Why Sing? Toward a Theology of Catholic Church Music.* Washington, DC: Pastoral, 1984.

Wolterstorff, Nicholas. "The Work of Making a Work of Music." In *What is Music? An Introduction to the Philosophy of Music,* edited by P. J. Alperson. University Park: Pennsylvania State University Press, 1987.

Woolhouse, Roger. "Locke's Theory of Knowledge." In *Cambridge Companion to John Locke,* edited by Vere Chappell. Cambridge Companions to Philosophy series. Cambridge: Cambridge University Press, 1994.

Wren, Brian. *Praying Twice: the Music and Words of Congregational Song.* Louisville: Westminster John Knox, 2000.

Wyckoff, D. Campbell, and George Brown, Jr. *Religious Education 1960–1993: An Annotated Bibliography.* Westport, CT: Greenwood, 1995.

Ylvisaker, John Carl. "The Two Streams of Congregational Music." *Borning Cry: Worship for a New Congregation.* Waverly, IA: New Generation, 1992.

Zajonc, Arthur. *Meditation as Contemplative Inquiry: When Knowing Becomes Love.* Great Barrington, MA: Lindisfarne, 2009.

Zatorre, R. J. "Pitch Perception of Complex Tones and Human Temporal-lobe Function." *Journal of the Acoustical Society of America* 84 (1988) 566–72.

Zentner, M. R., and J. Kagan, "Infants' Perception of Consonance and Dissonance in Music." *Infant Behavior and Development* 21 (1998) 483–92.

Index

academic rationalism, 16, 93, 135, 145–46, 148–49
acoustics, 64
Adam, 39–40, 74
aesthetics, 89, 93–94, 98, 141, 145
agonistic, 119
Alexander III, Pope, 30
Anabaptist Protestants, 164
Andernach, Tengswich of, 30, 36
angels, 36, 39, 42
Angier, Natalie, 65
apartheid, 187
apocalyptic, 35–37
architecture, 64
Aristotelian, 106, 124, 127–28, 131, 168
Art 2, 31, 49, 51, 54–55, 112, 134, 136, 139, 141, 143, 193, 195–96
artisanal, xi, 13, 17, 167–69, 171–77, 184–86, 188–91, 199–206
Atkins, Patty, 139
Atkins, Tim, 139
audiation, 15, 95–99, 101–5, 107–9, 121–23, 131
audiation stare, 108
aural perception, 15, 96, 99, 101
aural-oral phenomenon, 16, 96, 117, 131, 124, 130, 132, 167, 208

Auschwitz, 162
Bach, J. S., 18, 36, 81, 130, 160
Balthasar, Hans urs von, 5
Barbarossa, Fredrick, 30
Bass, Dorothy C., 125–26
Beethoven, Ludwig, 92
Begbie, Jeremy ix, 1–3, 18, 21–23, 25, 46–47, 50, 52–53, 93, 95, 106–8, 116, 123–24, 127–32, 208
being, 181, 206
Bell, John L., 64, 90–91, 93
Benedict of Nursia, 34
Benedictine 14, 28–29, 31, 33–36, 38–39, 41, 57–58, 61
Benzon, William, 96, 123
Berry, J. W., 78
biblical music, 19
Binet, Alfred, 76
Bingen, Hildegard of, 43–45, 47, 49, 51, 53, 55–57, 59, 61
BioMusic Program, 66
Blacking, John, 3, 23–5, 46
Body 15, 20, 22–25, 31–33, 38–44, 56–61, 71, 74, 79, 81, 85, 87–88, 99, 126, 152–55, 164–65, 168–69, 175
Boethius, 31, 33
Bondi, Roberta, 175, 189
Bourdieu, Pierre, 125
Brahms, Johannes, 18

Brethren in Christ, 164
British empiricist school, 76
Brody, Nathan, 76
Burt, C., 77, 79
Cady, Calvin B., 136
Caputo, John, 200
caritas, 179–80, 184
Catholic church music, 77
Cattell, James McKeen, 76
Cattell, Raymond, 77
cenobite, 35
certainty, 179–82, 186
Chalcedonian, x, 13, 17, 156, 193, 198–99, 201, 205
Chalcedonian method, 156, 193, 198–99, 201
Chambers, Norah, 160
character of music, 42–43, 143
Chittister, Joan, 33–5
choir, ix, x, 64, 90, 93, 102, 148
Christian hymnody, 143
Christian ritual music, 20
Christian spirituality xi, 1, 4–14, 17, 21–22, 26, 30, 137, 161, 168, 205, 208, 210–11
Christian tradition, x, 2, 20, 43, 126, 147–48, 177–78, 186, 209
chronos, 117
church music, 19–20, 89, 139, 142, 146
Church, Norval, 138
civil rights movement, 21, 187
Clark, Linda, 20
cognitive participation, 97
cognitive processes, 16, 49, 83, 96, 135–7
Cole, M., 78
Colijn, Helen, 159–60
Colossians, x, 147–8
compassionate companionship, 17, 167, 173, 187, 189
composition, 28, 41, 43, 83, 112

conflict-in-context, 156, 160
congruence, ix, 155, 158, 179
congregation, 20, 90, 93, 156, 194, 215
consummatory experience, 16, 135, 140–1, 151
contemplative x, xi, 12–13, 17, 27, 167–69, 181, 183–91, 93, 195–99, 201–3, 205–7, 209, 211
contemplative empiricism, xi, 13, 167–77, 184–86, 188, 190–207
contemplative inquiry 17, 27, 168, 170–72, 175, 179, 184, 99, 98, 201, 206
contemplative practice, x, 171
convictional knowing, 156
Cooper, B. Lee, 144
corporate worship, 18
correlation, 73, 77, 155, 168, 176–77, 179–80, 182–83, 190
correlational theological method, 167, 178
covenantal companionship, 173, 202
covenantal relationship, 168, 184, 197
creative spirit, 138
critical-correlational, 17, 166, 179, 184
crucial catechesis, 149
Dalai Lama, 169
Davison, Archibald T., 142
deconstructionist, 1
delight 13, 17, 19, 39–40, 165–66, 168–69, 171, 188–89, 198, 205–7, 211–12
descriptive-empirical task, 195
desert monasticism, 34
desire, 56–57, 59–61, 65, 91–92, 104, 170, 184, 201

developmental aptitude, 72
Dilthey, Wilhelm, 154
discernment, 126, 170, 192, 194–96
discretio, 14, 28–29, 38, 44, 47,
    57–58, 60–61
distal, 154
Divine Office, 35, 38–42, 44, 57
Doing, Ruth, 140
drama, 57, 174
Dronke, Peter, 30
Dryburgh, Margaret, 159
Dykstra, Craig, 7–9, 125–26,
    152–53, 185
Eastman School of Music, 69
ecclesial rationalism, 16, 146–49
ecclesiastical authority, 36
education 6–9, 16, 26, 29, 39,
    69–70, 74–75, 82, 92, 96–98,
    102, 104–5, 108–9, 126,
    133–51, 153, 155, 157, 159,
    161, 163–65, 185, 200, 203
educational theory, 7, 16, 26, 74,
    133–34, 137, 140, 160
ego cogito, 182–83
Einstein, Albert, 157
Eisner, Elliot, 135, 137–38, 140–41,
    145–46
Elvis Presley, 142
embodied epistemology, 16, 152,
    155, 166
embodiment 16, 22, 27, 32, 44, 54,
    59–60, 107, 117, 128, 170,
    178, 184, 189, 206, 208
Enlightenment, 26, 44, 54, 134
epistemic, 179, 180, 182
Epstein, Heidi, 32–33, 56
erotic phenomenon, 180–81
erotic rationality, 168, 176, 179–81,
    183, 185, 187, 197, 206
ethics, 141
ethnomusicology, 23–24, 26
Eucharist, 35

Fall, the, 39–40
Farley, Edward, 144–45
Fassler, Margo, 37–38
fear of the Lord, 34–35
feeling, 8, 14, 29, 45–56, 58–59, 70,
    82, 171
feminist theology of music, 33
Feuerstein, Reuven, 79
Frohlich, Mary, 11, 12
Gaebelein, Frank, 148
Galton, Francis, 76–7
Gardner, Howard, 15, 46, 68, 74–76,
    78–88
Garment of the Word of God, 32,
    40, 42, 59
gestalt, 47, 153–55, 193
Gestalt Field Theory, 139
God without being, 170, 179–81,
    184, 197–98
Gordon, Edwin, 15–16, 68–75,
    87–8, 94–112, 115, 121–24,
    131, 152, 164
Grainger, Percy, 160
Greek, 5, 111, 124–25, 130–31
Greenfield, P. M., 79
Guilford, J. P., 77–79
Habermas, Jürgen, 195–96
habitus, 168
Hargreaves, David, 47
Harrington, Karl Pomeroy, 146
Hart, Trevor, 49
Harvard Glee Club, 142
Havelock, Eric A., 112
Haydn, Joseph, 81, 160
Hebb, D. O., 77–78
Hebrew wisdom literature, 111
Heisig, James, 170, 198
Heitink, Gerben, 190–92
hermeneutical, 154, 177, 191–92,
    196–97
Hildebert von Bermersheim, 129
Holsinger, Bruce, 32, 56, 60

Index

Homeric Poetry, 112
Homeric studies, 111–12
horizon of ultimate value 4–5, 8–10,
    13–4, 17, 26, 134, 166, 168,
    179, 186, 197, 205, 208, 210
hospitality, 34, 44, 90, 126
human body 15, 20, 22–25, 31–33,
    38–44, 56–61, 71, 74, 79, 81,
    85, 87–88, 99, 126, 152–55,
    164–65, 168–69, 175, 196,
    202–6
human mind 1–3, 9–10, 14, 16, 20,
    22, 29, 39–40, 45–49, 52–58,
    60, 68, 74, 78, 79–80, 82–86,
    95, 97, 105, 107, 109–14,
    117, 118–27, 131–32, 136,
    148, 151, 154–55, 165,
    168–76, 179–84, 187, 189,
    196, 198–99, 202–3, 205–6,
    208, 210
humility, 3, 30, 34–35, 44, 164,
    175–77, 186, 209, 212
idealism, 170
Iliad, 112
imago dei, 33, 198
imitation, 15, 96–97, 103, 108
impassioned conviction, 168,
    185–87
Incarnation, 148
indwelling, 16, 152, 154–55, 163,
    165, 165, 175, 179, 201
innate musicality, 65, 68–71, 73,
    77, 87
insight ix–xi, 13–14, 16–17, 27, 29,
    33, 45–47, 49, 51, 53–62,
    107, 134, 141, 151–52,
    155–57, 159, 163–74, 176,
    180, 184, 199, 202–3, 205,
    208, 211–12
instrument, 18, 44, 90–91, 153–54
insufficient reason, 180, 182, 197,
    207

integration 5–6, 8–10, 12–13, 16,
    22, 26, 51, 87, 111, 115,
    140, 146, 154, 168–69, 206,
    209–10
intelligence tradition, 76
Interdict of 1178, 14, 30
interior illumination, 39–40, 43,
    56–57, 59, 61–2
interiorized, 154–5
interlude for scanning, ix, 156–57
interpretive task, 185, 194–95
intimacies of difference, 168,
    185–87
IQ test, 76
irreducible multidimensionality, 16,
    107, 129, 189
James, William, 171
Jensen, A. R., 77
Jerome, 5
Jesus, x, 5, 9, 14, 28, 40, 43, 147,
    156, 198–200, 205
John Dewey, 7, 8
Jutta von Sponheim, 29
Kant, Immanuel, 170
Kairos, 117
Keble College, Oxford, 113
Kegan, Robert, 10
Kiddush Club, xii, 161–64
King, Roberta, 139
kingdom of God, 136
Klein, Perry, 84
Knowing 4–5, 7, 11, 86, 92, 110,
    121, 126–27, 136–37, 145,
    152–58, 181, 183
Koestler, Arthur, 157
Langer, Susanne K., 2, 14, 25, 29,
    45–56, 58, 60–61, 82, 104,
    137, 214
language, 15, 20, 46, 49, 51, 53, 55,
    61, 63
Last Supper, 147
Latin Psalter, 29

learning from music, xi, 190, 101, 159, 162
learning in music, xi, 14, 28, 90, 104, 122, 151–52, 167
Leclerq, Jean, 5
lectio, 34–35
Lipps, Hans, 154
Listening 15, 32–35, 44, 58, 60, 90, 98, 100–101, 103, 114, 137, 139, 170, 176, 194
literacy, 110–18, 120–22, 135–36
literature of music, 19
liturgical music, 20
liturgy, 20, 39, 41–42, 57, 61
living light, 29–31, 36, 42
Locke, John, 170
Loder, James E. xii, 16, 112, 132, 134, 149, 151–52, 155–58, 185, 190, 193, 198–201, 203, 209
logos, 95, 106–7, 124, 131
Lonergan, Bernard, 113, 174
Lord, Albert B., 112
Love xi, 9, 63, 65, 90–91, 121, 126, 147, 179, 175, 179–84, 187, 189, 194–200, 209, 211–12
love without being, 170, 179, 183–84, 187, 197
Luria, A. R., 120
Macarena, the, 21
MacIntyre, Alasdair, 21, 106, 125
Magistra, 29
Marion, Jean-Luc, 170, 178–79, 197, 210
Mass (Christian), 31
May, Gerald, 169
McCant, Jerry W., 139
McGinn, Bernard, 4–5, 7, 13
McKinnon, James, 19
Mechthild von Bermersheim, 29, 83
medieval cosmology, 33
medieval worldview, 32–33, 59

Mendelssohn, ix, 18
Messiah College, 164
metaphysics, 180
methodologically relational, 172
MI theory, 80, 84–6
missio dei, 195, 197–98
Monastary of St. Disibod, 29
Moore, Mary Elizabeth Mullino, 190, 193, 202
Morsch, Vivian, 143, 147
Mount St. Rupert, 30
Mozart, Wolfgang Amadeus, 81
multidimensionality x, 12, 16, 22, 26, 51, 53–54, 58, 96, 107, 129, 134, 149–51, 155, 159, 164, 167, 185, 188–89, 206, 208
music as garment, 43
music's corporeality, 32, 60–1
musica celestis, 32
musica humana, 31, 38
musica instrumentalis, 31–2
musica mundana, 31
musical achievement, 68, 70–71, 87
Musical Aptitude Profile (MAP), 70–71, 75, 78, 102
musical harmony, 31
musical intelligence, 68–69, 74, 79–80, 82–84, 86, 88
musical learning theory, 15, 69, 75, 94–112, 121
musical notation, 66, 70, 90–91, 93, 98, 109, 116, 122
musical potential, 5, 61, 65, 67, 69, 72–73, 83
musical test battery, 69–71
musicality, 15, 33, 63–65, 67–68, 70, 81, 87–88, 90–92, 96, 98
musicking, 96
mystical experience, 171, 211
narrative quality of human experience, 21

natural discretio, 57
natural world, 30, 57, 81, 113, 128, 130, 185
Nelson, Ronald A., 148
Neo-Platonic, 33
Newman, Barbara, 35–38
non-correlational theology, 13, 17, 165, 176, 178–81, 184, 189, 192, 194
non-musical, 15, 63–65, 67, 69, 71, 73, 75, 77, 79, 81, 83, 85, 87, 89–93
normative task, 194, 196
numinous, 22
Odyssey, 112
Old Testament prophets, 37
Ong, Walter J., 16, 95, 107, 110–24, 131, 168
ontological, 22–23, 164, 179–80, 182
oral cultures, 114–19
orality, 16, 95, 107, 110–23, 131
orthoaesthesis, 170, 198
Orthodox Jews, 161–62, 164
orthodoxy, 170–71, 205
orthopraxis, 170–71
Osmer, Richard R., 190, 192–98, 203
Otto, Rudolph, 26
Page, Sue Ellen, 136–37
Papousek, Hanus, 83
Paradise Road, 160, 162–3
Parry, Adam, 112
Parry, Milman, 111–12
pastoral music, 20
patristic, 19
perfect form, 49
perfection of form, 49, 57
performative mode theology, 167–80, 184, 188–206
personal transformation, 169
phenomenon of music, 2, 19

phronesis, 124
Piaget, Jean, 77–78, 87
pneuma, 5
poesis, 128
Polanyi, Michael, 152–55, 157, 164, 201
post-critical, 152, 154, 198
postmodern, 31, 137, 200
poverty of spirit, 34–36, 189
practical theology, 4, 127, 185, 193, 197
practice x, 2, 4, 20–22, 31–32, 38, 41–46, 55, 57, 65, 71, 85, 87, 97, 103–6, 114, 119, 124–27, 139, 146, 151, 153, 155, 163, 171, 193–96
pragmatic task, 194, 196
prayer, x, 11, 29, 33–5, 39, 44, 148, 189
Prelates at Mainz, 14, 28–31, 35–37, 39, 41–45, 47, 49, 51, 53, 55–57, 59, 61
preparatory audiation, 108
Presbyterian, x, 159, 1
primary relationality, 200
Principe, Walter, 205
Progressive Education Association, 136
Project Spectrum, 84
proverbs, 111, 114, 119
Psalms, x, 14, 40–41, 44, 147
Psalter, 29, 39, 41, 43, 143
psychometric, 76–77, 80, 84
pure design, 49
pure form, 46–47, 49–51, 56, 60, 124
Pyle, David, 76–78
Pythagorean thought, 31
Qoheleth, 111
quest for assurance, ix, 179, 181–82, 184, 197
rabbi, 161–62

Ralph Tyler, 150
rationality of discernment, 192, 195
Ravel, Maurice, 160
reason 27, 40, 48, 50–51, 54–57, 97, 112, 151, 160, 168, 175–78, 180, 182, 192, 196–97, 207, 210, 212
reciprocity, 180–84, 210
reduced reciprocity, 182–84,
reflective orality, 35–37, 57, 64
reformer, 52
Reichling, Mary, 173
relational contexts, 173
relational logic of the Spirit, x, 13, 193, 198, 200–201, 209
relationally-formed, 17, 167, 172, 201, 206
release of energy, ix, 156–8
religious education, 16, 26, 133–51
religious experience, x, 93, 210
revelation, 57, 140, 176–78, 180
rhythmic imagery, 71
rhythm, 51, 58, 66, 72, 82, 99–100, 140
Ricoeur, Paul, 9
Rider University, 102
Ridley, Aaron, 2, 3
ritual, 20, 23, 25, 106
ritual music, 20
rock music, 143–44
Roehmann, Franz L., 65, 67–8
Rogers, William B., 148
ruah, 5
Rule of St. Benedict, 33–5
Sacks, Oliver, 67–68
sacraments, 42–43, 126
sacred discretio, 57–58
sacred music, 20–21
sagely wisdom, 195
Saliers, Don, 20–21, 46, 53, 137, 148–49
salvation history, 37, 39, 55

Sami (of Scandinavia), 67
Satan, 42
Schiff, Andras, 92
Schmidt, Margot, 37–38, 45, 57–58
Schneiders, Sandra, 5–6, 8–9, 11, 13, 161, 205, 209
Scivias, 30, 34–35, 37–38
Scott, Joyce, 63–64
Scripture, 9, 19, 41, 177, 186, 205
Seashore Measures of Musical Talent, 69
Seashore, Carl E., 69
Second Coming, 37
self-actualization, 16, 135, 140, 149
self-implication, 2, 5, 10–12
self-transcendence, x, 5, 8, 10, 16–17, 158
sensate, 92, 111
Sessions, Roger, 82
Seymour, Harriet Ayer, 138
Shabbat, 162
Shields, Elizabeth McEwen, 138, 140, 142
Small, Christopher, 2, 96
Smart, Ninian, 22
social reconstruction-relevance, 135, 141
social reconstructionism, 141
social relevance, 16, 141–43
somatic, 27, 32, 125, 152–53, 188
song of the people, 90
South Kensington Museum, 76
Spearman, Charles, 76–80
spirit x, 5, 9, 13–14, 20, 22–32, 25, 29, 34–37, 39–44, 57–59, 121, 125–26, 138–39, 146, 148, 156, 161
spiritual experience, 143, 149, 151
Springiersbach, Richard of, 36
St. Paul, 148
stabilized aptitude, 72, 74, 88
Stackhouse, Max, 141

Steiner, George, 26–27, 47, 106, 188
Sternberg, Robert, 76, 78–79
strategic, 176, 188, 191–92
Stravinsky, Igor, 18–19
Stromberg, Bob, 139
subsidiary, 154
suffering, 13, 17–18, 125, 166, 168–69, 187–88, 198, 202, 205–6
Sumatra, 159
Swan, Laura, 33–34
Sylvan, Robin, 22–23, 25–26
symbolization, 25, 45–50, 54–55, 58–61, 104
symphony, 67
systematic theology, 1, 3, 17, 127
systemic education, 7
tacit dimension, 152–55
Tanner, Kathryn, 125
technology, 16, 121, 137–40, 144, 149
theological knowledge, 57
theory of mind, 46–49, 54–56, 68, 60
Thomas, Edith Lovell, 146
Thurstone, L. L., 77–8
tikkun olam, 204
tonal imagery, 71
Torah, 161–62
Tower of Babel, 113
Tracy, David, 165, 176–8
Tramo, Mark, 66, 109
transcendence, 6, 8, 10, 12, 17, 23, 26–27, 47, 61, 144, 208–9
transcendental, 174, 177
transformative learning 4, 7, 9, 13, 16, 23, 94, 130, 134–35, 164, 208, 210–11
Trinitarian, 17, 123, 156, 196, 198, 205

Tuvan throat-singer, 18
Tyler Rationale, 150–51, 156
unconsummated symbol, 47, 49–52, 54, 56, 59
universal music, 67–68
University of Chicago, 177
Vallance, Elizabeth, 135, 137–38, 140–41, 145–46
vanity, 181–82
Ven, Johannes van der, 171
Venda (of Transvaal), 23
Vernon, P. E., 77, 78–79
Vinay, Gustavo, 5
Virgin Mary, 40, 42–3
Visio, 29
Visionary, 28, 30, 32, 35, 47
Voice 14, 18, 23, 28–29, 32, 35, 37, 39–41, 43, 45, 60, 67, 90–91, 123, 137, 156
Volf, Miroslav, 125
Vulgate, 5
Vygotsky, Lev, 79
Westermeyer, Paul, 19–20
Westminster Choir College, 102
Whitney, Thomas, 136
Wing Standardized Test of Music Intelligence, 69
Winter, MMS, Miriam Therese, 189
Wolterstorff, Nicholas, 129
world music, 63
world of audiation, 107–8, 121, 123, 131
World War II, 159
Worship 18–20, 45, 63, 90, 93, 126, 139, 141, 143, 146, 147–49, 187
Wren, Brian, 20
Wundt, Wilhelm, 76
Ylvisaker, John Carl, 89
Zajonc, Arthur, 211

www.ingramcontent.com/pod-product-compliance
Lightning Source LLC
Chambersburg PA
CBHW051053230426
43667CB00013B/2276